# EGYPTIAN THEATRE

*Perspectives*

*Nehad Selaiha*

Library of Congress Cataloging-in-Publication Data

Names: Ṣulayḥah, Nihād, author. | Carlson, Marvin, 1935- editor.
Title: Nehad Selaiha : selected essays / Nehad Selaiha ; edited by Marvin Carlson.
Other titles: Ahram weekly.
Description: New York : Martin E. Segal Theatre Center, 2020. | Includes index. | Contents: v. 1. New directions -- v. 2. Plays & playwrights -- v. 3. Perspectives -- v. 4. Cultural encounters, [pt.]1 -- v. 5. Cultural encounters, [pt.] 2. | Summary: "A collection of essays by Nehad Selaiha (1945-2017), distinguished scholar and prominent critic of Egyptian theatre. The essays gathered in the five volumes of Nehad Selaiha: Selected Essays are those selected by the author herself from the hundreds she published in the weekly journal Al-Ahram (The Pyramids). These collections, now long out of print, appeared in 2003 and 2004, approximately half way through Nehad Selaiha's remarkable career, and provide an impressive sampling of the range and depth of her critical insight and interest. The first volume is largely devoted to one of Selaiha's central interests, the modern Egyptian Free Theatre Movement, which has produced almost all of the significant young directors, dramatists and actors in that country for the past generation. The next two books report on productions of various Arab dramatists. The final two volumes, Cultural Encounters, discuss examples of international, primarily European and American drama presented in Egypt"-- Provided by publisher.
Identifiers: LCCN 2020045146 | ISBN 9781953892003 (v. 1 ; paperback) | ISBN 9781953892010 (v. 2 ; paperback) | ISBN 9781953892027 (v. 3 ; paperback) | ISBN 9781953892034 (v. 4 ; paperback) | ISBN 9781953892041 (v. 5 ; paperback)
Subjects: LCSH: Theater--Egypt--History--20th century. | Theater--Production and direction--Egypt--History--20th century. | Arabic drama--20th century--History and criticism. | Theater critics--Egypt--History--20th century. | Dramatic criticism--Egypt--History--20th century. | American drama--Appreciation--Egypt. | European drama--Appreciation--Egypt.
Classification: LCC PN2974 .S83 2020 | DDC 892.7/27--dc23
LC record available at https://lccn.loc.gov/2020045146

All rights reserved. Except for brief passages quoted in newspaper, magazine, radio or television reviews, no part of this book may be reproduced in any form or by any means, electronic or mechanical, including photocopying or recording, or by an information storage and retrieval system, without permission in writing from the publisher.

Professionals and amateurs are hereby warned that this material, being fully protected under the Copyright Laws of the United States of America and all other countries of the Berne and Universal Copyright Conventions, is subject to a royalty. All rights including, but not limited to professional, amateur, recording, motion picture, recitation, lecturing, public reading, radio and television broadcasting, and the rights of translation into foreign languages are expressly reserved. *Nehad Selaiha Selected Essays* © 2020 by Nehad Selaiha. Any inquiries concerning copyrights should be addressed in advance to the Martin E. Segal Theatre, 365 5th Avenue, 3rd Floor, New York, NY 10016. email: mestc@gc.cuny.edu

© 2020 Martin E. Segal Theatre Center
Marvin Carlson, Director of Publications
Frank Hentschker, Executive Director
Newly Indexed by Marvin Carlson
Dohyun Gracia Shin, Managing Editor and Cover Design
Stephen Cedars, Managing Editor and Page Layouts
Christopher Silsby, Additional Typesetting and Layout
Jacquelyn Marie Shannon, Original Books Scans

# Dedication

"But Oh for the touch of a vanished hand,
And the sound of a voice that is still"

Alfred Tennyson

*In remembranc of all those lovely artists who continue to enrich our days, though they have physically departed.*

# Editor's Preface

The essays gathered in the five volumes of *Nehad Selaiha: Selected Essays* are those selected by the author herself from the hundreds she published in the weekly journal *Al-Ahram* (The Pyramids). Her death at the beginning of 2017 left an enormous void in the Egyptian and Arab theatre world. She was not only by far the most widely read, widely informed and influential critic in this world, but was a figure of considerable international stature and the mentor and model for an entire generation of young Egyptian performers, playwrights and scholars.

These collections, now long out of print, appeared in 2003 and 2004, approximately half way through Nehad Selaiha's remarkable career, and provide an impressive sampling of the range and depth of her critical insight and interest. The first volume is largely devoted to one of Selaiha's central interests, the modern Egyptian Free Theatre Movement, which has produced almost all of the significant young directors, dramatists and actors in that country for the past generation. The next two books report on productions of various Arab dramatists, mostly Egyptian and mostly in Cairo, but Selaiha's wide-ranging interests take her often to productions in other parts of Egypt, and eventually to various festivals in other Arab nations.

The final two volumes, Cultural Encounters, discuss examples of international, primarily European and American drama presented in Egypt. Selaiha's view is a cosmopolitan, international one (her academic field was English literature, and she is as likely to quote Shakespeare, Wordsworth or Eliot as she is some Arab authority) but her view of even familiar classics, in the eyes of an educated articulate contemporary Cairene woman, bring to these a stimulating fresh perspective. Rarely does Selaiha confine herself to the parameters of a conventional review, though she does generally provide detailed comments on acting and staging, but she embeds these observations in more general essays on the physical, social and cultural context of each production, so that the reading of these essays provides a unique insight not only into the current theatre scene in the theatre capital of the Arab world, but into the cultural context that surrounds that scene and gives it meaning and resonance.

Marvin Carlson
Dec. 2019

# PREFACE

This book, the third in the *Modern Egyptian Theatre* series, is partly intended as a token of love and gratitude to all those brave women and men of the theatre who, through their work on and off the boards, have shaped the course and direction of the art of performance in Egypt since the 1920s.

Whereas the second volume concentrated on playwrights and their work, here the reader will meet performers, directors, dramaturges, producers, and pioneering critics. Some of them are still with us and some have gone; but in either case, the valuable work they have done will continue to inspire future generations. In a sense, this book is an attempt to stem the tides of oblivion and keep the memories green.

Nehad Selaiha<br>
Cairo,<br>
**June 2004**

# The Egyptian Theatre

## Perspectives

Sanaa Gamil
as Sheherezada

**Nehad Selaiha**

# Contents

|  | Page |
|---|---|
| Dedication | 3 |
| Editor's Preface | 4 |
| Selaiha's Preface | 5 |
| Original Cover | 6 |

**I. Performers:** 11
- Down Sunset Boulevard: Fatma Rushdi (1908–1996) ..... 13
- Age Could Never Wither Her: Amina Rizq (1911–2003) .. 21
- A White Flame: Sanaa Gamil (1930–2003) ................... 29
- Dancing Into the Twilight: Farida Fahmi (1940– ...) ....... 37
- The Frog Prince: Adel Imam (1940– ...) ..................... 45
- Rising From the Ashes: Mohamed Khayri (1945– ...) ..... 51
- Bright and Brittle : Aida Fahmi (1960– ...) ................... 57

**II. Directors:** 63
- Ripeness Is All: Karam Metaweh (1933–1996) ............. 65
- Exit an Unsung Hero: Salama Hassan (1945–1997) ....... 71
- Sa'd Ardash and Brecht ......................................... 75
- Samir El-Asfouri (1937 – ...): Five Takes:
    1. Floggin a Dead Horse ................................. 83
    2. Jangled Out of Tune ................................... 86
    3. The Call of the Wild ................................... 90
    4. A Wave of Nostalgia ................................... 95
    5. All That Glitters ........................................ 99

- Walid Aouni's Dance: Five Takes and a Footnote:
    1. Landscapes of Memory ............................. 103
    2. Mission Impossible ................................ 111
    3. In the Heat of the Night ......................... 115
    4. Songs of Innocen and Experience ................. 119
    5. A Homage to Mokhtar .............................. 121
    - Footnote: Aouni's Brood ........................... 125
- Hani Metaweh: A Director Turns Playwright (1944 – ..):
  Tow Ventures:
    1. Into the Undiscovered Country .................... 131
    2. Shooting Farouk .................................. 136
- Intisar Abdel Fattah (1955 – ...): Four Takes:
    1. A Street Cart Named Ghabn ....................... 143
    2. The Book of Outcasts ............................. 148
    3. Sonata ........................................... 152
    4. Lear, A Symphony ................................. 153
- Remembering Allula .................................... 155

**III. Fiction in Action: Dramaturges:**  159
1. From the Page to the Stage ......................... 161
2. The Brief Summer of Aton ........................... 179
3. Schools for Scandal ................................. 187
4. Home-Made Theatre .................................. 191
5. Anecdotes and Vignettes ............................. 199
6. A Secret History ................................... 205
7. Faces in the Mirror: Images of Sheherazade on the
   Egyptian Stage ..................................... 213

IV.  **Behind the Scenes:**                                      229
   – Tonight We Improvise: Ali El-Ra'i (1920-1999) .........   231
   – Rescue Operations:
      1. Samir Khashaba (1939 – ...): Interview ...............   239
      2. Huda Wasfi (1943 – ...): Interview .....................   249
      3. The National Theatre Conference .......................   255
   – Noblesse Oblige: Rashida Taymour .......................   259
   – A Rainbow After the Deluge: Nadia El-Shabouri and
      Husam Atta .................................................   263

**Appendices:**                                                269
   1. Down Memory Lane: Recreating the Splendour that Was
      Rushdi .....................................................   271
   2. Age Cannot Wither Her .......................................   275
   3. A Taste of Vintage ..........................................   285

**Index** ...........................................................   289
**Errata** ..........................................................   306

# I
# Performers

# Down Sunset Boulevard:
## *Fatma Rushdi*[*] (1908-1996)

And so she is dead – the legendary Fatma Rushdi, the Sarah Bernhardt of the east, as she was dubbed; and how she cherished the title. She made a smooth and graceful exit without the convulsive harangues and heroic declamations that usually accompanied her famous death scenes on stage. In fact, it was one such death-scene that indirectly launched her on her glorious career as the first woman founder of a theatrical company in the Arab world.

It happened in the mid-twenties when she was a member of the prestigious Rasmes Company, founded by the equally legendary actor and director Yusef Wahbi after his return from Italy. When the company's *prima donna*, Rose al-Yusef, left the company to pursue a career in Journalism and found the publishing house that still carries her name today, Rushdi became the female lead. Naturally, the choice incensed the young female members, some of whom had joined the company before Rushdi. There was a lot of spite and bitter back-biting. Amina Rizq, Rushdi's colleague at the time, admits to this. "She was the wife of the company's director, Aziz 'Eid, and we naturally thought this was behind her choice as leading lady", she says. "It was not until we saw her in the leading parts that we had to admit, however reluctantly, that she was truly great," she adds.

One night, however, just as Rushdi was coming to the end of an inordinately long dying speech and building up for a grand finale before

---

[*] 8 February, 1996.

collapsing into the arms of her four female attendants, one of whom was Rizq, she caught sight of one of the attendants, the beautiful actress Zaynab Sidqi, imperceptibly lifting a hand to her mouth to suppress what Rushdi thought a giggle but was in fact a yawn — induced by the long, silent vigil. She insisted that Yusef Wahbi kick the culpable attendant out, and when he refused (the actress in question being an asset to the company at a time when female acting talents were scarce) she walked out, taking the husband along.

Together, they set up their own company which carried her name. It was not easy, and, financially, it was an uphill struggle. At one time, they had to acution some of their furniture, and it is doubtful that the project would have taken off if a certain, wealthy gentleman by the name of Eli Adru'i had not suddenly and miraculously materialized. Rushdi has described their first meeting in her memoirs and in several interviews. She met him at a night club where she had gone to meet an acquaintance who had promised her a loan. She and 'Eid where down to their last penny. The loan was not forthcoming, but the acquaintance pointed out to her the rich, Jewish businessman and told her to try him. Proud as ever, though nearly a pauper, Rushdi insisted that he come to her table and introduce himself. By the end of the evening, he had agreed to sponsor her company and arranged to meet her the following morning to settle the matter. On reaching home, she discovered that he had slipped five hundred pounds (a fortune in those days) into her bag without telling her. The next day, Mr. Adru'i took his beautiful protégé round the shops, outfitting her as befitted her future status, and finished off by opening a 12,000-pound bank account in her name.

For seven years, the amorous sponsor continued to lavishly fund the company, not minding the heavy losses in terms of cash returns.

Thanks to him, Rushdi was able to indulge her wildest acting dreams, performing many classical female as well as male parts, including Cleopatra, La Dame aux camélias and Hamlet, and touring Egypt and the Arab world with her performances. Everywhere she went she was received with rapturous adulation and given red-carpet treatment. As her reputation grew, she began to become a legend. It was during those years that she was called the Sarah Bernhardt of the east; another cherished title was "the friend of students," which she earned on account of her giving free performances for students on certain days. She also became something of a patriotic figure for her attacks on the British occupation of Egypt which led to the closing down of her theatre once or twice. The poor, little Alexandrian girl who was driven by poverty to the stage at the age of ten had come a long way. She was the only actress in her time to receive bouquets tied with strings of real pearls, as the legend goes.

Sayed Darwish had been the first to discover her talent; he heard her sing one night in Alexandria with the troupe of Amin Atallah and advised her mother (who had joined the troupe with her three daughters after the death of her Yugoslav husband) to take her to Cairo, the land of golden opportunities. In Cairo, she presented herself to Naguib El-Rihani to work for his company and there she met Aziz 'Eid, her future tutor and husband, and life-long mentor, friend and loyal companion. 'Eid took to her at once and set about educating her (she couldn't even read or write) and polishing her talent; he brought her several teachers and coached her himself in acting and drama, lavishing on her his long experience. When he finished with her, she had perfect elocution and an impressive artistic range. Predictably, Pygmalion-like, he fell in love with his creation and they married when she was fifteen.

The marriage cost 'Eid his religion since she was a Moslem and he a Copt.

How 'Eid felt about the liaison between Rushdi and her newly acquired 'mobile bank' (as she, somewhat callously, described her rich patron in an interview) is impossible to know. He was much older than Rushdi, of course, and knew that however much she respected him as an artist and trusted him as teacher and friend, she had married him primarily to further her career. She admitted once that she had never been really in love, that her passion for theatre had engrossed her totally, leaving no room for any other passion. One tends to believe her. She seems to have regarded men as useful props that enhanced her performance, and Adru'i was no exception. 'Eid must have realized this. Eventually, however, as tongues began to wag, creating a malicious din, he was forced to make the difficult decision of divorcing her for both their sakes. But their friendship emerged from the crisis unscathed and their professional partnership continued until 1934 when the sponsor withdrew and the company finally went bust. The valedictory performance was *Salomé*, played by Rushdi (who else?) and directed by 'Eid.

Rushdi's company was not the only one to go bankrupt in the lean thirties. It was a period of real crisis for the theatre and most troupes were disbanded. There was suddenly a glut of out-of-work actors. To provide them with employment, the government founded the first Egyptian national theatre company; but Rushdi, too independent to be run by anybody but herself, did not join it and turned her talents to the silver screen. Her association with the celluloid world had started as early as 1923 when she produced, wrote and directed a two-hour silent movie called *Marriage* in which she starred with Mahmoud El-Meligi. Her first talking movie was *Faji'a Fawq al-Haram* (*A Tragedy at the Top of the Pyramid*) in 1926, and her last was *Da'uni A'ish* (*Let Me Live*) in 1955.

In betweem, she did 14 films of which the most important and memorable is *Al-'Azimah* (*Will Power*). During the shooting, she married the film's director Kamal Selim; but the marriage was short and turbulent due to Selim's violent, unreasonable jealousy. They broke up and she went back to 'Eid to resume the only stable and enduring relationship in her life. Their theatrical partnership, however, had come to an end. Rushdi's work in films had estranged her from the stage. Apart from a trip to Morocco in 1937-38, where she directed two plays, and a single stage appearance in an adaptation of one of Mahfouz's novels (*Bayn Al-Qasrein*) with the Free Theatre company in 1959, she stayed away from the theatre. A glamorous career had come to an end, and with it a whole way of life.

Unlike Amina Rizq, her old colleague in Ramses company, who is still very much active and around in films and on television, Rushdi could not adapt to the changing world around her, accept old age and, with it, smaller parts. Rather than play second fiddle, she opted for seclusion and led a frugal life on her measly pension from the Actors Union. The state honoured her twice, in the reigns of Nasser and Sadat, and the American *Life* magazine celebrated her achievements on four pages in 1964. But medals and magazine articles do not pay the bills. She had saved nothing, except her memories and her overriding sense of pride and dignity. When she could no longer afford a flat in Cairo she moved to Suez where she seemed to sink without a trace. She surfaced briefly in 1993 when Karam Metaweh, as head of the state-theatre organisation then, decided to honour her on The Egyptian Theatre Remembrance Day.

That night, she forgot her wrinkles and sat in her box, in a pink dress, with short, puffed sleeves, smiling and waving excitedly to everybody. It was heartening and pathetic all at once. In 1995, she was back in the news but, sadly, as a poor and aged actress who could not pay her hospital bills. It transpired that prior to her hospitalization she had been living for months in a shabby, dingy *pension* in down-town Cairo. It was shocking, scandalous, outrageous, many artists felt; they rallied round her and bought her a flat in Ma'rouf street, in what used to be the artistic downtown area. But three days after she moved into it, and after a long look at the old haunts of her youth out of her window, the magnificent Rushdi quietly slipped away. It was a peaceful, lonely death, behind the curtains; but, by God, what theatrical timing!

I was fortunate to meet Rushdi at the National theatre one month before she died, at a gathering held in her honour by the National Centre of the Egyptian Theatre. She looked shaky and fragile but deeply happy. She obviously enjoyed being surrounded by fans and admirers. I thought how cruel her lonely life in Suez must have been. But as I looked at her carefully henna-dyed hair, fully made-up face and bright green suit I found myself quizzically musing on the delightful, eternal vanity of actresses and divas. Then she started talking, retracing the past, and it felt as if she was growing younger by the minute, lightly shedding off the years as she went on. When we asked her at the end to act for us a short scene from her repertoire she paused for a few minutes, then reeled off, in a warm, full-blooded voice, eighty lines from the final scene of Ahmed Shawqi's verse drama, *The Death of Cleopatra* (which he had written especially for her), without a single error or hesitation. She held us in a spell and gave us a taste of the overpowering vitality and charisma that had enthralled her lucky audiences in the past. Looking back on that evening, I cannot help feeling that Rushdi was really then reciting her own farewell speech, not Cleopatra's.[*]

---

[*] See appendix 1 for a review of a production on her life and career.

# Age Could Never Wither Her:
## *Amina Rizq*[*] (1911-2003)

In the early afternoon of 25 February this year, a taxi drove into the courtyard of El-Tali'a theatre and pulled up in front of the wide glass doors leading to the main hall. At once, the artistic director of the theatre, Intisar Abdel-Fattah, who had been waiting on the steps otside, rushed to it, diligently manipulating a video-camera, with a crowd of stage-hands close at his tail, one of them holding a huge bouquet of flowers. Inside the cab, a frail, old woman in black, with a deeply wrinkled face and hands, looked out on the scene with hazy eyes in some amazement. The black scarf wound turban-like round her head accentuated her pallor, at the same time setting off her strong, compelling features and purposeful air. She was obviously in pain; she had fractured a knee in 1999 and had been having trouble with it since. Nevertheless, she beamed at everybody as they helped her out of the car, pushed the flowers in her direction and jostled with each other to kiss her hands. Supporting herself with a stick and leaning heavily on the arm of a hefty stage-hand, she limped up the steps and disappeared behind the glass doors. Inside, veteran director Sa'd Ardash with actor Fuad Selim were waiting for her. It was the first day of rehearsals for a revival of Ardash's 1964 Pocket theatre production of Tawfiq El-Hakim's experimental venture into the absurd, *O, Tree-Climber!*

*O, Tree Climber!* Opened on 23 April, after two months of intensive rehearsals, during which Rizq bravely battled against age and failing health. It was as if she knew it would be her swan song and

---
[*] 28 August 2003.

poured the remainder of her fast ebbing energy into it. Sadly, she could only manage 16 performances, spaced out over 25 days, before her health gave way. Sadly too, on many of the 16 nights, the auditorium was barely half full. The timing was bad, the tail-end of the season when all families start gearing up for the beginning of exams. Did she feel that her beloved audience had turned its back on her, that the times had left her behind? Mahmoud El-Hedeini speaks of the loneliness of her last years and how she left her flat in Zamalek, which overlooked the Nile, and moved to a small hotel to escape it. Was it also to escape it that she always turned up at El-Tali'a two hours before the performance to chat with the people there and inspect the stage before going to her room "to prepare," as she would say, and, perhaps, to pray for a decent house as someone once overheard her do aloud? Would the applause of large audiences have given her an extra ounce of strength to go on a little bit further or, at least, some solace and a final reassurance that theatre – the partner she had pledged her life to – had not deserted her or let her down? May be. All I am sure of is that a grand dame like Rizq deserved a far grander exit that the one she got at El-Tali'a.

On that April afternoon, however, Rizq was there in the flesh, eager to start work, and so was Ardash. "A historical moment to be recorded, the meeting of giants," Intisar shouted happily to everybody as he followed Rizq inside, plying his camera. I was tickled by the incongruity of the comparison: "giants" seemed hardly an accurate way to describe a man of nearly eighty and an ailing woman over ninety; but Intisar's childish excitement was genuine and infectious. I remembered how three years ago, on a mild night in November 1999, I experienced a similar thrill when I saw Rizq coming out of El-Tali'a's other, smaller hall next door; she was in the same homely, black get-up and also limping, but she looked elated and quite regal. It was after a performance of Abdalla El-Toukhi's *The Black Rabbit* which had brought her back to the stage after nearly a quarter of a Century. Though her part in it, that of an old, crippled woman who viciously abuses her meek daughter, was thoroughly repulsive and she executed it with faultless mastery and malicious relish, the audience loved her in it. Every night, they fllocked in hordes to the theatre, crowding the small auditorium of Salah Abdel-Sabour hall and overflowing into the corridor outside. It was a triumphant comeback which ran for two seasons, then toured in Kuwait where Rizq was received like a conqueror and showered with honours.* She was obviously happy with the enormous success of the play and grateful to director Isam El-Sayed and actress Sanaa Yunis (who played the daughter) for joining forces to seduce her back to her old love and real passion: the stage.

For years she hadn't been offered any decent stage-parts in the state theatre, or decent wages for that matter. She was also put off by the haphazard work conditions there, the lack of discipline and proper respect for directors and among colleagues, not to mention the general sloppiness and air of indifference which prevailed among technicians. In cinema and television, where the pay is better and the work less taxing, she had long been consigned to the niche of the affectionate, long-suffering, self-sacrificing, but morally strong and upright mother or granny. Though she never had any children, her warm sincerity and power of conviction in these parts were incomparable. So, the orders kept coming in, and however small the part, she rarely said no. She knew she could always work something memorable out of the smallest

---

* See Appendix 2 for a review of the play and a record of the meeting with Rizq after the performance.

parts; besides, they meant work, something she had done all her life and could never live without. They also kept her decently clothed, fed and sheltered and allowed her to put a little something on the side for a rainy day. She had seen so many famous and once fabulously rich colleagues reduced to beggars and having to live off charity. Fatma Rushdi, who had worked with her at Ramses company, was a particularly poignant example.

Nevertheless, for an actress of her wide and varied repertoire and broad talent, this stream of repetitive, marginal roles which offered no challenge and engaged only a fraction of her technical arsenal must have palled. She had started her career in drag, impersonating boys, played the 'damsel in distress' in countless melodramas as well as the romantic *vedette* in many local and foreign texts (including Shakespeare's *Romeo and Juliet* and *Othello* and Ahmed Shawqi's *Majnoun Leila*). As she matured in years, she began to tackle more complex and demanding characters, such as Anna in *Rasputin*, Cleopatra, in Ahmed Shawqi's *The Death of Cleopatra*, Gertrude, in *Hamlet*, Isis, in Tawfiq El-Hakim's play of that name, Sheherazade in both Aziz Abaza's *Shahrayar* and Ali Ahmed Bakathir's *The Secret of Sheherazade*, Shagarat Ad-Durr in Aziz Abaza's play on the life and tragic end of that great Egyptian queen and, later, in the early 1960s, the autocratic mother in Garcia Lorca's *The House of Bernarda Alba* and flighty Mme. Ranyevskaia in Chekhov's *The Cherry Orchard*. Her repetoire of roles also included the fallen woman, the seductive home-wrecker and the shrewish, domineering wife, notably in the stage version of *Bayoumi Effendi*.

In the 1970s, when the state-theatre lay in ruins, she made a few forays into the commercial sector, and though she soon became disgusted with its insipidity, cheapness, slovenly practices and view of the actor as commodity, she scored some memorable successes there. In one play in particular, *Innaha Haqan 'A'ela Muhtaramah* (It's a Truly Respectable Family), with star comedians Fuad El-Muhandis and Shwikar, she revealed what a wonderful knack for comedy she had and led some to declare that her talent for comedy was far superiour to that of many a seasoned professional comedian. Other comic parts followed, and in all of them she strictly avoided exaggeration and physical gimmicks; however funny the situation or absurd the lines she had to say, she would always deliver them seriously, with a straight face, and suddenly everyone would be in stitches.

The secret lay in that barely discernible hint of quizzical irony that laced her intonation and subtly coloured her general demeanour – a technique she only mastered and refined in the last stage of her career. It was a far cry from the old sensational, heavily melodramatic and declamatory style she had learnt in Ramses company and used in her early plays and movies. Curiously, the master who had drilled her into this way of acting when she first joined his Ramses company as an apprentice in 1923 had himself displayed in the later phase of his career a marked comic bent and a more technically sophisticated approach to acting. Wouldn't it be a horrendous irony if despite their pioneering role and great achievements in the field of serious drama both Rizq and her life-long mentor, Yusef Wahbi, were best remembered in the future for their comic parts? As Faten Hamama's hilarious mother in Dawood Abdel-Sayed's memorable film, *Ard El-Ahlam* (Dreamland) or the scatty, eccentric old woman in the recent television serial, *Opera*, opposite Yehya El-Fakharani, Rizq is pure joy to watch, and so is Wahbi as the hen-pecked husband in the film version of *Bayoumi Effendi* or the incorrigible, old philanderer in *Isha'it Hob* (Love Rumour).

Some historians have argued that Rizq's fanatical loyalty to Wahbi, which took the form of a monopoly contract, giving him exclusive control of her acting career both in theatre and cinema for many years, was ultimately detrimental. Had she been exposed to other influences and different directors and acting methods, the argument goes, her performance, whether on stage or the screen, would have gained in terms of subtlety, variety, depth and refinement at an earlier stage and the full scope of her talent would have been better exploited. Rizq invariably rejected this argument, even became angry if someone dared mention it in her presence. For her, Wahbi was almost a sacrosanct figure and she always spoke of him with a veneration approaching idolatry. Whether she ever loved him as a woman loves a man, no one will ever know. Not that she wasn't repeatedly asked. Every time, however, she would laugh off the idea and repeat the same thing: that she loved him as a father, teacher and benefactor and owed him an infinite debt of gratitude.

She was just a slip of a girl, in her early teens, when she turned up at his office in the Ramses company one evening and asked to become an actress. With her was a young aunt, Amina Mohamed, only a few years her senior and equally stage-struck. For a year, the two girls had secretly frequented the small theatres and music halls of Rod El-Farag, where Rizq's family had moved from Tanta[*] after the death of her

---

[*] A large town in the middle of the Nile Delta.

father, and wanted to go on the stage. Despite violent family opposition, they ultimately got their way and joined Wahbi's company, thanks to his active, personal intercession and the attractive salary he offered his two new proteges.

Provincial, ignorant and very green, Rizq learnt everything from him, not only about acting, but how to dress, walk and talk, and he was always kind, protective and very supportive. How could she not feel indebted to such a man or not stand by him in times of crisis? When the company ran into serious financial trouble in the mid 1930s and had to vacate the theatre for failing to pay the rent, many members deserted, joining the newly founded National Egyptian company. Though by now famous and very much sought after by theatre and film directors, Rizq was not one of them. It wasn't until the company was finally dismantled in 1944 that she joined her former colleagues at the National. But even then, whenever Wahbi could put together enough money to stage a few revivals from the company's repetoire for a short season, as he did in 1947, 1957, 1960, 1969 and 1970, he could always count on Rizq promptly dropping everything and turning up. And when the state television decided to record 23 of his plays in the summer of 1960, she was there as his leading lady.

But if she did not love him, why didn't she get married? She was on the verge of doing it twice, she told an interviewer in 1995: once during a spell of extreme depression, induced by sheer exhaustion; the other, under strong family pressure. In both cases, however, the prospective spouse insisted that she quit acting, stay at home and live as a dependent. She couldn't simply do it. She was "besotted" with acting and could not imagine living away from the stage; besides, she had been her own mistress for far too long and could not tolerate the idea of someone running her life for her. It was after breaking the second engagement that she decided to dedicate herself undividedly to her art and "become married to the stage," as she liked to put it.

It was to renew her bond with the stage that she insisted on going through with *Black Rabbit* against the strict orders of her doctors when halfway through the rehearsals she injured her knee. It was also to renew this bong that, three years later, in the autumn of 2002, she allowed Isam El-Sayed once more the honour of directing her in another play, *The One Thousand and Second Night*[*], also by Abdalla El-Toukhi, but this time at Al-Hanager centre. On the opening night, after the performance, Huda Wasfi, as head of the centre, held an elegant ceremony in Rizq's honour to mark the 78th anniversary of her first appearance on stage, as Dimitrev in *Rasputin*, in October, 1924. Seventy-eight years later, *O, Tree Climber!* was to prove her last. Between the two, she performed hundreds of parts, on stage and radio, in cinema and television, building a massive, glorious heritage over the years and gathering many laurels.

---

[*] See Appendix 3 for a review of her performance in that play.

# A White Flame:
## *Sanaa Gamil*\* (1930-2003)

Elegance was the hallmark of Sanaa Gamil as an actress and a woman. Off stage or the screen she was always dressed to the nines and more often than not in white. She seemed to favour this colour, or rather, non-colour, perhaps because its neutrality at once offset and softened the impact of her forceful presence and overpowering personality, or may be because it did not overshadow the natural beauty of the exquisite fabrics and delicately-embriodered lace she favoured. The first time I met her in the early 1980s, it was at a small dinner party in a posh hotel, hosted by the late dramatist Nehad Gad to discuss a project for a one-woman play (which, sadly, never materialized). She wore a fluffy, snow-white fur wrap which seemed in perfect harmony with her polished, aristocratic voice, the plate of pink smoked salmon and the glass of sparkling white wine she ordered.

I was not a little undaunted by such perfection of appearance and deportment which seemed somewhat 'unnatural' or too good to be true. The sense of awe deepened as the evening wore on and she warmed to the subject of the meeting. I came to the conclusion that she was the most uncompromisingly honest person I had ever met and that such honesty, outside the realm of acting or work, was not necessarily a virtue. But then, it was a working session and so, she spoke her mind openly, candidly, in a sharp, clear, unwavering manner, with a faint touch of impatient asperity, as if in a hurry to get straight to the point.

---

\* 26 December, 2003.

She never minced her words or made the effort to soften their sharp edges and it was obvious that though she might have had a heart of gold and a warm, affectionate nature, she was definitely short-tempered.

It occurred to me then that her elegance, impetuosity, together with her fluent French, traces of which remained discernible in her intonation till the end, were perhaps what had made her a perfect cast in such parts as Magdelon in Moliere's *The Affected Ladies* (in the early 1950s), the princess in Alfred Farag's *The Fall of A Pharaoh* (1957), Raqiqa Hanem, the Pasha's Wife, in No'man Ashour's *The People Upstairs* (1958), and the eponymous heroine in both Tawfiq El-Hakim's *Shams El-Nehar* (1965) and *Sheherazade* (1966). But Gamil had also acted the witty, crafty maid, Toinette, and the humble servant, Claude, in Moliere's *The Hypochondriac* and *The Miser* at the beginning of her career, and was successfully cast as the unprepossessing, impoverished and hardworking spinster twice when she was still only a little over thirty and by all reports an attractive woman. The first was in 1959, in *A House of Glass*, loosely adapted from one of Jean Cocteau's plays (it is not certain which), then as Gamalat, in Mikhail Roman's *Smoke*, in 1962, one year after she had scooped the best supporting actress award at the Moscow film festival with a similar role, as Nefisah, in Salah Abu Seif's memorable film version of Naguib Mahfouz's famous novel *A Beginning and an End*.

In other parts too – as Ragaa', in No'man Ashour's *The Female Sex* (1960), Lady Macbeth, in a production by Hamdi Geith in 1963, the woman, in Anis Mansour's full-length two-hander, *The Neighbourhood*, Samia, in Tawfiq El-Hakim's *The Fate of A Cockroach* (1966), the mercurial, multi-faceted, constantly changing

Nunu, in Yusef Idris's *Terrestrial Farce* (also 1966), Serafina, the nervous, sexually-frustrated widow and mother of a teenage girl in Ezzat El-Amir's adaptation of Tennessee Williams' *The Rose Tattoo*, retitled *The Lion Tattoo* (1972), the narcissistic, egotistical Awatef, in Rashad Rushdi's *The Light of Darkness*, 1971, and Alice, in Gamil Rateb's stage production of Strindberg's *The Dance of Death*, performed in French and Arabic in Cairo and Paris in 1977 — Sanaa Gamil brought to life many variations on the character of the wife and mother, ranging from the loving and cheerful, the humble and downtrodden, the flighty and feather-brained, the weak and nervously vascillating, the selfish, greedy and grasping, the strong-willed, obstinate and possessive, the pushy and nagging, the shrewish and domineering, down to the viciously vindictive and downright murderous.

In her last memorable stage appearance at the Opera house, in Mohamed Subhi's production of Friedrich Durrenmatt's *The Visit*, opposite her friend and soul mate Gamil Rateb as Alfred III, she seemed to draw inspiration from all her former stage parts. As the aged, seven-times married, infirm and vulgar Claire Zachanassian, who nurses a lethal thirst for revenge and still carries within her the pain of the young woman who was cruelly spurned by her lover, denied justice by the court, ostracized and hounded out of home by the villagers, she brought together different aspects of all the women she had impersonated before and wove them in a taut, seamless, and finely-detailed performance, alternately vulgar and pathetic, abrasive and tender, shocking and poignant, but always riveting and unfailingly mesmeric.

Eight years after *The Visit*, precisely last year, I had the chance to see her once more off stage; it was in Maadi, in a small but select gathering of theatre people, intellectuals and artists, at the literary salon of Lotus Abdel Karim and this time I found the courage not only to shake her hands but also to give her a big hug and kiss her on both cheeks. The occasion, as the invitation card mentioned, was "to honour the rich and lasting achievements of the great and gifted Sanaa Gamil" – or, rather, Thurayya, as she was christened by her father, Yusef Attallah, in Mallawi (a small town in Menya) in 1930.

Little did Mr. Attallah realize when he gave her this auspicious name (which means a lamp or chandelier) that he was intuitively reading the future. He could not have known, indeed would have been deeply offended if anyone had told him that his little girl whom he promptly consigned to the care of nuns to learn French, sound morals and etiquette and prepare for the leisured life of a gracious wife to a well-to-do husband, would escape to Cairo in her teens, illicitly join the Acting Institute recently founded by Zaki Tulaymat, take up acting while still a student under a new name – which nevertheless carried the same meaning (light) as the old one, live to make this meaning come true and become a veritable beacon to all aspiring actresses.

It was a daring risk the young Thurayya took and one doubts if she could have sustained it had not the Acting Institute in those days made the wise decision to pay female students a generous monthly allowance by way of encouragement and to help them survive since most of them were boycotted by their families. Veteran actress Samiha Ayoub mentions it was six pounds, the equivalent of what a respectable civil servant usually got in those days. The strength of mind, independence of spirit and determination which characterized the young Thurayya were carefully preserved and jealously guarded by the older Sanaa and she gave them new confirmation when at the age of thirty she met at a party the man who was to become her life-long husband, closest friend and sole love, writer and journalist Louis Grace. Trusting to her intuition, she rushed headlong, refusing to play the coy mistress, and made to him what amounted to a proposal. As he was leaving the party, which took place at her flat downtown, she accompanied him to the door and asked him if he had three half piasters on him. He was taken aback and befuddled, he remembers (she was by then a star at the National theatre and earning a good income); he fumbled in his pockets, coming up with two whole piasters which he offered to her. She quizzically smiled as she said: "Make sure you use them to phone me up tomorrow."

Though Sanaa Gamil was awarded the Order of Arts and Sciences by Nasser in 1969 and the Order of Arts by Sadat in 1976, Lotus Abdel Karim thought she merited more honours and held this small gathering at her *salon* to confer upon her a special medal in her capacity as founder and editor-in-chief of the literary magazine *Shumoo'* (Candles). As if not to disappoint me, Gamil, once more, came in a beautiful white dress with a long lace jacket embroidered with small pearls. And though obviously weak and ailing, she looked as elegant, proud and refined as ever. Her wit, scathing sense of humour and ironic turn of mind were also unimpaired. As she spoke her thanks in a tremulous voice, in Arabic, with the same distinctive French intonation which miraculously disappeared in acting, I found myself pondering once more this paradox, or "invention", as comedian Fuad El-Muhandis prefers to describe her, called Sanaa Gamil.

As a person, she could switch from chic French to the authentically pure southern (Sa'idi or Upper Egyptian) dialect in almost the same breath, enjoy smoked salmon and the most traditional southern dishes with the same relish, be fiery, rash and impetuous one minute and gentle and profoundly sedate and wise the next, strike you as a bundle of turbulent emotions one moment, then suddenly tense up and harden like an obstinate, impervious rock – a soft, cuddly kitten who could become a tigress at a moment's notice.

No less of a paradox as an actress, whether on radio, television, the stage or screen, she was at once a mistress of comedy and tragedy, playing both with the same zest, flair and competence and holding her grounds against the paragons in both fields. Like a champion tennis player, again Fuad El-Muhandis's description, she could fence and parry with stunning ease and in all the thrilling, delightful matches she played opposite comedians of the calibre of El-Muhandis, Abdel Moneim Madbouli, or Sayed Radi, or tragedians, like Amina Rizq, she never missed a ball, often serving smash-hits. Whatever she did, she approached with great fear and trepidation, studied with humility and care, then threw herself into with passionate abandon, alacrity and dedication, handled it with integrity and unwavering sincerity and lavished on it her vast store of technical and human experience. Though a craftswoman of the first order, her technique remains illusive, like a deeply buried secret, only discernible by the intense white flames it gives off and keeps feeding.

The last time I saw her was in the final ceremony of the CIFET last September, when she was honoured by the festival, drawing from her fans a fervent homage of loud cheering and tempestuous applause that lasted a full five minutes. And she was again in white, as elegant, distant, bewitching and elusive as ever. A true artistic aristocrat. Her frailty, however, left no one in doubt as to the state of her health and made many in the audience cry. Playwright Fatheya El-Assal who sat next to me whispered bitterly: this should have come earlier. Comparing her to the actresses of her generation who surrounded her after the ceremony, I suddenly saw why, on and off stage, she had inspired in me so much love and awe and why she was so special and also so frail.

Like an exposed power conductor, a naked, electric wire with not a shred of insulation, she responded immediately, spontaneously, ardently to life and the demands of her art, never sparing herself and shunning all protective shields. That is why her acting was always imbued with a such a sense of urgency, why she could play the fluffy kitten, the evil, rapacious female, the ugly spinster, the poor victim, the dangerous wild-cat and the clown with the ring of truth never missing, why one never noticed her physical attributes, or stopped to consider whether she was pretty, plain, beautiful (in the sense in which Anna Maniani is) or simply attractive — as if she were a disembodied spirit. Was this why her physical presence in real life seemed so disturbingly unreal, like a cunning and convenient fabrication, and why in acting her body seemed to melt and recreate itself in the image of the character and its feelings? Was this her secret? A tempestuous flow, momentarily arrested in the semblance of a cool, smooth, perfectly even, bright surface for a brief snapshot, only to dissolve afterwards and revert to its original tumultuous liquid state?

Like a pearl-fisher, with every part she took on, she had to sink her body to reach the hidden treasures and only surfaced to deliver them and sink again. Finally, the pearl-fisher became weary, cracked under the strain and went to rest, leaving behind the treasures of a lifetime of ceaseless toil. May Sanaa rest in peace: Technically, her acting had a cool, smooth, unblemished surface; its impact however was that of burning ice.

# Dancing Into the Twilight:
## *Farida Fahmi*[*]

In 1946, Hassan Fahmi, a lecturer at the Cairo university faculty of engineering, and his British wife, a fashion-designer whom he had married during his studies in Britain, sent their little daughter Farida, one of two, at the age of six to a private school to receive lessons in ballet and dancing, side by side with her regular schooling. This was not such an uncommon thing to do as it may seem now. Institutions of this kind, which also provided training in music and other artistic skills, were numerous in the 1930s and 1940s and were usually run by expatriate artists. Their customers came almost exclusively from other expatriate families, the shifting foreign community in Egypt, and Egyptian aristocratic or socially privileged families who adopted the western way of life and its modes and mores. In most cases, the reason for sending little girls to such schools was not to train them for a prospective profession; indeed, that was rarely the motive, particularly in the case of Egyptian families. Rather, dancing lessons were regarded as part of a programme to equip a future debutante with the necessary social accomplishments which would give her an edge on her peers in the marriage market.

In the case of little Farida though, those early lessons in ballet and other forms of dancing which continued over many years were to change her life and dramatically alter the course, concept, and social and moral status of oriental dancing and with it the image of the female Egyptian dancer.

---

[*] 21 October, 1999.

In 1957, Farida, still at school preparing for university, took part, perhaps by way of an escapade, in a grand national musical work of operatic proportions, produced by the state, and intended as a celebration of the triumph of the Egyptian people over the tripartite aggression of 1956. *Ya Leil Ya 'Ein* (a phrase which traditionally forms the prelude of all Egyptian *Mawwals* or ballads, and which in that musical provided the names of the hero and heroine) was an instant success; it achieved immense popularity with the public, the critics and, more significantly, the regime. The press described it as the first genuinely Egyptian opera and it was sent on tour to China and Russia, performing in Moscow and Peking among other cities.

Farida got part of the acclaim and was recognized as a budding dancer of unusual talent and immense promise. She was dark, slim, tall and willowy, with typical Egyptian features of the kind you come across in the paintings of Mahmoud Sa'id. And she danced with the grace and lightness of a nymph, seeming like an airy presence while leaving a very vivid impression on the senses. She seemed to have a natural gift for sinking her corporeality so completely into the movement that she became purely the dance while building up the abstract lines of the choreographic design into an ineffable poetic metaphor.

In the limelight, with all the acclaim and touring, it was a heady experience for 17 year old Farida, but also a kind of self-discovery. Her passion for dancing had continued to grow over the years, but *Ya Leil* was the catalyst which transformed it into a committment and a career. The following year, 1958, she decided to team up with the Rida brothers (Ali and Mahmoud) whom she already knew and who were in the process of setting up their own popular and folk dance troupe. It was a sensational decision which made the headlines in many of the arts pages in newspapers and magazines. For the first time ever, an educated young woman from a good family – with a father from academia at the head – was voluntarily embracing what had long been regarded as an immoral, degrading profession to which females were only driven by poverty and dire need.

It was universally believed then (perhaps is still now) that no respectable woman of whatever means would willingly stoop to this, the most demeaning form of public entertainment. Indeed, it was not unusual then, as many old movies testify, to hear oriental dancers contumeliously dismissed as *Ghawazi* – a word of controversial date and origin, but which denoted in the early 19th century (according to Edward Lane in his *Modern Egyptians*) dancing-girls who "perform unveiled, in the public streets, even to amuse the rabble." The force of the social and moral stigma that had long attached to the profession is eloquently manifested by Mohamed Ali's decree to exile all *Ghawazi* to Upper Egypt in the middle of the 19$^{th}$ century.

Acting was different: the founding of Ramses company by Yusef Wahbi, a member of the aristocrasy and the son of a Pasha, in 1923, the establishment of the National Egyptian Company for Acting in 1935 by the government, together with the insistently didactic view of theatre as a school for morals – fiercely blazoned by the critics of the first half of the 20$^{th}$ century as the only criterion – had made acting less of a social risk for females by the time Farida was born. Add to this that acting in those days was heavily vocal, with a lot of posturing and gesticulating but minimal physical contact, and did not involve any of the wiggling and wriggling, not to mention the extensive baring of the body that traditional oriental dancing required.

But perhaps Farida would not have been able to make her daring decision had she not had Hassan Fahmi for a father. He was a genuinely enlightened man, with a real respect for the arts, and with progressive views which he, unlike many of his generation, did not flinch from carrying out whatever the consequences. He stood behind Farida every step of the way, steadfastly defending her decision in the papers and firmly announcing that his daughter would go to university and continue her education until, as he hoped, she got a Ph.D. "When people see a dancer with a doctorate, perhaps they will begin to respect oriental dancing as an art," he once said. The remark caused a lot of satirical mirth at the time and triggered many jokes; but Farida did join the English Department of Cairo University in 1963, at the height of a brilliant and fiercely active career, graduating in 1967 without flunking a single year, then got a postgraduate diploma from Ein Shams University in 1971, and later, a masters in fine arts (M.F.A.) from the University of California in 1988.

Hassan Fahmi's active support extended to the Rida brothers and their burgeoning dance troupe: he blessed the marriage of his two daughters – Farida and Wadida – to Ali and Mahmoud respectively, wielded his influence to secure the theatre of the Engineers Union in Ramses street for the troupe's first season in 1960, and later, as dean of the Cinema Institute, gave them valuable assistance with their movie projects, all of which were directed by Ali Rida. Another invaluable asset for the new company was composer Ali Ismail who worked closely with Mahmoud Rida, the company's choreographer and lead dancer. Together, with creative contributions from Farida, the female lead, and her husband who managed the company, they started a new tradition in Egyptian dancing.

Using material from daily life – the movements and gestures of ordinary people, and drawing on the rich and diverse local traditions of dancing in different parts of Egypt, as well as on the various contributions, innovations and refinements introduced by such leading and original oriental dancers as Badi'a Masabni, Taheya Carioca, and Samia Gamal (all of whom sought the expertise of foreign dance-masters), they evolved strikingly fresh and authentic kinetic rhythms, patterns and combinations. Sometimes, to provide a programme of dances with structure or give it a dramatic form, they would use a thin narrative line to string the items together – usually a journey or a quest. In this, they were perhaps inspired by a well-known formula popularized by composer and singer Farid Al-Atrash in several of his films. In his short 'movie operettas', which usually came near or at the end of the film, Al-Atrash, as the lead singer, would embark on some kind of quest which involves wandering through several Arab countries and different parts of Egypt, displaying their characteristic dialects, music and dancing in refined or adulterated forms. Of the troupe's works which used this or other narrative formulae, the most memorable were *The Ring of the Anklet, Wafaa Al-Nil* (the annual festival of the Nile inundation), and *Ali Papa and the Forty Thieves*, based on the *Arabian Nights*.

In these, and several other works, many on patriotic themes, popular dancing of whatever variety, even *Ghawazi* dancing, was unearthed, researched and rid of its crudities, without severing its vital links with its origins, or sacrificing its invigorating sensuality and primitive exuberance. Whatever foreign serums were injected into the choreography, and this was done in carefully controlled doses, became part of its main blood stream which was then infused with poetic meaning, contemporary relevance and expressive energy. Through this process of pruning, blending and grafting, oriental dancing was reborn as a thoroughly Egyptian art, embedded in the body language and movement vocabulary of daily life, and eloquently expressive of Egyptians, their cultural richness and variety, their temperament and states of mind. Equally important in an Islamic society was the rehabilitation of dancing as a joyous celebration of life, history and the national identity, as well as of the human body in all its glorious vitality and sad transience.

The sixties were triumphant years for the Rida troupe: they produced their best work, were at the peak of their popularity at home, and often got rave reviews when they toured abroad. Invariably, Farida was singled out for special accolades, the highest of which was given in the French press. And yet, as early as 1963, the company began to lose momentum, and this coincided with – was perhaps caused by – its loss of independence. That year, due to deep financial difficulties, the troupe agreed to become one of the state-owned companies. And although the Rida brothers stipulated full control and no interference, artistic or otherwise, clashes and conflicts were inevitable. There was also strong competition from a new grand-scale national dance troupe created by the ministry of culture on the model set up by Farida and the Rida brothers but with Russian choreographers and coaches. Mahmoud Rida had acquired his training with European companies; and what with Farida's British mother and English education, the group was suspiciously regarded as pro-western. In those days the tide of socialism was at its height, and with it the influence of the Soviet Union in many spheres including culture and the arts. One therefore suspects a degree of bias in the government's treatment of both companies, at least in terms of funds and facilities.

As the years went by, the Rida Dance Troupe became one of several of its kind, spread over the country, and all funded, controlled and administered by the ministry of culture. The troupe struggled on through the seventies, trying to guard its individuality and independent identity and to salvage something of its former glory. But in 1983, Farida, disheartened, or simply tired (she was 43 then), left for the States and spent the next five years there documenting and analyzing the artistic development of Mahmoud Rida's choreography; it was the subject of her M.F.A. thesis.

She rejoined the company in 1988, but this time only as a costume-designer, a talent she inherited from her mother and cultivated during her years as dancer. Two years later, she was appointed manager and artistic director of the company but resigned the post in 1992, leaving the company. Mahmoud Rida too gave up dancing, restricting himself to managing the company, and choreographing and directing its shows.

The company still goes on, and is currently performing its latest work, *A Heart in the Junkyard*, at the Balloon theatre. But without the posters and billboards you could easily attribute it to any of the many popular dance troupes who perform there. With the withdrawal of Farida and Mahmoud from the scene, the company was virtually dead. Those who have not seen its earlier work and watch it today side by side with other popular dance troupes would be quite at a loss how to explain its prestigious artistic status and the size of its reputation. Apart from one dance, in which the traditional Egyptian wooden slipper (*qubqab*) is manipulated to create a local version of tap-dancing and initiate a musical dialogue with the live orchestra, the choreography in *A Heart* comes across as anaemic and dated. I searched hard for signs of the troupe's former effervescence, exhilarating freshness, lightness of touch and sparkling joy in the dance and could only find a few faint traces here and there.

Even the thin and by now quite hackneyed story-line was carelessly stitched, leaving many silly and ridiculous gaps. A fisherman goes to sea, is abducted and bewitched by a nymph or a mermaid (the costumes are vague) and deserts his sweetheart upon being released and coming back to the shore. In despair, the sweetheart gives away her heart to a rag-and-bone trader. When the fisherman suddenly recovers from the spell (how, nobody knows), he repents and sets out on a journey which takes him to the countryside, to Upper Egypt, to the desert, and again to the bottom of the sea, to recover the lost heart. He never finds it; nevertheless, he is united in marriage with his beloved and the story ends happily after a dancing match between the mermaid and the bride which the bride wins. Don't ask me how she can still love the fisherman without a heart. Even fairy stories have a kind of logic.

This does not mean that *A Heart* is not worth seeing. It is. It offers decent, relaxing entertainment with well-trained, competent dancers, some excellent singers, a reasonable score, played live (itself a treat in theatre nowadays) and efficient scenery with occasional clever manipulation of sheets of flimsy cloth to create the effect of waves. But gone ... gone is the magic.

# The Frog Prince:
## *Adel Imam**

Adel Imam is a super clown, and also a very different one. He has never donned the clown's characteristic motley, nor adopted his make-up and traditional routines. His broad bony face, his rugged but fascinatingly mobile features and his rich store of varied vocal tonalities are his only tools and props. He needs no tumbles, no slapstick or knockabout farce. It is enough for him to turn his head and look quizzically at the audience in the middle of a conversation with another character to send them falling off their seats with laughter. One glance can communicate many contradictory messages; and even when completely still, with his eyes closed, the subtle, almost imperceptible workings of the muscles of his face and his expressive posture are discernible. Suddenly, he flashes a froggy smile, from ear to ear, while blinking his eyes rapidly. The impact, unfailingly, is side-splitting. Imam also juggles with his voice and can perform impressive acrobatic vocal feats. He can swing suddenly, in a split second, from a deep, confidential bass to a high-pitched alto yelp. In terms of physical movement, he is carefully economical; this accounts for the exhilarating funniness of his abrupt, well-orchestrated outbursts of energy.

With a monkey-face, a froggy smile, a slight, narrow frame with the hint of a paunch, it is amazing the amount of charisma and sex-appeal this figure commands. We do not usually associate sexual attractiveness with clowns; but Imam is an exception. The fact that he is not only a great comedian, but also a great, all-round actor, may

---

* 4 November, 1993.

account for this paradox. The provenance of his art is multiple and ambiguous; he seems to belong to some special world that intersects the realms of comedy, tragedy and romance, and combines them. This, perhaps, explains why he was able to upgrade the clown to the status of *jeune premier*. Over the years, in many films, television serials and plays, he promoted the image of the down-trodden, marginalized, passive and somewhat cowardly underdog as romantic hero – a kind of battered and vulgarized Robin Hood. But however, tragic or romantic he became (sometimes in a Rambo-like fashion), the froggy grin of the clown was never absent and it never failed to communicate that exhilarating sense of liberation that only the parodic antics of clowns can generate. Whatever he did, Imam was always able to wring laughter out of the heart of suffering and remained firmly linked to the community of wise fools and sagacious, albeit outrageous, mockers.

Having said that, I must hasten to add that until recently my attitude, and that of some other meticulous (carping, some would say) critics, to Imam's indubitably great talent had been vexingly ambivalent. He seemed to purchase his success at an exorbitant price: the work of art itself, no less. His monumental egotism left him in complete disregard for the integrity of form. He would rampage into a play, walk all over his fellow actors, ransack the plot, disrupt the rhythm and walk away with a triumphant performance, having laid the work to ruin. The verdict on his work in the theatre, therefore, was always mixed: 'a great performance in a sprawling, ramshackle work' about sums it up.

In cinema and television, of course, he was more controlled because of the nature of the medium, and the *monteur* or 'editor' was always at hand to repair whatever damage he wreaked. In the theatre, however, there was no controlling his ad-libbing; he would, not infrequently, interrupt the action for half an hour or more to quiz, hector, or banter his fellow actors without prior agreement,. or to provide a satirical, running commentary on topical matters. It was like watching an interesting one-man show, but not a proper play. And when you consider that his plays usually ran into three and a half hours, you can imagine the sense of futility, boredom and inane rambling that, inevitably, made a part of the evening.

Luckily, however, this rare comedian seems to be embarking on a new phase. It needed the firm hand of a young and gifted film-director to keep him in line. In *The Leader*, Sherif Arafa created a taut, fast-flowing production. Strangely, or rather logically, this helped to foreground Adel Imam's genuis even more; his charismatic presence drew added charm from the overall elegant directorial design. Director Sherif Arafa enlisted the talents of stage-designer Nihad Bahgat and musician Moudi Imam and together they translated the sequence of events in the plot into a series of rapid, eloquent and aesthetically pleasing scenes, rich in nuances, intelligent lighting and sound effects. Every detail was carefully studied, with not a single colour or tone or costume out of harmony with the rest. The sets were sumptuous or shabby as the plot required, but whether they were realistic or expressionistic, whether they represented a suite in a presidential palace or a poor quarter of Cairo, they were uniformly of a sophisticated beauty.

Nothing here of the haphazard sloppiness, the vulgar tattiness, the slatternly cheapness of the run-of-the-mill commercial theatre product. Upholding the famous American motto that "it takes money to make money," producer Samir Khafagi, the founder and head of United Artists, roped in the best artists, on the market, spared no cost, and spent lavishly on the show. It must have cost him a pretty penny, and that 'pretty penny' could not have come easy since had just invested most of his capital in giving Cairo, sorely starved of theatres, a new playhouse.

At this new playhouse, El-Muttahidin's Haram Theatre, *The Leader* opened three weeks ago, the new building symbolically marking the transition in Imam's career to a more responsible, more controlled and maturer stage. The story of the beggar who becomes king for one night is neither new nor unfamiliar; it originates in the *Arabian Nights* and has since inspired many works, the most famous of which are Naguib El-Rihani's *Salama Fi Kheir* (*Salam is Well and Thriving*) and the Syrian Sa'dalla Wannus's *Al-Malik huwa Al-Malik* (*The King is King*). Imam declares that the story haunted him for a long time; maybe he wanted to pitch his own performance against El-Rihani's, the great predecessor to whom he is frequently compared. Farouk Sabri's new treatment partakes of both the political intent of Wannus's version and El-Rihani's comedy-of-errors formula.

Zeinhum, a simple, passive, struggling hack-actor, with no interest in politics whatsoever, is suddenly drawn into the tangled web of high-power politics simply because he happens to be the spit image of the president. The despot, who rules over some unspecified third-world country(though the sets firmly locate the action in present-day Egypt, especially in Zeinhum's roof-top accommodation scenes), suddenly and untimely dies before signing an important treaty granting some foreign superpower the right to dump nuclear waste on his soil. The military junta who stand to gain fat commissions from that foreign power, to be spirited away immediately into Swiss bank-accounts, pounce on the unlucky, naive Zeinhum for a substitute. Once the treaty is signed, he is to be summarily despatched to the other world.

In the presidential palace, Zeinhum becomes completely engulfed in a sea of sensual pleasures. Sex here, with its trappings of beautiful girls in revealing costumes, obscene jokes, play on words and scatological innuendoes, is, for once, put to good effective dramatic use. It becomes an indispensable functional element and is, therefore, neither shocking nor disgusting. The benighted consciousness of the lackadaisical Zeinhum, however, is suddenly jolted into a sudden awakening when he goes out one day to open a new hospital and is showered with bullets in an assassination attempt. With the help of one attractive female member of the opposition, he comes to understand why, as the president, he was targeted, and how his going to open the hospital was nothing but a theatrical charade and a publicity stunt.

In a series of delightful gimmicks and ruses, he manages not only to avoid signing the treaty but also to set the members of the junta at each others' throats. He does not, however, emerge triumphant, nor does he succeed in dismantling the gargantuan gorgonian military dictatorial system. In the monologue which he delivers as he prepares to leave the palace before the finale, he acknowledges the inability of any one individual to change any system single-handed. The romantic age of heroism, of individual saviours and wandering knights in shining armour has departed, never to return. Wistfully, he admits that whatever he has done will ultimately change nothing. Another appointed leader will sign the treaty and the pollution of dictatorship and nuclear waste will overtake us all in third world countries unless — and this is the theme of the musical finale — we make a concerted effort to achieve real democracy and a multi-party system.

This level-headed conclusion which does not seek comfort in romantic heroism or facile optimism, together with the meticulously interwoven choreographed musical scenes (an integral part of the show and no mere addenda) and the superbly controlled performance of Adel Imam, and the no less impressive performance of Ahmed Rateb, make this play a triumph of art and artifice, an elegant musical comedy well worth seeing. In the space of three weeks, it has already proved a box-office blockbuster. And if you go, watch out for the inept and good-natured apprentice-burglar, hitched up on a drainpipe and constantly falling off. He threads a delightful and telling motif throughout the play.

# Rising From the Ashes:
## *Mohamed Khayri**

I had nearly forgotten there was an actor called Mohamed Khayri. The once highly promising handsome young man who made his debut in cinema as the male lead opposite Magda in the 1970s in *Life Is But A Moment* was not destined to make it as a star. He stumbled through a few more major and supporting roles in films then seemed to diminish, recede to the background, and pale out of sight. He continued to act, and one occasionally came across his voice in radio plays or serials, or caught fleeting glimpses of him on stage in tawdry commercial plays or on television in small, lacklustre parts in trashy soap operas. But few registered his presence, or continued to remember him once his image went off the small screen or he withdrew off stage. He seemed to have become that most unfortunate of things: an eminently forgettable figure.

When I heard he was playing the leading part in a revival of Mikhail Roman's earliest play, *Smoke*, it took me sometime to put a face to the name. When I did, I groaned in a mixture of dismay and disbelief. Hamdi, the central character in the play, is an extremely complex and often baffling character who needs a really tough actor to cope with his wide range of diverse, often contradictory emotions, his constant vacillation and sudden, extreme changes of mood. Combining aspects of the typical romantic and existentialist heroes, Hamdi is at once an anarchist, a nihilist, a dreamer, an escapist, a social rebel, a poet, an egoist, a warm, affectionate man, a selfish brute, a weakling who blames his failure on fate, society and others, and a man of integrity and

---

* 4 Mach 1999.

determination who takes full responsibility for his tragedy and recognizes his suffering as part of the human condition. Nauseated by the dullness and triviality of his existence and the ugliness, vulgarity and injustice of reality, and haunted and tormented by a vague, strong (almost incestuous) attraction to his elder sister, Gamalat, whom he at once adores and deeply resents, this almost pathologically sensitive character takes refuge in drugs. *Hashish* and opium become his solace, and his way of literally giving life the slip.

The play traces graphically his gradual deterioration and relentless descent into the darkest pit of despair — to the lowest depths of physical degeneration, social degradation and moral disintegration. When he hits rock bottom, the shock proves a turning point. He begins his arduous ascent towards the light alone, rejecting the help of his family and refusing medical assistance. Taking his destiny into his hands at last, he sets out alone on a perilous journey 'through hell' – as he says – to achieve his salvation. The play ends at the beginning of the journey and we are denied the comfort of knowing how it ended.

This character was too deep for Khayri, I thought, and felt almost certain he would drown in it. When the play was first performed in 1962 at the National, Salah El-Sa'dani, a brilliant actor even then, played the part, giving a highly acclaimed performance. But, even so, the production, directed by Kamal Yaseen, failed to please the leading critic at the time, Lewis Awad, who referred to the play disparagingly in an article in *Al-Ahram* as *"that thing* called *Al-Dukhan (Smoke)."* Another source of worry was Khayri's age. In his late fifties, wasn't he a little too old for the part? He may be still handsome, but Hamdi is not suppose to be more than 35 in the play, or 40 at the outside limit.

I grew even more sceptical about the production when I heard it was that vexing thing: an adaptation. Adaptation is all very well when it is a question of turning a novel or a story into a drama. But I am always wary of plays billed as adaptations of other plays, especially when those 'other plays' are by dramatists of acknowledged talent and technical expertise. In nine cases out of ten, the word 'adaptation' is used as a camouflage term for messing up an original drama, simplifying and diluting it in the name of making it more relevant, up-to-date and accessible, or stuffing it with topical references and issues, as well as songs and dances, until it becomes overblown and bursts at the seams, or simply subverting its artistic meaning and direction. In the past, when writers plagiarized foreign plays, they either kept the fact a secret, trusting to the ignorance of the public, or honestly admitted it, calling their versions 'adaptations'. The practice continued in the 1960s but remained confined to foreign drama, and only comedies for that matter, like *Topaz* and *My Fair Lady*. Since the 1980s, however, it has spread like a plague, infecting all plays, local and foreign, so that it has become nearly, if not quite impossible to see a play – even at the National – the way it was originally written.

More worrying still was the choice of venue. I could not see Roman's three-act realistic drama, with its two detailed, realistic sets (one representing Hamdi's lower middle-class family home, and the other, a cave – the hideout of drug-dealers – in the Muqattam hills) could be squeezed, together with an audience, into the cramped space of the Abdel-Rehim El-Zurqani Hall at the National. What did the adaptation do to make this possible? And how will Khayri, who is tall and well- built, manage his part in that tiny space.

I went to see the play mainly to satisfy my curiosity on those points and did not expect to have an enjoyable, let alone memorable experience. As it turned out, those who went to scoff stayed to applaud. Within ten minutes of the beginning, I became wholly engrossed in Khayri's performance. Standing in a soft pool of bluish light, he seemed like a man emerging from the shadows of the valley of death, and staring around in utter bewilderment and growing panic at a world at once hostile and engimatic. The tiny, semi-circular performance space, fenced in with panels representing an old, dilapidated wall, with a forbidding stone gate in the middle, intensified the sense of constriction, becoming a concrete stage metaphor for isolation, alienation, and imprisonment. Gazing at us with those tortured eyes – the eyes of a haunted man, a wounded animal, a man tormented beyond human endurance by shame, guilt and self-loathing – he communicated to us vividly, almost physically, his terror, making us wonder what horrors lay behind that mysterious door. At this moment, it did not matter what age he was or how he looked; he was ageless and could be a baby just out of the womb, or an old man gazing into his gaping grave. The actor had bared his soul to us, or grown so physically transparent that we could see through his body and look directly into his soul.

The intense immediacy and urgency of Khayri's performance was truly stunning. He had obviously made a thorough study of the nature and causes of addiction, its phases, physical and mental effects, and the psychology of the addict. It is possible also that he resorted to intimate observation of addicts. But he did not stop at giving us just an accurate and meticulously detailed portrait of a man enslaved by drugs, but went on to transform this image, through a masterful management and control of voice and body language, into a powerful theatrical metaphor for the human condition, and a metaphoric embodiment of the tragic sense of life. Actors often speak of "a once in a lifetime performance", and for Khayri, this is it. Facing a really physically and mentally taxing part, perhaps for the first time, his latent acting talent rose to the challenge and burst forth with unbounded energy and devotion.

But this could not have happened had *Smoke* been given the way Roman wrote it. For once I find an adaptation that does not alter or spoil the original text, but, rather, improves it substantially. Guided by Roman's extensive experimentation with dramatic form in his subsequent plays, and his frequent recourse to expressionism and other non-realistic modes, Nagwa Abdel Rahman shrewdly realized that rather than help the drama along, the realistic mode and framework chosen by Roman (perhaps because it was fashionable at the time or to dress his shocking theme in familiar robes) hampered its progress, obstructed its psychological flow, obfuscated its central themes, landed it into many contradictions, and cluttered it with many unnecessary and tedious details. With a firm, unfaltering hand, she dismantled the outer realistic frame, removed the paraphernalia and trappings of realism, promptly excised the characters and scenes which she regarded as mere deadwood obstructing the course of the drama.

In her hands, *Smoke*, became, as perhaps Roman had intended it, a taut, intense psychological drama, with clear metaphysical reverberations and a tragic, cathartic impact. The setting of the drama and its stage becomes Hamdi's mind which expands under the pressure of his agony to encompass heaven and hell, and the space inbetween, and embrace the existential suffering of all humanity. To achieve this,

Nagwa changed the original, chronological order of the scenes, replacing it with a stream-of-consciousness state of flux, shaped by subtle resemblances, echoes, repetition, contrast and association. The characters and events materialized as Hamdi remembered them, flowing in and out as if borne on waves. The world of the play became an internal space inhabited by memories and shadows which merged, separated and overlapped – a world that embodies in its spatio-temporal fluidity the tragic elements of life and the ineluctable existential loneliness of wo/man.

With such a beautifully distilled, stirring script, and Khayri's magnificent performance, the director, Asim Ra'fat, would have been well-advised to adopt the principle of austerity and do without the offensively banal songs which fitfully intruded on the show, vexing both the actors and audience, the strange contortionist movements and inexplicable postures he foisted on the actors, and many of the props which were distracting and completely redundant. However, no amount of directorial impurities could have spoilt my enjoyment of such a superb brand of 'Smoke'.

# Bright and Brittle:
## *Aida Fahmi**

That performers, however competent, personable, dedicated and even charismatic, can never hope to achieve fame, let alone make a living by the stage alone, is one of saddest and most depressing facts of our contemporary theatrical life in Egypt. Even when employed by the state-owned theatre companies (originally launched to guard actors against penury and unemployment), and supposing they manage somehow to make do with the measly stipend dispensed to them at the end of every month, actors can never be sure of regularly getting work, or ever having the chance to realize their full potential. The lucky ones make it in television, though usually in small, supporting roles – mostly stock characters. The unlucky, or those who lack the knack for self-promotion, or are unwilling to compromise their art, end up at home, frustrated and despodent, and progressively lose shape and grow fatter as the seasons go by without a single order.

"Where are you my dear girl?" I exclaimed at Aida Fahmi as we warmly embraced in the foyer of Al-Hanager at the end of *Optical Illusion* where she played the lead. I had not seen her for years and had really missed her on stage. "At home, where else?" she answered laughing and I was glad to see once more that sunny, infectious smile of hers I so well remembered from the past. She had put on weight, but seemed to have lost none of her former youthful zest or joyous, irrepresible high spirits. "I am always there for the asking," she added,

---

* 19 April 2001.

and I vaguely registered something forced in the gaiety – a faint trace of bitterness, perhaps? A hint of disillusionment?

In the early 1980s, Aida Fahmi seemed confidently set for a brilliant career in theatre. She was young, enormously attractive, with a chubby, baby face, small, twinkling eyes and a mischievous smile which disarmed everybody and endeared her to all; and, on stage, her striking presence, impressive figure, vocal range and technical skills (amply demonstrated in such varied parts as the bereaved, aged Maurya in J.M. Synge's *Riders to the Sea*, the gay, voluptuous Polly Peachum in Brecht's *The Threepenny Opera*, and the vengeful, embittered Electra in Euripides's eponymous play) led many to view her as the rightful successor and natural heiress apparent of the great 1960s' National theatre star (and Fahmi's professed model) Samiha Ayoub.

Then the Itinerant theatre troupe (a branch of the Youth Theatre), of which Fahmi was a member, fell foul of the theatre administration, purportedly for financial and managerial reasons, but more likely, as one suspects, on account of its political outspokenness; it was summarily dismantled in 1987, only four years (the most fruitful in Fahmi's career) after it was founded. Since then, Fahmi's stage-appearances have been distressingly few and far between and at times she seemed to completely pale out of sight. I expected that, like many of her peers, she would drift into television. But somehow, and despite the ceaseless demand for new faces imposed by the torrential flow of television soap operas, Fahmi rarely appears on the small screen. The reason, I guess, is that she belongs to that tribe of performers who, like opera signers, are intrinsically, intensely theatrical and larger-than-life, and can only come into their own on a stage, before a live audience; put them in a studio and they immediately wilt and droop or burst the walls around them.

I went to see *Optical Illusion* with no expectations except one – to enjoy Fahmi's acting, and for that I was willing to forgive anything. As it turned out, there was little to forgive – at least where Amir Salama's text and Amr Dawwara's direction and choice of cast were concerned. Salama's play, though it involves six dramatis personae in a realistic, contemporary setting, is essentially a one-woman psychological drama set on the borderline between illusion and reality, fact and fantasy — an arid mental desert haunted by phantoms and infested with mirages.

The set (by Fadi Fukeih) represented a garish waiting-room in some famous psychiatrist's clinic. On a red plush sofa, a glamorous woman sits, obviously waiting, smoking a cigarette and leafing through a glossy magazine. When Zaher, the handsome and strangely refined clinic attendant, ushers in a dishevelled, tense and harrassed-looking, middle-aged bank clerk, called Hamdi, in the company of his sick, teenage daughter, Maggy, who at once recognizes the woman as Magda Saleh, the famous film, stage and TV star, the drama begins. The star who acts neurotically, speaks disjointedly and aggressively flirts with the dazzled, dazed and drooling new comer, fitfully confusing him with her ex-husband and father of her aborted child, who was also called Hamdi, turns out to be not a patient, but the psychiatrist's wife.

Through a series of poignant revelations and harrowing confrontations, punctuated with a rehearsal of a planned elopement with the attendant, two attempted seductions – one real, the other imaginary – and two suicides (which dispose of both Hamdi and his daughter), we gradually discover that the woman at the centre of it all is no more than a 'ghost', as her husband describes her, an empty shell, the mere husk of a person. Having bartered her real identity, her true love, marriage and motherhood for a plethora of screen images and stage characters, the bright star has become the victim of a chronic sense of guilt and spiritual emptiness. We see her in the last stages of her mental disintegration, just before she completely loses her grip on reality. Like a drowning person, she desperately reaches out for anything she can hold on to and this makes her dangerous – like a voracious, treacherous vortex that engulfs and devours anyone who comes near her. She drives her first husband into loneliness and exile, her second to drink and unethical conduct with his patients, kills her unborn baby, and unwittingly destroys a family, causing the death of two innocent people.

In the hands of a less skilled craftsman, such stuff would have made the play a prime candidate for melodrama – and corny, gory melodrama at that. What saves *Optical Illusion* is the subtle, intriguing suggestion that, perhaps, despite the realistic veneer, the characters we are seeing do not exist at all except in the mind of the star – are only projections of her splintered psyche and deranged imagination; in other words, optical illusions. The suggestion is enforced by the end which links up with the opening scene, bracketing off what happens inbetween and tentatively consigning it to the realms of fantasy, memory and day-dreaming. The beginning shows the star waiting for her husband to finish attending to his patients; the end shows the couple still in the clinic, one hour later, preparing to go out to celebrate their wedding anniversary with other celebrities. But just as they are about to leave, the woman slumps lifelessly down in a chair and stares stonily into space. Whether anything really happened during that hour remains a teasing question.

As the pervasive, overriding, all-engrossing consciousness of the play, Aida Fahmi gave a virtuoso performance, displaying to the full her amazing emotional mobility and control of voice. Her startling change of mood and tonal shifts were uncanny; but every word and gesture had a faint hysterical edge and communicated an ominous sense of danger, of growing strain, of something about to snap. But to give her best, Fahmi needed good, experienced actors in the supporting roles and she was lucky that director Amr Dawwara could rope in such fine talents as Mokhles El-Beheiri, in the part of the second husband, Mahmoud Mas'oud as the hapless bank clerk, and Ashraf Tulba as the clinic's attendant. They were a great asset to both Fahmi and the show as a whole; and though Karima El-Hifnawi and the young, sylph-like Nisreen made brief appearances in very small parts (as the bank clerk's wife and daughter), they were fully in tune with the rest of the cast. The only discordant note and source of irritation in the play was the salmon pink, pistachio and red velvet set. But with Aida Fahmi on stage at long last, and in such a rich, complex part, to complain of this would seem like ungracious carping and wilful, gratuitous nitpicking.

# II

# Directors

# Ripeness is All:
## *Karam Metaweh*[*] (1933-1996)

As a person Metaweh never left you much choice: you either loved or hated him. But whichever way you felt, you could not help acknowledging, however begrudgingly, the overwhelming presence of the man, the colourful vividness of his character and his powerful charm. He walked and moved with the sinuous grace of a cat and even in a subdued mood and very sombrely dressed, he made everyone around look drab in comparison. Like an aristocrat among plebeians, he made people feel slightly uneasy and apprehensive, and the elusive hint of quizzical irony that always tinged his voice could prove disconcerting.

He was theatrical all right, but always in an elegant, subtle way; you could never imagine him gushing, violent or sentimental. Romantic, yes — in a distant, pensive way, but never mushy. In life, as well as in the theatre, he was a master of mood and intonation. If he chose, he could charm the light out of your eyes; but the next moment, as likely as not, he could switch off with a sudden, sardonic remark and turn away, shrugging his shoulders. I often wondered if he was not constantly playing a game, indulging a passion for acting that his reputation and achievement as director never allowed full scope. He had the makings of a star — good looks, charisma and sex-appeal; and he made a good beginning on the screen, playing the lead in a film on the life of the famous singer and composer Sayed Darwish. But he never made it as a film star; possibly he was far too theatrical, and the camera

---
[*] 12 December 1996.

does not take kindly to that, or possibly he was far too involved in the theatre to give much time to films. My own guess is that his personality, sharp intelligence and artistic perspicacity were in the end responsible for making film producers and directors shy away from him. He was difficult to approach, let alone lead and direct. With only 15 film appearances, did it rankle to see so many of his students, of far lesser talent than his, far outstrip him?

Ironically, for most ordinary Egyptians and Arabs nowadays, and particularly for those who were not around in the sixties, Metaweh is known primarily, and often solely, as a TV actor. A series of romantic roles in soap operas in recent years established him as a household name and a clear favourite with the ladies. After one such soap opera, *Bardees* (the name of the heroine), it was common to hear it jokingly said that half the women of Egypt were in love with Karam Metaweh; and the remark carried more than a grain of credibility. It sounded flattering and doubtlessly gave its object some pleasure: it is no mean achievement for a man in his middle fifties to be seen as the romantic hero of soap opera *par excellence*, especially when he had been regarded as unfit for the part when young. But there was something shamefully reductive in all this. Television may have brought Metaweh fame and possible fortune; but it is not for his parts on the small screen that he is going to be remembered. To know the full size and value of the man, one has to look to his career in the theatre.

Born in 1933, Metaweh combined the study of law and theatre as an undergraduate, matriculating in both in 1956 and 1957 consecutively. In those years it was good to be young, talented, ambitious and of the Left. Ideologically, Metaweh was a socialist revolutionary and an enthusiastic supporter of the Nasserite regime. (He remained a socialist till the end, albeit a disillusioned one.) He embraced the revolutionary project proposed by Nasser wholeheartedly and with it the notion of the politically committed artist. Like the majority of leading intellectuals then, he believed that the primary function of the arts, and of the theatre in particular, was to revolutionise society and heighten social consciousness. Fortunately for Metaweh, the cultural policy of the regime then aimed at developing a new, revolutionary intellectual leadership and generously invested in scholarships abroad. Within a couple of years of graduation, Metaweh found himself in Italy, at the age of 25, studying theatre. If this had not happened, would his talent have survived the stifling grip of dogma? One wonders.

Six years in Italy corrected the balance between art and ideology. He came back in 1964 as revolutionary as ever, but he had gained a deep and wide experience of a large variety of theatre and developed an intense, meticulous consciousness of the aesthetic side of performance. He plunged headlong into work, creating a veritable furor with his production of Yusef Idris' *Al-Farafeer* (The Underlings). For the second time, he had proved the favourite of fortune. It was a glorious start and gave him just the right kind of push at the right time. It was a stroke of luck his stumbling upon Idris at the time. After three plays, Idris had tired of realism and spent some time mulling over the question of dramatic form. In three articles, published in 1964, he explored the possibility of arriving at an authentically Arab theatrical mode based on the traditional forms of popular entertainment. To hone his ideas and by way of experimenting, he wrote *Al-Farafeer*. The experiment paid off and blazed a trail for a whole theatrical trend that is still with us today.

As the director of Idris' pioneering work, Metaweh was caught up in the blaze and it carried him, instantly, to the top. The production process was predictably tempestuous: both the playwright and director were young, willful, confident and proud. Soon, they were at loggerheads, each insisting he knew better. What kept them from splitting was their deep appreciation of each other's talent. In the battle of wills, Metaweh won, omitting the whole of the third act from the text and producing a much more taut and less rambling play. The version that played at the National and was subsequently authorised for printing by Idris himself is a credit to Metaweh's artistic and critical sense.

Despite their much-publicised differences and disputes over *Al-Farafeer*, Idris and Metaweh were essentially similar in their attitude to theatre and shared a common artistic and ideological ground. Both were keen experimenters and innovators and, at the same time, quite paradoxically, passionate fundamentalists, intent on discovering an authentic identity for theatre rooted in the Egyptian soil. In the case of Metaweh, this double pursuit of authenticity and innovation became evident when he took over the management of the Pocket Theatre on 13th July, 1964. In a series of productions, he brought the latest trends and techniques in directing to bear on texts ranging from Aeschylus' *Agamemnon*, Goldoni's *Servant of Two Masters* and Chekhov's *Cherry Orchard*, to an epic poem by the contemporary Egyptian poet Naguib Sorour, based on a popular, peasant love story, and a peasant drama by Shawqi Abdel-Hakim, based on a popular ballad.

In these productions, as well as in his overall managerial policy, whether as head of the Pocket Theatre, or the National, or the State-theatre sector, Metaweh established, perhaps for the first time in Egypt, the complete authority of the director over the performance and his right to interfere with the text. The notion of the theatre director as creative artist, rather than as executor of the author's will, was born then, starting the long feud between dramatists and directors. In these productions, too, Metaweh developed and clarified his distinctive directorial style, which is his great achievement. It is an elusive style that shuns gimmickry, decoration and any gratuitous details, and concentrates instead on powerful lines, clear contours and sculptured formations. On the visual level, his productions carry a kind of dignity that is rare in the Egyptian theatre, and their austere simplicity is invariably imbued with a sense of urgency and pent-up passion. But the visual simplicity is always countered by aural richness, and I have never known an Egyptian director to expend as much care and attention on the sound and vocal texture of his productions as Metaweh did.

The last years of Metaweh's life were turbulent. Politically, and on the public level, he was at peace with the regime at last; whether out of conviction or cynical lassitude is anybody's guess. The time of active, violent dissent which had driven him out of the country for years had gone by and he had settled into a kind of mellow melancholy underneath a theatrical mask of cynical, languorous nonchalance. But, on the personal level, and perhaps as a sign of deep, spiritual malaise, there were storms and upheavals: after an exemplary marriage that lasted nearly 25 years and was regarded by many as a marriage of true minds, he suddenly divorced his wife, actress Sohair El-Murshidi, fell in love and quickly remarried, and one month before he died he was single again, with only his sister beside his sick bed. I only hope that in his final hours he could draw some consolation from remembering those glorious days in the sixties.

# Exit Another Unsung Hero:
## *Salama Hassan*\* (1945-1997)

The National was packed though it was a Wednesday, the theatre's day off. Some of the faces I knew very well, and the rest were all vaguely familiar. They belonged to people I had met at different times during my trips to various regional theatrical pockets up and down the country. Most of them have never had the chance to tread the boards of the National (and, perhaps, never will); and for some, it was the first time they had ever set foot inside that venerable building. Some brought along their wives and children, and somehow, the presence of children among so many sad grown-ups made the sadness more bearable. The shock and bitterness I had felt upon hearing of the untimely death of Salama Hassan at the age of 52, just as he was becoming recognised as one of the leading directors and shaping forces in regional theatre, had not abated; but as I shook hands with poet Fouad Hajaj, Hassan's closest friend and life-long comrade and ally, my rage against the unfairness of life suddenly evaporated, giving way to a warm, comforting sense of continuity, of human solidarity, and to renewed faith in the value of what such unknown theatre-fighters like Hassan have done and will continue to do to bring theatre to the poor and culturally deprived masses all over the Nile Valley.

The occasion had the air of a family reunion, a celebration: people had gathered not to mourn but to remember and pay tribute to the heroic struggle of a courageous, self-made man who had let neither illness nor poverty stand in the way of his talent. The story of that struggle was

---

\*   15 May 1997

told from the stage that evening in a series of biographical, dramatic sketches written by Fouad Hajaj and directed by Abbas Ahmed, another close friend and associate of Hassan and a veteran fighter in the cause of regional theatre. As it unfolded, many of those present could recognise themselves in that story.

Hassan's background was remarkably inauspicious and his childhood was particularly harsh and deprived. He came into the world on 25 December, 1945 with no social or economic advantages whatsoever: his father was a poor field hand in a tiny, insignificant village called Shober, in the middle of the Delta, and the atmosphere in the humble household was marred from his birth by constant domestic strife. When Hassan was six, his parents broke up and the father moved to another village, in another governorate, where he settled down, found work and remarried. Two years later, Hassan was forced to leave his home, his mother and the village school (where he had spent only a year and a half) to join his father in Bahteem. There, his new life took on a shape closely resembling that of a typical Dickensian boy-hero. He never went back to school and his father and step-mother put him to work in a factory for making matches where he stayed for the next six years.

The dangerous work, the long hours and the unhealthy conditions soon took their toll on the boy's health. It was during those years that he, like millions of other Egyptians, contracted bilharzia — that endemic Egyptian curse that has claimed the lives of a long line of Egyptian writers, scholars, intellectuals and artists, including the singer Abdel-Halim Hafez.

The chances of someone in Hassan's situation then getting properly cured were very slim. He got the treatment available to the poor and the result was that the schistosomes or flukes continued to eat into his liver until they caused his death last month. The cancer and terrible headaches he suffered from during the last 12 years of his life were also part of the legacy of those early years. But those long grim and drab years at the match factory were not without moments of hope and comfort. It was during that period that Hassan discovered the magic of acting through the movies and developed an overpowering passion for it. This sparked off a long process of self-education which started at the age of 14 and continued until the last day of his life.

The break came when he left the matches factory to join the work force of a large textile company and could find the time to attend the literacy classes available at the branch of the National Union (Al-Itihad Al-Qawmi) in Bahteem. Soon, he was a voracious reader, devouring books on all aspects of theatre, and when he felt he was ready, he formed a theatre troupe out of the company's workers and set about directing his first play. When the textile company suddenly withdrew its support for the project (either because it, or the chosen play, was too daring), and closed the rehearsal area, Hassan was not discouraged. He announced that his group would compete in the national youth centres' theatre contest and found a sympathetic headmaster who agreed to host the production in his school.

The costs of the production were paid out of the pockets of the group who also constructed the stage (with a bedsheet for a curtain) while the rehearsals took place at Hassan's home. The troupe survived and thrived against great odds and performed five more plays over the next eight years; and all the time its leader and members were doing their eight-hour work shift at the factory each day and spending most of their earnings on their productions. Indeed, one evening (23 May 1977), a member of the group called Hassan Uqda sold the gold bracelets of his wife (kept for a rainy day) when the company ran short of money and could not pay for the Bahteem movie house they had rented for three nights.

From his modest, but brave beginning in Bahteem, Salama Hassan went on to direct more than 24 productions in various cultural palaces, homes and centres all over the country (winning several regional prizes), set up and train many amateur theatre groups, and establish for himself a reputation not only as an artist of great integrity and a gifted, hardworking director, but also as a man of great strength and determination and as a gentle, affectionate, warm and unassuming human being. The evening held in his memory by his friends, students and admirers last Wednesday at the National, together with the small commemorative book about his life and work issued by the Cultural Palaces Organisation were fitting tributes not only to Salama Hassan, but to all the unknown soldiers and forgotten heroes of the regional theatre, to that army of men and women who work so hard and give so much in return for so little in terms of fame, wealth, and critical recognition.

# Sa'd Ardash and Brecht*

In his brilliant book, *Brecht: A Choice of Evils*, Martin Esslin astutely observes that while Brecht intended his theatre to be popular and address the masses and the working classes, he ironically ended up as the pet of the elite theatrical circles and "the daily coinage of dramatic critics." This actually describes the situation in the 1960s, when the first Brecht play ever performed in Egypt burst upon the scene. *The Exception and the Rule* (translated by Abdel Ghaffar Mekkawi and directed by Farouk El-Dimirdash) was presented in 1963 at the Pocket theatre, which catered for a small, elitist audience. It would have been even more of an irony had Brecht received his Egyptian premiere at the Royal Automobile Club, the Pocket theatre's former home. Luckily (for Brecht), it had burnt down a few months earlier. The company's new home, at the Pharaonic Garden theatre in Zamalek, where the play was presented, was equally small, but, at least, it was not forbiddingly smart, and overlooked the Nile to boot. (The building still stands but is used at present as a TV studio.)

The person responsible for bringing Brecht to Egypt and popularizing his theories is director Sa'd Ardash (1924-    ). He first came across Brecht's works in 1961 while on a scholarship in Italy. "I felt I had stumbled upon a treasure," he says describing the impact of the discovery; "his theatre seemed perfectly suited to the needs of the moment and the national goals of the 1952 revolution." An inveterate socialist, with a deep-seated belief in the political role of theatre, Ardash still maintains that Brecht's epic theatre, with its pronounced socialist

---

* 11 June 1998.

slant, is the most appropriate theatrical mode for the third world "where people are still fighting for their freedom and rights."

It was at Ardash's instigation that El-Dimirdash undertook the production of *The Exception and the Rule* in 1963 (it opened in December the same year). At the time, Ardash was the artistic director of the Pocket theatre (which he was instrumental in founding) and had launched the company, a year earlier, with the Arab premiere of Beckett's *Endgame*, which he directed (in a tragic vein); it was followed by the Arab premiere of Ionesco's *The Chairs*, directed by Mohammed Abdel Aziz. Two absurd plays in a row seemed a curious choice for a socialist and committed artist, and the word "turncoat" was whispered. But then, Ardash's commitment was not of the bigoted, narrow-minded type. "When I came back from Italy," he says, "there were two things I wanted to do: to introduce new trends in world theatre by way of experiment through the Pocket theatre, and to try out the epic theatre to test its potential and appeal to the audience here."

— Why *The Exception and the Rule* in particular? "It is short and straightforward; for an audience bred on traditional realistic drama, it would not be too shocking or taxing, we thought."

But social realism, which had established itself on the Egyptian stage (at the hands of No'man Ashour and Saadeddin Wahba, among others) as the theatrical mode most favoured by the public since the beginning of the 1950s, put up a good fight. It was not until three years later, after Brecht's theories had been translated, explicated, controverted and propagated (and quoted in support of a multitude of contradictory causes), that another Brecht play found its way to the

Egyptian stage – precisely to the stage of the Pocket theatre – and two years after Ardash had resigned his post as its head.

*Drums in the Night* (translated by Abdel Rahman Badawi, to whom we owe most of our Arabic versions of Brecht's plays, and directed by Kamal Eid) appeared in 1966, and gave Egyptian critics and audiences a different glimpse and taste of Brechian writing. The play, which was written in 1918, belongs to Brecht's early nihilistic, anarchic stage: the critics could relax, take a holiday from ideological criticism and dwell on the novelty of its expressionistic techniques. The production was like "a big stone thrown into stagnant waters," Ardash says. Its must have been wonderful not having to talk about propaganda and didacticism, but about theatre art and expressionism.

Ardash was quick to capitalize on the success of *Drums*; within a few months he was staging Abdel Rahman Badawi's translation of *The Good Soul of Setzuan (Der Gute Mensch von Sezuan)*, with that redoubtable actress, Samiha Ayoub, in the lead, and with a prestigious artistic crew which included Salah Jahin (lyrics), Sayed Mekkawi (music), Awatef Abdel Karim (sets) and Layla Gad (choreography). Reading through the old, 1966 numbers of the *Theatre Magazine*, one is infected with the same sense of urgency and excitement that marked the reception of this play so long ago.

Brecht's precepts, Ardash admits, were not adhered to to the letter. "I was aware I was dealing with an Egyptian audience, well-tuned to realism." So, as one gathers from the reviews (I did not see the production), Brecht's "Alienation-Effect", particularly where acting and stage-design were concerned, became the focus of critical controversy. As Farouk Abdel Wahab, who translated Brecht's *A Short Organum for*

*Theatre* and published it the same year, says: "Critics and academics squabbled over the method of acting chosen by Ardash: was it too emotional? Too naturalistic? Or simply "demonstrational" as Brecht had advised?"

Brecht's essays on acting were diligently consulted by some and glibly quoted, parrot-fashion, by others; but since no one at the time had actually seen a production by Brecht or had first-hand experience of how this new technique of acting works, the controversy could not be resolved. Lewis Awad, however, a prestigious, influencial critic, highly commended the show and, more importantly, the audience loved it. Unlike the two former Brecht plays, *The Good Soul* was presented at the much larger and more popular (now defunct) El-Hakim theatre in Emadeddin Street.

By that time, the influence of Brecht's theories had already begun to manifest itself in the work of Egyptian directors and playwrights, such as Karam Metaweh, Alfred Farag and Naguib Sorour. In 1965, Farag's epic play *Suliman Al-Halabi* was followed by Sorour's *Yasin and Baheya*, a long, narrative poem, staged by Metaweh. The same year, Ardash gave Sophocles's *Antigone* a pronouncedly Brechtian production and two years later, Mahmud Diab, who had displayed in his earlier plays a marked bias for the kind of drama evolved by the Italian Pirandello (another important influence on Egyptian drama in the 1960s), switched loyalties and joined Brecht's disciples with his magnum opus *Bab Al-Futuh (Conquerors' Gate)* which Ardash directed. The production, however, fell through midway on account of the Censor's intervention. It wasn't until 1977 that Ardash able to give it a public performance. In 1971, another semi-Brechtian play by a leading playwright – Yusef Idris's *El-Mukhatateen* – mounted by Ardash was banned on the opening night. None of these works, and many more, would have been possible without Brecht's liberating influence and Ardash's championing of it. Of his generation of playwrights, Farag says: "Realism had begun to pall on us, and we had two alternatives: the theatre of the absurd and Brecht's epic theatre. We opted for the latter. We needed a theatre that could grapple with our social problems and such hot political issues as capitalism, fascism, colonialism and justice. We rejected the absurd on ideological and artistic grounds. Brecht offered us a new theatrical formula that enabled us, without direct preaching or hectoring, to make the spectator adopt an attitude of inquiry and criticism and, in Brecht's words, to purge the stage and auditorium of everything magical and hypnotic."

There was also the natural affinity between the type of theatre Brecht advocated and the indigenous Egyptian forms of popular entertainment, as Ardash perceptively adds. The Egyptian temperament has a natural inclination for comedy, song and dance, and Brecht's theories sanctioned their use and made them ideologically respectable. No wonder Brecht's recipe for a popular theatre was eagerly embraced by the regional companies and has been functioning quite well up until now. For many provincial theatres, such essays as *On Unprofessional Acting, The Street Scene, Notes on the Folk Play, Theatre for Pleasure or Theatre for Instruction, The Popular and the Realistic* provided the kind of legitimation they needed and were the stuff out of which they spun their manifestos.

In 1968 Ardash wanted to give the Egyptian theatre a further, and stronger injection of Brecht; a theatre director from East Germany ("his name was Kurt Viet, if I remember correctly," Ardash says) was invited to direct *The Caucasian Chalk Circle* for the Pocket theatre. But soon enough, the German's punctilious sense of time clashed with the Egyptian lax and elastic comprehension of time; he left in a huff, and Ardash ended up directing *The Chalk Circle*.

It was not until the 1980s that another Brecht play was performed in Egypt. *Mother Courage and her Children* was premiered at the Citadel, and Ardash tells me that Layla Abu Seif's production was quiet riveting. Others whisper that she had a hard time putting up with the loud calls for prayer vociferously issued during the performance by the *mu'azzin* of the mosque nearby. I was not in Egypt at the time, and by the time I came back, Abu Seif had left for the States for good.

Nevertheless, Brecht survived: not just in Naguib Sorour's Egyptian version of *The Three-penny Opera*, rechristened *The King of Beggars (1968)*, which was readapted by poet Izzat Abdel Wahab and directed by Abdel Rahman El-Shaf'i in 1986, and re-adapted once more by Farag in his *Atwa Abu Matwa (Atwa, the Jack-Knife)*, which Ardash directed in 1995, but in a multitude of plays, including a provincial production of *He Who Says No* and *He Who Says Yes* (directed by Husam Atta for the Children's Theatre in Assyout) and, more recently, in Hani Ghanem's controversial production of *The Seven Deadly Sins* at the House of Zeinab Khatoun in 1997.

One has to admit, however, that Brecht in Egypt has been adapted almost out of recognition. What Egyptians have consciously or unconsciously chosen to forget was his insistence that moral values are historically determined. In a deeply religious country with a deep-seated hang-up about absolutes, this was, perhaps, inevitable. Rather than use humour, song and dance and ham acting to provoke a mood of critical thinking and inquiry in the audience, a plethora of provincial productions have reduced Brecht to an Islamic Communist propagandist. More importantly, his great talent as a poet is, almost always, nearly forgotten.

# Samir El-Asfouri:

## Five Takes

## *1. Flogging a Dead Horse*[*]

Some productions lack the quality of mercy, turning political protest and self-criticism into the worst form of self-flagellation. Samir El-Asfouri's current modified version of his previous triumphant musical *Honey is Honey and Onions are Onions* (at the Puppet Theatre in Ataba) is one such production. Not that one ever expects wine and roses in a work by El-Asfouri: he is notorious for his acrid cynicism and caustic humour and barbed invective is his forte.

The fact that he was the one single major theatre director to have resisted the lure of oil-soiled money and the temptation of migrating to Iraq or the Gulf during the lean seventies, hoisting the quixotic (and rather suspect) banners of political rejection, as many have done, might explain his sourness. But that is meat for a sociologist or a biographer. What concerns us here is the palpable effect the political events in the Arab world have had on the deep-seated cynicism of this brilliant director.

He was busy preparing for a new production of Eugene Ionesco's *Macbett* when the Gulf crisis hit him, snuffing whatever last flickers of hope had remained in the dark alleyways of his mind. He put the project aside. "It would look like a facile parody of Saddam; a cheap cashing in on the situation," he explained, tacking on a wry comment on the

---
[*] 5 May 1991.

National Theatre current *Macbeth* as an afterthought. (It wasn't verbal; he mumbled something under his breath accompanying it with an eloquent wave of dismissal. *Macbeth* was damned forever.)

His turbulent soul, however, wouldn't give him peace; an outlet for his rage must be found. *Honey* was close at hand and a further run was planned. It was then that he began to display worrying signs of hidden suicidal tendencies. The Gulf crisis had aggravated his already advanced state of misanthropy, and rather than Dionysius, Thanatos presided at the rehearsals. I attended one and watched in disbelief and horror a magnificent well-balanced show being slashed about and savagely mauled. The gentle satire and witty sarcasm of the original, concocted out of Bayram El-Tunsi's *Maqamat* (verse dramatic situations and anecdotes) suddenly grew claws and fangs and ripped off, tearing at everything and everybody. On the opening night, the corpse of the once vibrant musical had already rotted and the smell of decay clung to the very seats. The naughty, tantalizing hint of bawdiness that colours the typical Asfouri production here thickened and coarsened into repulsive obscenity. In the previous show, equally iconoclastic, the taste of honey was palpable despite the stinging smell of onions. The dish on offer was sweet and sour. In the modified version, nothing but the slop of kitchen sinks and the sludge of sewers is to be had.

With over ten years first-hand experience of the British theatre, five of them in the sixties, I am hardly shockable. I have gone through the horrors of Kenneth Bernard's *Dr Magico* with his cannibalistic sexual fantasies without turning a hair, and compared to that, my earlier experience of *Amédée*'s sprawling, ever-expanding corpse and the huge mushrooms sprouting between the rotting boards of his dank living room in Ionesco's play seemed like a childish game of peek-a-boo. The nausea that attacked me during *Honey is Honey*, particularly the salacious 'Arab Summit' new sequence (rendered as a series of gambling sessions, slanging matches and homosexual encounters), sprang, I suspect, from a rampant nihilism, an excruciating sense of utter futility: no logic can ever explain what has happened, the show seemed to argue, and all we can do is splash about in the muck and oil slicks left behind, hurling obscenities at everybody, like a flasher baring himself to shock the world, or a person cutting off his nose to spite his face. Apart from three or four memorable scenes salvaged from the old version, the whole was infected with this spirit of obscene self-laceration.

Coming away from the show, I, an Egyptian who once cherished the hope of Arab unity, felt violated, besmirched with mud. It was as if someone had sadistically rubbed salt into my raw wounds, as if El-Asfouri's whole purpose in reviving his once frothy and scintillating lampoon was to deal us all a deadly blow. The *Honey* has become polluted by too real a despair. Mankind cannot bear too much reality, T.S. Eliot has said. Can art?

## 2. Jangled Out of Tune[*]

Samir El-Asfouri has a knack for transforming what usually passes for vice into virtue. He has been known to unconscionably plunder whatever material comes his way, literary or otherwise, and retailor it to suit his own immediate artistic purposes, usually with stunning, if controversial, results. A prime example of this is his latest production at the Tali'a Theatre of Tom Stoppard's *Every Good Boy Deserves Favour*. The title is simply the mnemonic device used to remind music students of the names of the five lines in musical notations, using the G clef.

Stoppard's original text, "a play for actors and live orchestra", was commissioned by André Previn and played for the first time at the Royal Festival Hall on 1 July 1977, with the London Symphony Orchestra, directed by Trevor Nunn. El-Asfouri stumbled on it when it was published in translation a few months ago in the *Cairo Theatre Magazine* and it fired his imagination, all too predictably, one might add. El-Asfouri's last production, *The House of Spinsters*, yet another free adaptation, featured a mental hospital-cum-concentration-camp where all the female inmates were victims of social, sexual and political coercion. In an earlier production too, back in the 1970s, El-Asfouri dramatised Chekhov's short story, *Ward Number 6*, rechristening it *The Cell*, and transformed madness into an all embracing metaphor for a world out of joint.

---

[*] 19 August 1993.

With such a deeply-engrained fear of incarceration and such long familiarity with the metaphoric potential of insanity as a dramatic theme and visual setting, Stoppard's *Every Good Boy*, which presents madness as the scourge inflicted in totalitarian societies on dissenters and nonconformists, was bound to touch a deep chord in El-Asfouri. He commissioned a poet, Omar Nijm, to prepare a colloquial version of the text and provide some appropriate lyrics. Then he proceeded to work on this material, reforging it, so that the end result bears unmistakably his individual mark and only a faint resemblance to Stoppard's original text.

The surprising and puzzling thing is that he did this without changing Stoppard's plot, characters, settings, or central themes. He even retained a good deal of the original dialogue as well as its equivocal manipulation of the image of the orchestra. In his production, as in the text, the image stands paradoxically for both freedom and oppression, dissent and conformity.

Wherein lies the difference then? It lies neither in the basic composition nor in the individual palette of each artist — to use a helpful analogy from painting — but, rather, in their distinctive styles. Whereas Stoppard uses light and even brush-strokes to achieve a smooth polished surface, El-Asfouri tends to apply his paints thickly on the canvas with a knife, occasionally sticking on foreign and discordant bits of material. The result is a cracked, rough surface and a raw, gritty look. This rugged style has a charm all its own and bespeaks a quirky, almost Baudelairean fascination with all *fleurs du mal*.

Stoppard's live, full-size orchestra, which occupies the whole stage, leaving only three cramped acting areas, was here replaced with a down-and-out scanty oriental band encased in a huge construction of metal bars and hardly visible. When the flimsy draperies hanging down the sides of the bars were parted, they revealed not the musicians, but shadowy scenes of torture and bare, limp torsos hanging upside down. Flanking that forbidding structure which occupied the centre of the stage on either side were the cell and the psychiatrist's office, while the front stage housed the school scenes. In Stoppard's text, only two characters engage the school area: the dissident's son and the strict party-line school teacher. In El-Asfouri's, however, it was crawling with kids of all ages and on two occasions a choir-master was added.

New scenes were tacked on to the original sequence in odd places, with startling results. These occurred mostly in the second part of the production; there Stoppard's smooth and subtle transitions from school to cell to office were rudely broken up with a shot of the military dictator (the Colonel at the head of the asylum in the play) taking a bath in his boots while munching a beefburger, with a cynical song from the school-teacher in her bath robe, with a funeral procession, a children's choral song, a fashion show with a hippy announcer, a monologue about shoes, enumerating the virtues of each kind as a beating instrument, not to mention a crazy couple in evening dress who wander on and off the stage and a grotesque scene with puppets, featuring the dictator as conductor.

The intermittent intrusion of these discordant notes was meant to give the show a touch of insanity and expand the metaphor of an aberrant world even more forcefully than Stoppard does. And to this end, El-Asfouri provided a lighting-plan, seemingly crude but highly suggestive. It would have all worked beautifully had the acting matched the other ingredients. Sadly, it didn't. Abdel-Ghani Nasser gave a competent enough performance as the mad maestro. His appearance certainly helped: with his thick white hair flying in every direction and a suitably dazed and crazed look in his light blue eyes, he at once suggested Beethoven and a man who has just put his finger in an electric socket. Raouf Mustafa was insufferably sentimental as the political dissident accused of madness and his scenes with his son were particularly embarrassing. Sawsan Rabi', as the teacher, was more petulant than austere and since the role of the dissident's son was given to a teenager much taller than she is one could hardly credit her seriousness as a menace. In any case, she quickly exchanged her severe outfit for a pink flowing dress with deep slits and proceeded to prance about blithely as a fashion model. As in many Egyptian shows, the intentions were good, but the acting marred all.

# 3. The Call of the Wild*

In Egypt, our censorship moves in mysterious ways. Originally, Samir El-Asfouri's latest venture into commercial theatre was billed *Hazimni Ya Baba* (roughly: tie the scarf round my hips Daddy – with "Daddy" here used in the sense of "man"; the verb "hazzim", in this sense, has no equivalent in English and the phrase which serves as the play's title is used both literally – by belly-dancers – and figuratively to indicate a general collapse of moral values). But, a few weeks later, the reference to the patriarchal figure in "Baba", or "Pappa", had disappeared from the title, leaving a suggestive, enticing gap. The impulse to fill it with more salacious appellations than the relatively innocuous original 'Baba' is almost irresistible — especially in view of the status, fame (or notoriety?) of its leading lady, Fifi Abdou, who is the most expert and sought after belly-dancer in Egypt today.

But regardless of whether it is 'Baba' who is alloted the delicious task of tying the lucky scarf round the dancer's hips (to enhance their latent energy and wriggling powers) or some other male personality, the *spectacle* (difficult to call it a play) has already proved a smash hit — even though the holiday season has ended and most of the Arab tourists have departed. The new, rich (*nouveaux riches*?) Egyptian middle classes, conspicuous by their veiled, bejeweled women, nightly flock to the Gezira theatre (formerly Minoush) on the Nile in Manyal El-Rhoda. The men and the young people love the show, and Fifi Abdou's spectacular presence, feminine allure and seductive art leave them gasping and bright-eyed. The women mostly hate it.

---

\* December 1995.

Leaving the theatre at the relatively early hour of 1 a.m. (I had opted for the Saturday matinee which starts at 8.30 p.m.), I overheard the women's comments. They boiled down to one word, "cabaret", curtly spat out and bespeaking volumes of moral indignation. A short, stocky woman protested primly to her husband: "all the Egyptian theatres have turned into cabarets" – betraying a long familiarity with such institutions and a habit of frequenting them. By "cabarets" she meant "nightclubs" of course, as most Egyptians do when they use the word. She was not absolutely wrong and had many grounds for her complaint. But I would have sympathized with her more had she excepted some private sector shows from her sweeping condemnation, including the refreshingly honest one she had just watched, or had she used a morally innocuous term like music-hall or variety show instead of the morally-loaded cabaret. Her tone of moral uprightness made me flinch.

Indeed, whenever I go to the commercial theatre now and watch the thinly-clad dancers on stage avidly scrutinized by the many veiled women in the auditorium I experience a sensation close to nausea; more and more I become convinced that the bond between stage and auditorium in such performances is one of mutual scorn and exploitation – a sick mixture of repulsion and attraction – and that this poisonous relationship is what nourishes our commercial theatre. I keep remembering how a student of mine once told me that what ultimately decided her against the veil (which her family had been pressurizing her to wear) was the blatant hypocrisy of those who "spend most of their leisure hours watching videotapes of commercial plays, condemning their immorality while lapping them up; and all the time they derive a ghoulish satisfaction from the conviction that all those voluptuous women will burn in hell while they, they smugly believe, are heading for paradise. It does not offer a very flattering image of God. Sadly, the concept of the "slave-girl" who is denied any claim to virtue but used to entertain the rich and respectably virtuous is still deeply entrenched in our Arab cultures and would loom large in any psycho-sociological study of the dynamics that keep our commercial theatres going.

But sociology apart, *Hazimni Ya* ..., despite the ridiculous title, has proved a very good show of its kind and a very blithe and refreshingly unsentimental one at that. The flimsy plot is based on an all too familiar stock situation which features a standard Mafia-type tycoon locked in mortal conflict with an impoverished middle-class family (three brothers and one sister) over the land where the family's generations-old villa stands. On the site, he plans to erect a high-rise building. To underline this conflict and its subsequent development visually, stage-designer Nihad Bahgat provided a series of eloquent, quick-changing sets, alternately featuring the small villa and its garden beseiged and dwarfed by an awesome wall of high-rise blocks, a typical, glittering, garish night club (satirically studded all over with heart shapes) and a lavish and studiedly vulgar red interior of a courtesan's boudoir.

The plot itself holds little interest and, indeed, once the sister (Ms Abdou), a young nurse, decides that only her feminine weapons and wiles will win them the battle against the tycoon and joins a night club as a dancer (at the end of act one), the plot grinds to a standstill. What fills the subsequent two acts (and, indeed, engages a substantial portion of act one) is a series of cleverly embroidered comic sketches with a lot of punning, parody, burlesque and some highly imaginative 'stage business' – the contribution of the director, of course. My favourites are the wiring of the villa with explosives by the tycoon's stooge (Mohamed Hineidi) prior to blowing it up (he kept popping up everywhere most unexpectedly as 'the man from the telephone company'); the unexplained visit of the same stooge, in a different disguise, to the ruins of the villa carrying a water melon and the deliciously nonsensical conversation he holds with the elder brother (Hasan Husni) there; and last, but not least, the hilariously funny transvestite scene where the two younger brothers (Sherif Munir and pop singer Midhat Saleh), together with the captivatingly versatile Hineidi, dress as vamps, complete with long cigarette-holders, low-cut, slashed evening gowns and make-up, and camp it up in an exaggeratedly ludicrous manner.

Needless to say, all these sketches are completely redundant. Here, as in most commercial plays, the plot exists solely as an excuse to provide as many gags, farcical sequences, songs and dances as possible. What makes *Hazimni Ya* ... different, however, is its director's imaginative flair and his penchant for the absurd. In most of his productions he manages to project an image of a crazy, topsy-turvy world where the rules of logic and the coordinates of time and place, of cause and effect, have dangerously become frayed, if not completely broken down. The same vision exists here and acts as a unifying power, binding the diverse, disconnected elements into a semblance of artistic coherence. The same spirit of zany absurdity infected the actors as well; they seemed to revel in the game and their zest and playful high spirits communicated themselves to many members of the audience.

Teamwork among the actors was the rule of the day; none of the all-too-common attempts here by one actor to upstage another; it felt as if we were watching one big family bungling their way through life, notwithstanding Ms Abdou's overpowering presence. Indeed, El-Asfouri managed the insuperable task of containing, without curtailing, her; he gave her ample space to display her genuinely wonderful and great talent as a dancer without letting her overrun the performance or spoil its delicate balance of comedy and show-biz. An added bonus was the absence of the usual hypocritical, squelchy moral tirades which have become almost a fixed feature in the majority of commercial plays. Since the sister decided at the end (quite realistically) to keep the fruits of sin (her earnings from the night club and the fortune she wheedled out of the tycoon before denouncing him to the police), we were mercifully spared the usual, melodramatic preaching on the virtues of being poor and the stupidly facile equation of wealth with evil. Such preaching in the commercial theatre which is solely patronized by the well-to-do can be unbearably embarrassing.

With a generous budget, El-Asfouri was able to enlist the talents of composer Farouk El-Sharnoubi, stage-designer Nihad Bahgat, our by-now-familiar 'imported' troupe of excellent Russian dancers, and to pick and choose his actors. But money alone, or the contributions of those artists, could not have made this show what it is. Its life and soul is El-Asfouri's direction. Stripped of all illusions, he deserted El-Tali'a theatre, his home-base for years, and opted for a life of vagrancy in the private sector. In his vagabond's bundle, however, he did not forget to pack his tools of the trade: his magnificent talent, his tough wit and superb ironical sense, together with the debris of broken dreams and the dry husks of cherished memories. Something of each has gone into *Hazimni Ya ...*, which perhaps explains that faint shading of resigned despair one fitfully glimpses in the show despite the zest, the energy and the tinsel glitter.

# 4. A Wave of Nostalgia[*]

At the National, marriage, rather than romance, is the subject of Ahmed Shawqi's *El-Sit Huda* (Madame Huda) — one of the great poet's two attempts at writing realistic verse comedy. The play is set in Cairo, in 1890, and revolves round the numerous marriages of the title character who is the exact opposite of the traditional romantic heroine. She is a wealthy, vain old hag, thickly painted, gaudily dressed and heavily bejewelled; with no children to remind her of the reality of her age, she insists she is twenty and conducts herself accordingly. She is not without charm, however, and under this ridiculous exterior we gradually discover a warm, generous woman, with a shrewd mind, a keen sense of humour and a vast appetite for life, men and human society.

She is something of an artist too, with a rare talent for drawing verbal satirical sketches of the people around her. In our age, she would make a wonderul cartoonist. In the long opening scene, her master-scene and the best in the play, we find her talking to a neighbour, chatting about the nine husbands she married (and buried) in the course of her life, and Ahmed Shawqi exploits the scene to satirise most of the respectable professions of his day, giving us through her a series of delicious caricatures. Here, rhyme and rhythm are used to enhance the wit and humour of the character-sketches and classial Arabic loses its habitual formal tone, acquiring the flow and intonation of everyday speech.

---

[*] 30 May 1996.

Unfortunately, by the end of this scene, Ahmed Shawqi seems to lose inspiration and steam. It is not just that the following scenes lack the crisp wit, natural fluidity and pictorial vividness of the initial one; they are also flimsily connected and shabbily built. One fails to see the point of them since they neither add up to a plot nor develop the central character or any other. In one scene we are introduced to her current husband, a greedy, foul-mouthed, drunken lawyer who, like the rest of her former husbands, is only after her fortune. In another scene, we see her with some young female visitors; but though the verse here recovers something of its initial liveliness and bite, and despite a sharp dig at the traditional mode of conducting marriages in Egypt then (when prospective brides were never consulted), the scene remains largely pointless. The first act ends with Huda rushing off, in all her finery, to do some visiting herself.

Act two begins with the attempts of the drunken husband to coax her into selling her land to cover his debts; she obstinately refuses and he breaks into a violent rage. Soon enough, the scene develops into a full-blooded slap-stick farce, with both spouses chasing each other, waving sticks, and with the female neighbours pitching in to chastise the loafer and beat him off the premises. In the following scene, which brings the play to a close, we are suddenly faced with a completely new character; it is Huda's last husband — the one she married after divorcing the lawyer. More startling still, we hear that she is dead. As the surviving husband sits, talking to himself, gloating over her death and rejoicing in his good fortune, a new bunch of characters arrive: the condolers. These represent a lower order of society and professions than we have encountered so far in the play and Shawqi seizes the opportunity to satirise their callousness, avarice and hypocrisy. Finally, a messenger arrives to announce what we have suspected all along: Huda had donated all her money and land to charity. Though in her grave, she has managed to out-wit this last husband.

Obviously, as it stands, *El-Sit Huda* is more of an amusing anecdote (albeit over-long and rambling) than a proper play. Its structure is deeply flawed and lacks cohesion. But then, dramatic structure was never Shawqi's strongest point and all his serious historical verse dramas manifest this weakness in varying degrees. It shows more glaringly in this comedy because in the other plays the historical order of events gives a semblance of artistic order. In previous productions of *El-Sit Huda* (it was first performed at the National in 1940-41 with a male actor, Fuad Shafiq, in the title-role), directors, awed by Ahmed Shawqi's status as poet laureate, or 'the prince of poets' (as his contemporaries crowned him), turned a blind eye to the play's faults and never interfered with the text. Director Samir El-Asfouri, however, is made of different stuff and is rarely awed by anything. He is born with a congenital suspicion of all haloes and auras and belongs to the rebellious sixties when many socialists could mockingly dismiss the aristocratic Shawqi as 'the poet of princes'. But if Samir El-Asfouri hates pomposity in art, he detests sloppiness even more. This explains his extensive restructuring of Shawqi's comedy when the National Theatre commissioned him to direct it to mark the 60th anniversary of the company and also the opening of the Ahmed Shawqi Museum in Giza.

El-Asfouri's solutions to the formal problems of the play were both simple and ingenious. Instead of springing Huda's last husband and the news of her death at the audience in the final scene, he opened the show with the funeral, a ritual that has vast theatrical potentials which he fully exploited. In his hands, it turned into a wild pageantry, a festive, riotous carnival with equal measures of mirth and dirge, song and wailing, dole and dancing. The funeral brings most of the characters of the play together in a natural way as mourners and introduces them to the audience; it also dispels the gloom that surrounds the idea of death from the start. The will, however, is kept a secret till the end.

Having begun with the funeral, El-Asfouri had to find a way to introduce the heroine and rather than resort to the obviously indicated technique of 'flash-back', he opted for fantasy. Without changing the set (which features a huge white tomb at the back above a flight of steps) he shifts the second scene to the underworld. Huda enters in a cloud of smoke, in a white mantle, with a beautiful bunch of female spirits fluttering around her. Within five minutes, however, she is inspecting herself in many mirrors, receiving friends and callers, chattering about her husbands and generally reliving her former earthly life down to its smallest details. As likely as not, El-Asfouri seems to be saying, the other life will turn out to be a copy of this one. What a prospect.

Another major alteration made by El-Asfouri was recasting the play in the mould of a musical comedy in collaboration with composer Ali Sa'd and lyricist Gamal Bakheet. This allowed him to counterpoint classical and colloquial verse in a most entertaining way and also to counterpoint the past and present and give the show topical relevance. The huge cast (numbering over seventy), all carefully picked, included some of the best specimens of comic talent in Egypt and was led by the magnificent Aida Abdel-Aziz in the title role. She made Shawqi's Huda an unforgettable stage character — a rare combination of shrew, earth-mother and glamour-puss.

## 5. All That Glitters[*]

Normally, I am not one for musicals, least of all what passes in Egypt under that name. But, last week, I had a sudden craving for one or, to be more accurate, I longed for something blatantly, flagrantly escapist – something light, bright and fanciful, preferably, "born of an idle brain, begot of nothing but vain fantasy" and "as thin of substance as the air" (to plagiarize Mercutio). In other, less poetic words, a glitzy, frothy, razzle-dazzle farce was what I needed. The commercial theatre was indicated; where else would one be sure to find a spectacular show, gorgeous sets and costumes, jokes galore and plenty of dance and music? Lightness of touch could not be guaranteed of course – it is notoriously heavy-handed – and anything resembling wit would be a very tall order. But of idle brains, at least, there would be no shortage — that for sure.

I first considered *Iddala'i Ya Dousa (Be Coquettish Dousa)*, starring Fifi Abdou, a dancer I greatly admire. In a different mood, I could find her atavistic celebration of the human body, its sensuality and erotic energy stimulating, even invigorating – a strong antidote to sickness, death and despair. But with so many people starving and freezing up in the mountains of Afghanistan and so many corpses on the ground, I didn't want to think of bodies, alive or dead; they carried the stench of mortality. Abdou's physical presence would provide more 'substance' than I could handle at the moment, I decided. There was also Ahmed Adawiya on the cast list, I remembered – a more difficult proposition; I would have to cope, not only with his raucous, rough-

---
[*] 18 October 2001.

hewn voice, his monotonous, coarse, so-called *sha'bi* songs, but also with the painful memories of the 1967 defeat he was bound to stir. He shot to fame in those black days and his inane, cacophonous songs were pronounced (by foes and fans alike) as symptomatic of the nihilistic/cynical mood of the nation then – a true expression of its disillusionment and sense of absurdity and betrayal. No thank you, I said to myself; I had enough mental bruises as it was and did not need that on top.

*That's (Kida) OK* seemed a safe bet. Luckily, it was still running, if only two nights a week (Thursday and Friday), and had not had to close down, like many others, for lack of audiences. Its director, Samir El-Asfouri (artistic director of El-Tali'a state theatre company for over a decade before he fled the public sector to take refuge in the private one) has a penchant for whimsical humour, fanciful wit and cannot abide attitudinizing or cant of any kind. His knack for smelling out and defusing the moral pretensions of any text is rare in the commercial theatre and makes his productions refreshingly free of the usual, almost mandatory, dose of sentimentality and hypocritical preaching typical of most commercial fare. I remembered how at the end of his memorable box office hit, *Hazimni Ya Baba*, he made the heroine (Fifi Abdou), a low-paid nurse who takes up dancing in nightclubs and makes a fortune, refuse to give up her 'ill-gotten gains' and live in chaste, honorable penury, as her virtuous brother advises, robustly declaring she would be more use to herself and life rich and powerful than poor and helpless and that, unlike many respectable wealthy people, she had really worked hard for her money, literally, sweated for it. "Ask all these lovely, respectable people here," she told her sanctimonious, rosary-fingering brother, winking facetiously at the audience; "they have paid money to see Fifi dance, not retire."

Like *Hazimni*, even more so, *Kida OK*, is not something one could call a play and make any sense; it is mostly gags, puns, mimicry, badinage, physical buffoonery and wild verbal exaggerations that make the most humdrum thing appear droll, fantastic or grotesque; and, of course, a song or two for every star and lots of dancing. There is also smoke, plenty of it, billowing in thick clouds from the stage to mark the first entry of every star, accompany the dancers, or frame the mock-political-riot scenes – not to mention the sound of loud gunshots and deafening explosions which made one actor, the night I was there, wonder if he hadn't lost his way coming to the theatre and gone instead to Afghanistan. There are also flashing lights, booming speakers and lots and lots of glitter: gleaming sets, glistening props, sparkling backdrops, heavily sequined costumes, it makes you blink after a while; even the most humble character in this escapist romp, the down-at-heel peasant girl (Mona Zaki), arrives on the scene in a shiny *galabiya* that dazzles the eyes.

The story line, what I could make of it in this heady orgy of sound and colour, features a serious-minded TV writer, terribly honest but naïve (Hani Ramzi), forced by his iniquitous, unscrupulous boss who owns the TV channel (Sherif Munir) to betray his principles and turn into a cheap and vulgar (phenomenally popular and fabulously rich) *sha'bi* singer, à la Adawiya in the past or Sha'ban Abdel Rehim in the present. He yearns for his long-lost bosom friend and university-days hero (Ahmed El-Saqqa), a left-wing political activist and something of a blockbuster, who left the country when things got too hot and moved to

Paris to pursue the struggle for freedom there. Predictably, once back, the idealized hero is discovered as a frivolous, loud-mouthed, self-seeking, pleasure-loving charlatan and a bit of a thug. Interwoven into this are several love-stories, involving courting scenes, sexual rivalry, passionate declamations, slapstick tussles and vigorous chases – all conducted in a highly farcical vein. Finally, after four full hours (not counting the interval) of high-voltage energy discharges on both sides of the orchestra pit, the lovers got sorted out somehow – but don't ask me how; halfway through the second part I completely ran out of steam though the actors continued full blast (there is something to be said for having an all-young cast); I felt so exhausted with all the laughter, the noise, the smoke, the glaring lights, I began to drop off. I tottered out of the theatre marveling at the talent, versatility and amazing vitality of those brilliant young stars, but also feeling as if those lusty young people had held me over a balcony ledge, shaken me like an old, dusty rug and, for four hours, beaten me clean of every thought and feeling. That night I slept as I had not done for weeks, without any pills and, for me, "kida" was definitely okay.

# Walid Aouni:
## Six Takes and a Footnote:
## *1. Landscapes of Memory**

Since 1990, when he arrived in Cairo to direct *The Rhythm of Generations* for the Cairo Opera Ballet Company, director, choreographer, dancer and scenographer Walid Aouni (a Lebanese expatriate, with a French passport, then living in Belgium) has been the target of many venomous jingoistic barbs and the subject of heated controversy in Egyptian theatrical circles. Some directors and choreographers resented that this much coveted lucrative commission (a kind of annual 'fatted calf') should go to a 'foreigner'; others simply regarded the matter as a slur on their professional capacity and status.

The resentment mounted in the following year, reaching ridiculously hysterical heights, when Aouni returned to do two more works for the Cairo Opera: *Three Nights of the Sphinx* and *The Book of Exiles*. Curiously, and quite paradoxically, he was now doubly resented on account of being both a 'foreigner' and an 'Arab' – "just like us, only with a foreign passport." Some felt the insult would be less galling if he had been 'really' a foreigner, French, British, or American for example.

With Aouni's *Tanakodat* (*Contradictions*) in 1992, however, there was a marked change in the Egyptian theatrical atmosphere. It was not simply that the theatre professionals here had got used to his presence or had tired of jeering and sneering at his work. *Contradictions* was

---
* 9 May 1996.

quite incontrovertibly the work of a vastly talented and innovative all-round artist and walked off with the Egyptian Critics Award at the 4th Cairo International Festival for Experimental Theatre. Subsequently, the Cairo Opera offered Aouni a long-term contract to found and train the first ever permanent modern dance theatre company in Egypt or the Arab world. Aouni accepted and a year later he launched the company with *The Fall of Icarus*.

Henceforth, the anti-Aouni lobby changed their tactics and their attacks took a different angle. The target now was not his 'foreignness' but his art and, occasionally, his personal life. Aouni once sadly remarked that the kind of 'racism' he met with here far surpassed any racial prejudice he had ever encountered in Europe. He has been called a show-off, a flouter of taboos and alternately accused of being shallow and superficial, prurient and peurile, gimmicky or deliberately tortuous. It was said that like a typical foreigner he neither understood nor respected our heritage and was simply manipulating it for exotic effects. The metaphoric density of his elaborate scenography and sound-tracks proved opaque and baffling for many and his mode of composition, which relies heavily on the technique of montage, was described as confused and rambling.

What made it worse for Aouni was the fact that his work lacked sufficient public exposure (his shows have extremely short runs – an average of six nights per run with virtually no publicity), was never seen on a large scale by young people or students, and that his limited, scanty audience of the regular clientele of the Cairo Opera main hall consisted mostly of smug, middle-class, middle-aged people with settled tastes and deep-seated prejudices, or simply people ill-equipped to receive and appreciate this new kind of theatre. Aouni often longed to break free of the heavily garrisoned main hall of this forbidding art 'mausoleum' and seek fresh audiences elsewhere. But being financially tied to the Opera, he had no say in the choice of venue. It was lucky for him that the Cairo Opera took over the Gomhoria theatre downtown. It is more accessible to the ordinary theatre-goer and the young. Despite the superior technical facilities of the main hall, he fought to have his latest production on the life and work of the great Egyptian painter, Tahiya Halim, shown there and got his way – albeit only for six nights. Did the choice of venue have anything to do with the fact that this production has been almost unanimously voted the clearest, warmest and most accessible of all Aouni's work in Egypt? Or was it the choice of subject that did the trick?

Tahiya Halim (1919– )*, as she herself admits in the recording which accompanies the performance, is loved and respected by everybody. "It is true," she says, "that those whom God favours, He endows with the love of everyone." Even those who are unfamiliar with her work or know it only slightly venerate her name. She is something of a national figure – a woman who has carved for herself a unique and distinctive artistic niche and with it a prestigious international reputation.

But rich and exciting as Halim's art is, her personal life does not strike one at first as the stuff dramas are made of. She was born into an aristocratic family of Turkish and Upper-Egyptian origins, studied art privately, met a young painter two years older than herself (Hamid Abdalla) who helped her discover Egypt, the world and herself, fell in

---

\* She died on 24 May 2003.

love with him and eventually married him. Together they studied in Paris for three years, living in very straitened circumstances on a meagre stipend supplied by her mother, then, twelve years later, the marriage broke down. Abdalla remarried and settled in Paris and she remained in Egypt, close to the springs of her inspiration, living independently on her earnings from painting and teaching, nursing her talent and her beloved cats. She never remarried and if she ever fell in love again she never told anybody.

She travelled widely, exhibiting in the major cities of the world (New York, Stockholm, Paris, Berlin and Rome), was honoured both abroad and at home (winning the Guggenheim international prize in 1958 and the Egyptian state award for oil painting in 1967), spent a month in Nubia on a state-organised trip before the waters of the Aswan Dam flooded the region, another month at a nunnery near the village of Akhmim with her fellow painter and friend Inji Aflatoun, and, like all humanity, she had her share of the heart-ache and the thousand natural shocks that flesh is heir to. Her constant companions throughout her life were her beloved cats. She never had any children.

"Why Tahiya Halim?" I asked Aouni. In his cosy, but distractingly crowded study in Zamalek, where hardly an inch of the wall is left clear of old and recent posters and photographs, he frankly admitted that "after *Coma*, the second part of my trilogy which took for its subject the work of Mahfouz and the attempt on his life, I wanted a female subject. I had already done the life of the historical female mystic Rab'aa El-Adawiya in Brussels in 1985 and thought it was time to do the life of another important Arab woman."

The trilogy which started with *Excavations of Agatha* in 1993 is meant to be an imaginative and highly personal reading of all the forces and images – past and present – that make up the consciousness of modern Egyptian history. In the *Excavations*, he romantically invoked four famous female figures who became connected with Egypt in different degrees and capacities – Agatha Christie, Rita Hayworth, Maria Callas and the Lebanese singer Asmahan. They float in and merge, creating a dreamlike fabric that carries us to the Pharaonic past, the tombs of Luxor, the land of Nubia and the *Book of the Dead*. In *Coma*, the second part, Mahfouz, as a young man, occupies the stage with his fictional characters to grapple with the conflicts of the present and its evil threats. Nubia and ancient Egypt, however, are never very far. For the third part of the trilogy Aouni wanted a female.

But, again, why Halim? "She is great and, more importantly, still living (God grant her health and long life). One can talk to her and record her voice." He needed the living voice of the character: "I had considered other figures and consulted with friends," he went on to say, "but finally decided on Halim after reading about her life, especially her story with Hamid Abdalla, her passion for Nubia and for cats."

He interviewed her extensively in her flat in Zamalek and came away with thirty hours of stories, views and reminiscences on tape, together with valuable slides of old family and personal photographs and of many of her inaccessible paintings, including the one called *War* which was stolen from the Egyptian embassy in Paris. Of the thirty hours, only fifty minutes – all approved by Halim – went into the show and of the many slides, he chose nearly thirty, including two of her photos with Abdalla, two of her alone, in youth and old age, one of her mother, another of her father and about twenty seven of her most famous and maturest work.

With her soft, nostalgic voice gently rippling into the auditorium and all those paintaings and photos flashing on the gigantic screen that formed the back-drop of the stage, her presence was vividly and intimately felt and it seemed as though we were at a larger than life exhibition of her work. This in itself, alone, would have made the evening unforgettable. Knowing that nothing he can put on stage can match the beauty and power of those paintings (which included, among others, *A Boat on the Nile*, *A Song for the Nile*, *The Woman and the Lamp*, *Nubian Hairdressing*, *The Lute-Player*, *The Mother*, *This Land is Ours*, *Bread Out of Rock*, *Four Nubian Girls in a Boat*, *The High Dam*, *War*, *Peace*, *Nubia Welcoming Nasser*, *Man* (or *Suffering*) and *A Girl and A Cat*) or achieve the moving dignity of her sculpture *The Pyramid of Ants*, Aouni reduced his set to the minimum of bare essentials. The only fixed feature of the set was an old-fashioned wardrobe which occupied one corner of the stage and was used both realistically to hold the various costumes of the dancers (they changed in full view of the audience) and, metaphorically, as the store-house of memories wherein the ghosts of the past resided, occasionally emerging then withdrawing. The props which were carried in and out by the performers were few enough, functional, and extremely unobtrusive: an ironing-board that transformed into a mummified baby, a plastic doll, a few matresses, polystyrene blocks and triangular frames, a low wooden bench, some sticks, umbrellas, masks and the like.

Despite many expressionistic touches and a few abstract ones, the choreography was predominantly representational, following the direction of the recorded voice and the projected paintings – but without resort to crass or vulgar mime. The rich and varied musical collage from east and west, nevertheless, gave Aouni ample scope to exercise his inventive imagination and come up with a richly variegated choreographical tapestry that draws on various sources and traditions, from classical ballet to Nubian folk dancing. Such movement designs are invariably taxing and in this show Aouni put his dancers (eight men and six women) through a gruelling test. They all passed it with flying colours and Nancy Tonsy, who undertook the role of the painter, has proved that not only is she an inspired dancer, but also a sensitive actress and a charming presence on stage. The eight male dancers, all endowed with magnificent physiques (enhanced by the near nudity of the erotic costumes designed by Aouni), together with Reem Sayed Hijab (who recently starred in *Woyzek* at Al-Hanager) and the four female dancers in Nubian dress played various parts, impersonating the characters from Halim's past, her cats and the Nubian men and women, the peasants, soldiers and boatmen who inspired many of her paintings.

The performance opens with a stirring *tableau vivant*: Halim's voice speaks to us of art and the task of the painter to the strains of Anwar Ibrahim's lute while Tonsy (as Halim) stands silhouetted, with poised brush in hand, facing an empty canvas marked out in a grid, ready for painting; at her feet, the eight male dancers lie in a heap, like dead matter waiting for the touch of her brush to be shaped and come alive through art; it slowly happens. The subsequent scenes vary in tone, mood and rhythm; they run the whole gamut of emotions from zest and vitality to gentle sorrow and wistful nostalgia. Of these, my favourites are the ones which develop, interpret or further explore the meaning of the scenes captured in Halim's paintings or visually fill in the gaps in her reminiscing voice-overs.

As we draw near the end, Aouni creatively contrives a gripping contrapuntal sequence which, more than anything else in the show, expresses the depth and power of his affection for the painter. Here Halim (Tonsy), who had at an early point in the show glimpsed the silent shadow of an old woman with a stick crossing the stage behind the screen while she was folding a white sheet (shroud ?), comes face to face with her aged self (Reem Sayed Hijab) and recognises in her the same old woman with the stick. The young and old Halim perform a farewell dance on a totally empty stage before they part. As the cats move in to carry the old Halim, now dead, off stage, holding her up high, as if carrying a coffin, we hear the real Halim's voice telling us how much she would like to paint just such a picture. The young Halim, however, the eternal artist, is undefeated; she performs a jubilant, light-hearted dance in accompaniment to some Andalusian Maqamat, which date back to the 12th century, enchantingly chanted by Lebanese singer Fadya El-Haj. As the male performers join in, now openly wearing cat masks, with one impersonating her absent lover Abdalla, the mood becomes positively festive and even carnivalesque; the shadows of death are completely routed.

The very final scene is a real coup de theatre which puts all that has gone before in focus: the stage is bare and empty and all the performers have gone. (Those our actors were only spirits and are melted into air, into thin air – one remembers.) A photo of Halim, now in her old age, smiles at us from the screen; we hear her saying, while the curtains begin to slowly close:

> "I have never been afraid of death. I have lived and travelled and laughed and cried, and will accept my fate when it comes. We are like actors. We play our parts. When the play is done, we leave the stage."

## 2. *Mission Impossible**

As I sat in the sparsely occupied auditorium of Al-Gomhoria theatre last week, on two successive nights, watching Walid Aouni's impassioned tribute to Shadi Abdel Salam – that richly gifted artist and film director who despite, or, perhaps, because of his tragically premature death has become something of a myth – I could not help thinking that there comes a time in the life of all genuine artists when they have to pause, take a long, honest look at the path they have traversed so far and ask themselves the excruciating question: where to and what next?

Ironically, this time never arrives before the artist has reached intellectual and aesthetic maturity, mastered his craft, and developed that elusive, intangible, but nonetheless very real thing called a style of his or her own. Over the years, and against great odds, Aouni – the pioneer of modern dance theatre in the Arab world par excellence – has evolved a style of production at once richly sensuous – even flamboyantly so – and ardently spiritual, and a composite, dazzling visual vocabulary drawn from a variety of cultural sources and intricately interwoven. His choice of music too displayed a similar eclectic tendency. This curious cultural potpourri, together with his mode of composition which, at its best, as in *The Fall of Icarus* (1993), *The Excavations of Agatha* (1993), or *Elephants Hide to Die* (1996), appropriates the strategies and techniques of poetry and music and relies on metaphor and paradox as structural tools, has intrigued some, baffled others and frustrated many. Few could deny the riveting beauty and evocative power of the images

---

* 20 March 1997.

he projected on stage. But the internal logic of his unsettling combinations of discordant elements was not always easy to grasp. Aouni provided some clues and hinted at frames of reference, but the demands his best productions made on the imagination of the audience were many and disturbingly unfamiliar.

It did not help, of course, that modern dance itself was practically unknown to the majority of Egyptian audiences. As early as 1933, John Martin had defined modern dance as "the expression, by means of bodily movement arranged in significant form, of concepts which transcend the individual's power to express by rational and intellectual means." Nevertheless, people continued to ask Aouni to define verbally what he 'meant'. In the heated critical controversy that surrounded his early work in Egypt he was accused, among other things, of muddle-headedness and a facile hankering after the strange and exotic for its own sake. Few, however, were sufficiently perceptive to realize that although the apparent fragmentariness and absence of a clear sequential narrative in these works points in a modernist direction, their total emotional and imaginative thrust bespeak a clear romantic quest for the validation of an intensely personal vision: a thirst for wholeness, belonging and, above all, a sense of continuity with the past. This explains, perhaps, Aouni's choice of themes — his fascination with myth and ritual, the lives of artists and the legacy of the Pharaohs.

How long can an artist, already burdened with a deep sense of alienation, tolerate the animosity of an uncomprehending audience and the loneliness that comes with it? Predictably, and perhaps inevitably, Aouni began to waver. I am not using the word pejoratively to mean that he sacrificed his artistic integrity to win the audience. He simply made his art more accessible by treading more familiar ground and providing clear narrative lines. In *Coma* (1995), based on the works of Naguib Mahfooz and sparked off by the criminal attempt on his life, *The Last Interview* (1996), based on the life and works of the painter Tahiya Halim and, finally, in *The Desert of Shadi Abdel Salam*, few could complain of not 'understanding', and for those language was used as an extra aid to understanding.

No one could quarrel with Aouni's choice of material for this last work. The artistic world of Shadi Abdel Salam, his personality and the quality of his imagination and response to life can be a wonderful source of inspiration for any artist. In handling this material, however, Aouni set himself the impossible task of reproducing on stage, in the third part of the work, Abdel Salam's inimitable film, *The Mummy*. This does not mean that there were not some ingenious touches and solutions – like the haunting music and back projections, the addition of the figure of death in the form of a seductive succubus with a mummified head and the use of the orchestra pit as a tomb. But Abdel Salam's *Mummy* is such a perfectly finished artistic product that to use it as material one has to break free of its spell and put it at a safe distance. I doubt if anybody can do this. What happened in this part of the production was that one kept remembering the film and comparing it to what was happening on stage and the comparison was definitely not in Aouni's favour.

He was on much safer ground with *The Chair of Tutankhamen*, the documentary film on which he based the first part, and *The Eloquent Peasant* (Abdel Salam's film version of a famous ancient papyrus) which formed the basis of the second part. Indeed, these two parts of the performance formed a self-contained unit. Here, Aouni succeeded in establishing a dialogue with his material, looking beyond the films to embody in simple, vivid images of striking clarity and economy, the process of their creation. In both, the presence of Shadi Abdel Salam (performed by the gifted dancer Mohamed Shafiq) was at once ethereal, emphatic and arresting. Even those who had never set eyes on the great film director felt as if they intimately knew the inner workings of his soul and mind. There were no concessions here, no frills, dazzling embellishments or redundancies, but a meticulous attention to form and structure and great austerity in the choice of colour, sound and movement. Perhaps a similar approach would have saved the third part.

## 3. *In the Heat of the Night**

It was a sweltering night with the temptrature soaring to 42°C and upwards. On my study floor were huge piles of exam papers waiting to be corrected: I had spent the whole morning and afternoon trying to wage a war of attrition on those piles and failing dismally. All I could think of was cool beaches, rural retreats and mountain resorts. As the day wore on I became more and more depressed and by eight o'clock I decided to call it a day and seek some relief outdoors. But where could you go on such a sultry night?

The last thing I wanted was to watch people doing strenuous musclar and physical work: the sight of someone pushing as much as a wheelbarrow or a light handcart was enough to send me reeling and make me collapse with fatigue. But there was no choice: it is the off-season, and in this drab, lustreless period of theatrical drought there is nothing on in Cairo in the way of theatre but a depressingly brash commercial, (so-called) musical comedy and Walid Aouni's selection of dances from his company's repertoire. There were other extra-theatrical options of course and my daughter reeled off a list of attractive suggestions, but they fell on deaf ears. She finally dismissed me as a hopelessly dogged and blinkered theatre-addict but agreed to dump me at Al-Gomhoria theatre.

The roads were absurdly impassable and we were stranded on the October bridge for nearly half an hour. Inhaling all that delicious car exhaust and feeling progressively dizzier and more benumbed, it occurred to me that perhaps I should not blame my students for writing

---

* 29 June 1997.

in the fragmentary, decentred style they do; I momentarily became convinced it was the effect of Cairo's pollution, not of their exposure to postmodernist art and writing. This pollution, I said to myself remembering Lear, will make fools of us all and, perhaps, postmodernists, even though very few have heard of the term or know what it means.

In the foyer of Al-Gomhoria the heat was suffocating; I took refuge in the cool auditorium, foregoing the pleasure of smoking one last cigarette before the show. It was scantly occupied and most of the occupants were either foreigners (predominantly French and American) or young Egyptian theatre professionals and amateurs. All the other Egyptian young people who love and usually flock to Aouni's shows were cooped up at home, preparing for tomorrow's exams. The idea depressed me; the performance was intended as a celebration of the fifth anniversary of the company's foundation – a kind of birthday party; why choose such a difficult, 'dead' time for a celebration when you know that most of the guests cannot make it?

But the performance soon dispelled all my fatigue, depression and unreasonable sense of guilt. When the curtains parted to reveal a bare stage, completely stripped even of the back partition which hides the back-stage and wings, I experienced a sudden and exhilarating sense of openness and liberation. It was like stripping off your clothes to plunge into the sea or rolling up the carpets at the beginning of summer to enjoy the cool tiles or wooden floor-boards. At the back we could see the cool inside of the building, its inner walls, and the long staircase leading up to the dressing rooms and various working and administrative areas. At the top of the staircase, Aouni appeared, casually dressed, and started coming down, his head turned towards the audience, in step with the music. The dancers followed, in shorts, slacks, sweat suits or workaday clothes and once down took their places at the barre, at the extreme back edge of the stage, and started warming up. After a very short solo dance, which seemed like a demonstration by a dance-instructor to his pupils, Aouni withdrew and the dancers advanced to occupy the stage and perform the 'Dance of the Beginning' from *The Fall of Icarus* (1993).

In the absence of costumes, sets and make-up, the effect of this opening scene was to superimpose the image of a rehearsal on the performance proper, foreground what takes place behind the scenes in the prenatal period of any performance and create a metatheatrical framework within which the miscellaneous dances are deployed. In the presence of this frame, the performance was no longer merely a selection of dances from previous productions, but became a dramatic, representational piece about theatre and performers, dance and dancers.

The relationships of the dancers to Aouni (who occupies the centre of the opening and closing scenes) and to each other provided a kind of dramatic thread on which the various dances (twenty-five in all) were strung. It showed through in the facial expressions of the dancers, their gestural exchanges, their choice of partners, their poses and attitudes at the barre as they watched others perform and their reactions to the solo numbers. One became dimly aware of emotional undercurrents and hidden tensions, and also of individual character traits and temperaments. The atmosphere was competitive, but in a light-hearted vein, with many humourous touches. In this quasi-dramatic context, it did not matter if you did not know which production each dance came from; the dances had detached themselves from their original sources to form a pastiche intended to showcase the art of dance and the hard work it entails. This reminded me of the American performer Karen Finley who once said that she strives in her performances to impress upon the viewer the fact that performance is really a very hard thing to do.

In *At the Beginning*, Walid Aouni is doing something similar, sharing with us his experience with his group over five long years of hard, back-breaking work, of joy and frustration, and proudly parading his achievement before us without any theatrical riggings or garniture. And the dancers did him justice: the night I was there they performed with great skill and zest and admirable control. It was an extremely refreshing performance, like a cool breeze, and ended on a highly comical note when Aouni appeared on stage after the last dance, as if to take his bows, then suddenly assumed the role of the hard, critical, impossible-to-please dance-master and was eventually chased around and off stage by his pupils. All too soon, we, the audience, suffered a similar fate and were shooed out by the ushers to face the heat once more.

## 4. Songs of Innocence and Experience[*]

Why should anyone want to watch a modern dance show where all the dancers are for the most part carefully hidden under a huge green cloth and only fitfully seen in silhouette? Only Walid Aouni could dare do such a thing and get away with it. The first time I saw his *Underground* I kept expecting the dancers to cast off this slimy looking green thing and emerge into the light. They never did; the only thing one saw of them, apart from their swaying, rising and falling bodies under the cloth, were arms, thrust through little holes and waving serpent-like. Occasionally, a rag doll would emerge, or the hands would turn into little palm trees, or sprout pistols pointed at the hidden heads, or hold up miniature models of the world trade centre in the face of a barrage of little paper airplanes shooting from the wings. The sight of stage hands, dressed like monks, with a faint suggestion of something Pharaonic about their postures and general demeanour, was a welcome relief. What could Aouni be thinking of carving a show out of absence? Was it another sadistic manifestation of the age-old hatred of directors and choreographers towards actors and dancers? Or was it a sign of infinite love? Of that impossible dream of making the dancer into the dance? A line from T.S. Eliot's East Coker in *The Four Quartets* floated in my head: "The dancers are all gone under the hill."

Was it this that made me revisit Aouni's *Underground*? I honestly do not know. It is one of those rare shows that puzzle and irritate you and yet keep tugging at your nerve cells. There was something about that big green sheet, the rag doll and paper rockets which took me back

---

[*] 5 September 2002.

to the distant, long-forgotten world of the nursery. The sense of security one enjoyed under warm bed sheets ... the protection and the many games we played. And the echoes of big disasters, menacing but not fully comprehended, which sent us scrambling under those sheets. Was Aouni giving us a view of what we must have looked like to all those grown-ups around us when we were children? When at the end of the show Aouni threw himself on stage and squirmed his way under the green cloth to join his dancers it was a moment of overwhelming pathos. The child in all of us, who never leaves us however old we grow, was there and opting out of our murderous, insane grown-up world. "O dark, dark, dark. They all go into the dark," another Eliot echo. Was *Underground* a swan song?

## 5. *A Homage to Mokhtar**

The idea of arresting the flow of time, of conquering the painful ephemerality at the heart of life, of defeating mortality or netting a few precious moments from the stream of days to fix them eternally, for all time, lies at the heart of many works of representational art. But more than painting or photography, three-dimensional sculptured figures or expressive forms seem to contain within them a latent dynamicity, a potential for mutation, the power to come to life. When the pharaohs asked their sculptors to preserve their likeness in imperishable granite, they believed the statue would work its spell when they were dead and help the soul to keep alive in and through the image. One of their words for sculptor was actually "He-who-keeps-alive." The same meaning has continued to inform our experience of great sculptural works in later times. Standing before Michelangelo's *Dying Slave* in the Louvre in Paris, E.H. Gombrich found it "difficult to think of this work as being a statue of cold and lifeless stone ... It seems to move before our eyes, and yet to remain at rest."

Paradoxically, the sense of awe this illusion generates is always accompanied, in my experience at least, with a pitiful awareness that the other side of this power is mortality – that were the arrested life to break free of its stone or bronze confines, it would inevitably sink back into the fluid temporal state we call life and dissolve into its transient flux. Lifelike figures in paintings or photographs seem less threatened; they are part of a scene, of a spatio-temporal constructed world – a virtual reality which, however illusory, exists on a different plane of experience where motion is not synonymous with finiteness and the paradox of mobility in eternity is admissible.

---
\* 27 March 2003.

Lifelike statues are not similarly framed; whether they are placed in a public square or a museum, or dumped in a storeroom or a backyard, the background against which they stand, the context in which we view and experience them is *our* world, *our* reality. Their stillness, which sets them apart, seems a forced, temporary freezing, like the stillness of Sleeping Beauty or the Biblical Seven Sleepers. Looking at Mahmoud Mokhtar's peasant women drawing water from the river, standing on its shore, crouching in sorrow, sitting with a knee drawn up against the chest, a bent arm resting on it to support a sleeping head, or forging ahead, like ships with swelling and billowing sails, against the *Khamaseen* storms, you experience an overpowering feeling that at any moment they will come alive and speak to you or simply straighten up and walk away.

This powerful suggestion of latent life, of motion momentarily arrested, brings representational sculpture, as well as the more recent spatial and kinetic varieties of that art, very close to theatre as a contingent, multi-disciplinary representational art, constructed out of the movement of human and inanimate forms and sounds in space and time. Walid Aouni draws on this connection and foregrounds it in his latest work, *Mahmoud Mokhtar and the Khamaseen Winds*. Unlike his earlier choreographic/scenographic tribute to painter Tahiya Halim, which featured both her life and work, the present piece concentrates solely on the living art of the dead master, drawing on it for both artistic form and content. Mokhtar's historical contribution to Egyptian culture was the recovery and reinstatement of the forgotten art of sculpture which the rise of anti-representational creeds had suspected and discredited as a leftover from paganism. His human figures, in stone, plaster, bronze, or marble, hark back quite vividly to Ancient Egyptian sculpture, linking the present with the past – Isis and the Bride of the

Nile with Umm Kulthum and Saad Zaghloul – across a gap of centuries; whatever posture they assume and whatever the emotion the shapes of the bodies express, their outlines always remain firm, simple and restful, reflecting that combination of geometrical regularity and keen observation of nature characteristic of all Ancient Egyptian art.

Mokhtar's contribution to the evolution of the idea of "Egyptianness" as a national identity through his restoration of Egypt's pre-Christian, pre-Islamic past in his works inspired the conceptual framework, simple narrative line and characters in *Mahmoud Mokhtar and the Khamaseen Winds*. Drawing on the image of the Pharaoh as a deity and on the ancient African worship of ancestors, it focusses on the idea of creation and tells a simple story. A Pharaoh-god, in the shape of a dark, sinewy figure with a jackal-like gait (Mustapha Haroun), descends from the top of a mountain at the back, holding the symbols of his creativity – a sculptor's chisel and mallet – and wades through what looks like a swirling amorphous mass of matter (created by the dancers' bodies). Gradually, he shapes this chaos into human figures and breathes life into them, then singles out one (Hani Mahmoud), dresses him as Mokhtar used to dress and, in a symbolic gesture, hands over to him his sculptor's tools, thus endowing him with the creative power to immortalise himself and others through his art.

From that moment on, the performance unfolds as a series of manifestations of this divine gift in sculptural feats in which the dancers first represent the real-life figures who inspired Mokhtar, then the sculptures which immortalised them. With the help of Aouni's costumes and lighting, the empty stage, bounded at the back by dark, rugged mountains and flanked on either side by electric fans on high stands and dangling lamps with straw shades, strongly evoked the feel and atmosphere of an old village at the edge of the desert in Upper Egypt.

In this figurative setting, Mokhtar meets, simultaneously or in succession, singly or in groups, the originals of many of his statues – graceful peasant women carrying their water jugs to the Nile, going to market with goods to sell, or returning from it, veiled Cairene women, wives of village dignitaries or aldermen, framers and Cairene men of the lower classes, as well as Saad Zaghloul, Umm Kulthum and Huda Sha'rawi. With the help of white stretch sacks and voluminous white sheets which flutter and billow in the wind created by the fans, and against a stirring soundtrack which combines African and Western music and old Egyptian songs, the dancers, guided by Mokhtar's hand and his chisel, with the Pharaoh looking on and occasionally assisting, transform themselves into many of his most famous works: *Fallaha, La Fiancée du Nil, Retour du Marché, Saad Zaghloul, Renaissance d'Egypt, Idylle, Au Bord du Nil, A la vue de l'homme, Le Gardien des Champs, Retour du Fleuve, Vers l'Aimé, Tireuse d'eau, Isis,* and *Vendeuse de fromage* and, of course, *Al-Khamaseen* which winds up this wonderful kinetic display.

The choice of *The Khamaseen Winds* to figure in the title of this homage to Mokhtar was an ironic and telling reference to our own time. Part of the show's impact stemmed from the timing of its performance, in the maelstrom of turbulent events and violent upheavals that are shaking the very foundations of this part of the world. With a painful irony, the Khamaseen winds of backwardness and bigotry which Mokhtar – like the figures in his Khamaseen statue – fought against in the hope of ushering in a new Egyptian Renaissance of art, science, enlightenment and tolerance, and thought he had conquered, are still with us, more stifling than ever.

## 5. *Footnote:*
## Aouni's Brood[*]

Small children, in my experience, seem attracted to any enclosed space that can hold them inside — cupboards, cabinets, crates, or underneath a table with the cloth draped to the floor. Wardrobes, however, particularly those of parents, seem to hold a special fascination for them. Is it the thrill of secretly invading a forbidden adult space? All those big, empty shoes, the clothes hanging down limply from the rail high up like fearful, disembodied apparitions, but faintly breathing familiar, reassuring smells? Is it a feeling that for a time you have all those grownups – alternately loved and feared, needed and resented – all to yourself, without rivalry, distractions, or the rigours of discipline, in a world more secure and less confusing than the one outside?

The sight of a solitary wardrobe standing on the empty stage of the small hall at the opera house as we waited for *The Wardrobe* to begin triggered these musings. It never stops to amaze me how, once on stage and properly framed, even the most ordinary and mundane of objects seems to spring to life, acquire a magical potency and becomes a protean sign. Even before the lights came on, that silent wardrobe, which I recognized from an earlier Walid Aouni production (*Tahiya Halim* I think), started working on me. A memory from the very distant past suddenly floated up – a conglomerate of sounds, sights, smells and painful childish emotions vividly recreated in the present.

---

[*] Spring 2002.

I remembered how my youngest sister used to hide every morning in my mother's enormous brown wardrobe when she first went to school. After the first two days her hiding place was an open secret; but though she was invariably discovered, dragged out of it, and bundled off to the hateful place in floods of tears, she never changed it. It was for her own good, they blithely said; but this didn't make the pain any less or alleviate my shameful, guilty sense of utter helplessness in the face of terrible oppression. This went on for a year. Then, suddenly, one day, she stopped hiding altogether and never went near that wardrobe again for years. Why she obstinately stuck to that imaginary sanctuary though it failed her every time and why she suddenly dropped it and didn't seek another puzzled me for a long time. When I asked her years later, she only laughed and said: "What can I say? Plain stupidity I guess." But was it that? Or do we need a psychiatrist to solve this riddle of the wardrobe?

The nine young performers (Heba Fayed, Sayed Ali, Ahmed Abou Zeid, Karima Bidair, Ahmed Abdel Ati, M. Mostafa, M. Mostafa Zein, Samah Saeid, and Mustafa Haroun), who choreographed and put together *The Wardrobe*, all by themselves, came up with a similar wardrobe riddle, equally teasing, but more profound and formally sophisticated. Notwithstanding what they say in the pamphlet about the theme of the "incomplete crime" and the figures of Alfred Hitchcock and Agatha Christie – a conscious throwback to Walid Aouni's work and possibly a sign of love and gratitude for having been given this golden opportunity to exercise their creative imagination as artists – the riddle that ultimately confronts the audience is not a detective one.

It is true that the brief, startling final scene which ends with a murder tends (is intended?) to make what had gone before appear in retrospect as a kind of explanation – a visual playing out of all the hidden emotional forces and sexual motives and prejudices behind it; nevertheless, it ultimately remains a purely formal device, at once forced and reductive – a concession to narrativity and intelligibility. It consists of five actions: Walid Aouni and Karima Nait walk in arm in arm, in formal evening dress; they stop centre-stage where he suddenly bends her backwards and kisses her on the lips; she slaps him and walks to the wardrobe stage-left where she bends down to pick up something while he remains centre-stage; she turns to face him, pointing that something, which turns out to be a pistol, at him and shoots him; he falls down while she freezes in the same posture. End of scene.

What had gone before, however, cannot be contained in a narrative. It had sought to 'detect' a different web of relationships and explore their psychological effects and shifting implications: how the human body relates to space, to other bodies, male and female, and to different, including gender-specific garments; how garments define or erode identity, character-type and social role. Left to themselves to improvise, with no directorial authority to guide or curb their body memories, and with five music albums by Tarek Sharara, the young performers spun their movements out of their memories, dreams and desires, giving free reign to their imagination. Basic to the structure of the performance they finally came up with was a complex dialogic relationship between the small, enclosed space inside the wardrobe and the open, empty space outside it – which comprised the whole stage.

As those gifted, vibrant, highly-trained performers moved between the two, in varied numbers, moods and guises, offering a wide spectrum of human interactions, emotions and states of being, subverting traditional norms and treading forbidden areas, they set in motion a dialogue between the two spaces. It was a physical, musical dialogue, in the archaic language of the body, and it addressed us at a level deeper than any verbal language can reach – save for poetry. As it developed, generating a series of paradoxes, it transformed both the wardrobe and the empty space outside into richly ambiguous metaphors. Alternately, the wardrobe became a womb and a tomb, a home and a prison cell, a playhouse, a public gents toilet, a sardine can, an actors' dressing-room and, ultimately, that repository of all which has to be repressed in the process of growing up and conforming we call the unconscious. Similarly, the empty space outside was successively an open, free space, a lonely exile, a playground, a sphere of violence, a street in a red-light district, a boudoir, a dormitory and, of course, a stage.

To be able to hear this dialogue, one has to listen with one's whole body, with one's whole being; for to each of us, it will tell a different story. The story it told me had no detectives in it, not even in the sense in which we sometimes describe Oedipus as a detective who finally discovers that he himself is the murderer. It spoke to me of the instability of identity and meaning and wondered why people were so keen on fixing them eternally. It argued that since the notion of fixed identities and functions was no more than a socially-constructed fiction, since signifiers were ever sliding and signifieds forever deferred, we should celebrate the fact and use it to resist stratification, liberate creativity and, in Julia Kristeva's words, "open the norms towards pleasure."

It also spoke to me of my childhood, its joys, terrors and vague feelings of guilt; of those forgotten archaic memories of our link with the maternal body and the trauma of birth which threw us out into the world, lonely and naked; of the vague sense of loss which settles upon us and continues to haunt us as soon as we are old enough to be sucked into those arbitrary, tyrannical sign-systems, where difference is the presiding principle, and those ideological/socio-economic structures where power is the only ethic. In the name of culture, they cripple and tame us, then either train us to run in the rat race, or drill us in the art of war to murder each other and become fodder for cannons.

Perhaps my sister's tenacious clinging to her wardrobe, despite daily evidences of its ineffectuality, was not a sign of backwardness, excessive shyness or inordinate spoiling as people judged at the time. Naïve and mulish as it looked, it could have been an unconscious ritualistic protest against what 'coming out' and growing up entails. But she had to come out, and like those wonderful performers planted into the company and nurtured by Walid Aouni until they flowered, find through art a new mode of protest, a more effective way to elude the tyranny of systems and a route back to the space she loved: inside a wardrobe spun out of fancy and the free play of the imagination.

My experience of *The Wardrobe* was at once intensely personal and artistically exhilarating; and judging by the response of the audience during the show on the two nights I saw it – the sense of excitement building up in the auditorium by the minute and infecting everybody and the rapturous applause at the end – I knew it had touched hidden springs in most of them and released many secret fantasies and buried tensions. Just as it had set free the imaginative energy of the performers and the memories and longings of their bodies, for the audience too, it proved an act of liberation.

# Hani Metaweh: A Director Turns Playwright
## First Venture:
## *Into the Undiscovered Country*\*

Barring a couple of shows, up until three weeks ago, the current theatrical season offered by the state companies had promised to be dismally dull and boring, with little to capture the imagination or move the spirit. Then *Ya Misafer Wahdak* (Lone Traveller) opened at the National, and *Khafyet Qamar* at Al-Hanager, and suddenly there was an air of excitement. In its last leg, with only one month of it left, the so far sickly pallid season seemed to shake off its sluggish, pedestrian existence, take on a new life and boldly soar on the wings of poetry.

Interestingly, though not surprisingly perhaps, both productions had the same woman behind them: Huda Wasfi, the director of both venues. For years, and in the face of great opposition, many slanerous campaigns and some very harsh and often unfair criticism, she has assiduously pursued an artistic policy rooted in a deep conviction that the only way to rejuvenate the Egyptian theatre is to continuously inject it with new blood, encourage new talent, restore the missing links between the older and younger generations, question and defy the established concepts and conventions and create a scope and opportunities for sharing experience with foreign and Arab artists. She was the first to introduce and popularise the idea of workshops in the state theatre, to arrange a successful string of them, mostly at Al-Hanager, and to host artists of international renown (such as the

---

\* 19 Mach 1998.

polish director Jozef Szajna, the Austrian choreographer Eva-Maria Lerchenberg–Tony and the Iraqi director Jawad Al-Asadi, to name but a few) to conduct them. She took many risks encouraging new experiments and launching new artists and, naturally, there were disappointments; but her faith has remained unshaken.

In the public debate over the future of the Egyptian theatre recently held at The Cairo International Book Fair she fiercely defended the right of the younger generation of theatre artists to learn by doing and improve through experience, even if they make serious and sometimes costly mistakes. She reminded those present that in the 1960s, artists like Sa'd Ardash, Karam Metaweh, and Galal El-Sharqawi were given leading posts in the theatre and made heads of companies at the age of thirty or even less; to be given your first opportunity at fifty, as sometimes happens now, she added, means that you are finished before you start and that your best creative years are already behind you.

Naturally, not everyone sees eye to eye with Wasfi, particularly the old veterans whom she sometimes intrepidly accuses of wanting to impose a monopoly on theatre. This angers many and she is sometimes accused of carrying outspokenness to the point of sheer blunt tactlessness. But however much people may disagree with Wasfi, no one can fail to recognize her zeal or respect her passionate commitment. And the last two productions she has sponsored at the National and Al-Hanager (one professional and the other with a cast of amateurs) plainly confirm the wisdom of her policy and vindicate her conviction.

The two productions, though vastly different, are similar in many respects; both are adaptations by their respective directors of well-known literary texts, one a fascinating Egyptian novel by Mohamed

Nagui called *Khafyet Qamar* (published by Dar El-Hilal, January, 1994) and the other, the famous, anonymous medieval morality play, *Everyman*. In both cases the rewriting goes beyond the mere dramatisation of a narrative in the former or the updating of old material in the latter and becomes a process of deep questioning, re-reading and interpretation of the original text — a process which deftly and quite imaginatively manipulates the rich resources of theatre and its multiple language to project a profoundly intense and personal engagement with the agonising paradoxes of existence on the moral, religious, material and even biological levels.

In the case of Hani Metaweh's *Ya Misafer Wahdak* (the title of a famous song by Mohamed Abdel Wahab), the straightforward and most unsubtle moral quest of Everyman, the hero of the medieval play, to find someone who would willingly accompany him into the nether world — a quest which yields a series of sad let-downs by all the (personified) values that presumably support human life and give it meaning, such as love, beauty, friendship, strength, wealth, knowledge and family — is transformed into a series of nimble, rapid scenes which mix with disconcerting agility all the known theatrical conventions, blithely blending them together, adding occasionally a generous splash of parody and burlesque, in the form of snatches of old songs and movies, and finally creating a crazy, dizzyingly surrealistic and deeply nostalgic potpouri in which fact and fiction, illusion and reality, life, dreams and hallucinations are indistinguishable from each other. But despite its incongruous ingredients, which include quotations from Descartes and Schopenhauer, Hani Metaweh's strange and exotic brew has a distinct, unmistakable Shakespearean flavour. What holds it together and gives it body and shape are the Bard's twin images of life as both dream and theatrical pageant.

The Shakespearean underlining shows through quite plainly more than once, but especially at the place where Everyman (or Unsi, as he is rechristened in the play) quotes in full Hamlet's famous "To be" soliloquy, stressing his bewildered fear of the dreams that may come in "that sleep of death" and his dread of the journey into that "undiscovered country from whose bourn no traveller returns."

In the case of Unsi, however, the lone traveller of the title (a self-made rich man, a political writer, and a bit of a womanizer), the return is made possible at the very last minute thanks to the grace and understanding of the angel of death (a seductive, luscious blonde, dressed to kill) who allows him a short reprieve to find a companion. But as he journeys back through his former life, it slowly dawns upon him that it has all been a charade – a big illusion. As wealth ( delightfully represented by Nohair Amin as a fleshy, vulgar belly-dancer in a heavily sequined gown), knowledge (superbly played by Mokhlis El-Biheiri as a doddering, retired professor of philosophy completely gone gaga), strength (farcically impersonated by Munir Makram Wilson as the tottery, delirious owner of a seedy gym, heavily bedecked with knives and guns), beauty, love and friendship (competently played by Yasmin El-Naggar, Reem Izzidin and Zein Nasser) are emptied out of meaning and life is revealed as a dream, an insubstatial pageant, Unsi becomes more than willing to withdraw into the dreaded, undiscovered country. The fact that his parents forgive him his long neglect and welcome his return like the prodigal son, or that Hassanat (Good Deeds), the beggar whom he had earlier saved from the clutches of her thuggish master just before he was shot at his wedding by some mysterious gang, does not lighten the sense of desolation that envelops the end.

The certain, overtly moral tone of the final monologue and its simple, comforting message are undercut and enveloped by an anguished sense of uncertainty as to the reality of anything. In the penultimate scene, the angel of death (Nada Basyouni) openly orders the stage hands to quickly change the set and prepare for the final scene and performs a cabaret number while they are doing it. One expects a view of the other world; instead, we find ourselves with Everyman and Good Deeds in a shadowy, eerie railway station, with angels on skates, with wirewings, and many of the characters flitting by, in and out, like phantoms. At the back, we dimly glimpse the silhouette of a train, waiting, then Nada Basyouni proceeds, slowly and mournfully, to draw the stage curtain closed. I remembered Prospero's "those our actors were only spirits and are melted into air" and did not want to stay and applaud. It is the kind of end after which the auditorium lights should be dimmed and the audience withdraw quitely.

But how could one leave without telling Nur El-Sherif what a really magnificent *presence* he is. I hesitate to use the word actor because for him acting comes as naturally as breathing. Though a star, and a super one, he glided through the show like a benign spirit, never pushing himself forward, never upstaging anybody and always helping everyone to give their best. Like a maestro, he wanted his players to perform with all the zest and vigour they could command while carefully orchestrating them to preserve the delicate balance between the varied moods of the play and its total effect.

# Second Venture:
## *Shooting Farouk**

Hyped as a play on the last days of King Farouk in Italy (he died in Rome in 1965 at the pathetically premature age of forty-five, thirteen years after he was forced to abdicate his throne and go into exile by the 1952 revolution), *The Last Whisper* — scripted and directed for the National by Hani Mutaweh — turned out to be an intricate theatrical prank, a highly contrived imaginative hoax which sticks up two fingers at audience expectations and unabashedly, indeed, quite gleefully, sports the (in this part of the world) much frowned upon post-modernist slogan that history (with biography subsumed under this rubric) is simply a narrative, a fictional construction with no better claim to truth than a novel. Mutaweh's devastating Pirandellian skepticism about the possibility of knowing the truth, or even obtaining a clear and accurate factual account about anything or anyone, blows like a hurricane through this show, almost splitting it asunder, scattering and sweeping before it the very last shreds of any belief in historical veracity. Sunk beyond any hope of retrievability are all the old cherished rational dams between legend and fact, history and rumour, life and art.

Farouk is there all right ... in a way (and a very queer way it is) and so is Italy, or rather Rome, as a setting. But in this hazy, chimerical no-man's-land, nothing is quite what it seems. Tall and elegant film star Hisham Abdel-Hamid (the last person anyone would cast as Farouk) is grotesquely padded and made up to look faintly like the cartoon image

---
* 5 October 2000.

of the fallen king, popularised by the press as a symbol of depravity, debauchery and corruption. But the fabricated image deliberately leaves a wide margin for disbelief — enough to accommodate the dozen other characters, factual and fictional, whom Abdel-Hamid masterfully evokes by sudden and startling shifts of tone, voice and physical demeanour and superimposes on Farouk. These characters, who include Zaki Rustum (as we know him in old movies), Yusef Wahbi (in his famous declamatory melodramas), Othello and Hamlet, among others, are craftily linked to some of the dubiously known facts about Farouk's life, particularly his relations with women, and are manipulated to suggest a subtle link between the many shifting masks of Abdel-Hamid, making his grotesquely theatrical multiple figuration of Farouk a comprehensive symbol for many states of being.

To further frustrate and obfuscate the audience who came expecting to see Farouk satirised, romanticised or convincingly analysed in pseudo-objective dramatic terms, Hani Mutaweh eschewed all traditional dramatic forms and any pretence to realism, opting for a highly fantasised version of the familiar picaresque novel. But Farouk here is no ordinary picaroon, though in the course of the play he nicks a watch, money, a gold pendant and fires a number of shots at imaginary spies and assassins. In his flight, he constantly finds himself inadvertently crossing over into fictional worlds, wandering through and partaking in famous scenes from old popular movies, TV soap operas and well-known plays. For company, he is given El-Masri Effendi — the cartoon figure devised and popularised by Armenian cartoonist Saroukhan for the national newspaper, *Akhbar El-Yom*, during Farouk's reign (deliciously brought to life by Sami Abdel-Hamid) – and Kishkish Bey, the *omdah* (mayor) of Kafr

Al-Ballas — a theatrical character created and popularised by the great comedian Naguib El-Rihani in the twenties. It was dizzying to watch the lavishly talented Mokhles El-Beheiri impersonating at the beginning an ex-*omdah* in 1965, then gradually looking every inch like Naguib El-Rihani impersonating his *omdah* of the 1920s. I wondered afterwards if this magnificent actor would be able to peel off his triple mask and find his way safely home.

As this delightful trio, like three lackadaisical musketeers, skip and cavort, and often whizz through this thick, bristling forest of references and cross-references, heedless of the fast-changing elaborate sets, the painted flats descending from the flies or props pushed from the wings, one experiences a dangerous sense of chaos, a painfully disconcerting awareness of the utter fragility and basic theatricality of that flimsy, artificial construct we call reality. The surreal crescendo reaches its climax when finally the trio find themselves in a cardboard Italian villa where a film about the life of King Farouk is being shot. Here, we meet Queen Farida, Queen Nazli and other members of the court and royal family, with the late famous comedian, Ismail Yassin, acting as chorus and master of ceremonies.

When Farouk, who enters the villa under cover, disguised as a peasant woman with a big wicker basket on his head, is asked to play the star role and impersonate himself, and as the short, quick takes flash before our eyes, like memory-pricking needles, hinting at the crucial psychological events and watersheds in King Farouk's life (as far as the layman knows them), we feel as if we are about to be tipped (three hours after the play started) into a turbulent, psychological drama. But in the nick of time, and just as picaroon-Farouk with his many theatrical masks seems about to fade away and dissolve into this new drama, a newspaper vendor arrives shouting 'Farouk morto'. Kishkish Bey, himself a theatrical fabrication, begins to wonder if the other highly theatrical fabrication he has all along taken for King Farouk is not an impostor, impersonating the real (by this time the word means nothing) king. Hisham Abdel-Hamid roundly denies the press reports of Farouk's death and the play, which has resuscitated Egyptian-Jewish actress Camelia (or Lillian) after her death in a plane crash, tantalisingly withholds comment, leaving the audience to work out this teasing conundrum.

The impulse behind this fantastically mad, technically magnificent theatrical enterprise called *The Last Whisper* (in a clear nostalgic/sarcastic allusion to Farid El-Atrash's vastly popular, perennial song, *The First Whisper*) is shatteringly anarchic and poignantly nihilistic. The general impact, however, is perilously exhilarating, as if one is cunningly led to gaze on the dread of freedom. Strangely, however, it is completely free of even the slightest trace of hard-hearted cynicism. Neither a tragedy, a lyrical elegy, a satirical skit or a comic romp (and, definitely, thanks to its constant semiotic prevarication, not a political propaganda sheet), *The Last Whisper* is thoroughly non-committal and wholeheartedly egalitarian, sinking all distinctions between the myriad images, thoughts and sensations we are fed by popular culture, giving them equal, ambiguous status and warning us all along that making sense is ultimately a question of ideology.

A "son of the revolution" who would not have been educated without it but who, like most of his (and my) generation had to pay for it by digesting the mind-boggling experience of watching history reborn and rewritten over and over, and having his memories as a school kid and adolescent constantly wiped out, like the classroom black-board, and then inscribed with contrary information and denied the right to question or protest, Mutaweh inevitably faced the shattering discovery that, rather than Sisyphus bearing his burden up and down the mountain if only to prove the undefeatable toughness of the human spirit (an infinitely comforting and morale-raising myth in the 1960s), he had been all along labouring under the weight of a soap bubble.

Since 1967 Metaweh has taken every opportunity to voluntarily exile himself, spending years in the US then in the Gulf. The few years he spent here were arid and hopelessly barren. It was only in exile that he could begin to sort out his kaleidoscopic conglomeration of splintered images and piece them together in thoroughly subjective works — subtle autobiographies of consciousness if you like — beginning with *Lone Traveller* a few years ago (also at the National) and now with *The Last Whisper*. *Lone Traveller* also took its title from a famous popular song — Abdel-Wahab's *Ya Misafer Wahdak* — and, using the framework of the old English morality play *Everyman*, launched a deeply anguished investigation into the meaning of life and death. What remains for a person at the end of the day was the irking question. In *The Last Whisper*, life is left behind and we are plunged into a world beyond life and death. The question here is what remains of a person after the fall of night.

Old movies broadcast on TV after the 1952 revolution had to undergo a purgation operation; any allusions to Farouk or his Alaweya family were excised and in any scene where the picture of the deposed king appeared you were sure to find a mysterious black blotch flickering somewhere in a vulgar bid to blur and obliterate history. For us, as children, those awful black blotches were fearfully forbidding traffic signals blocking all thoughts and questions. Farouk had been erected as a bogey and we felt that if we ever dared peep behind the blotch he would jump at our throats.

Now the blotch has gone but the scar on the imagination remains. Was it in such a scar that *The Last Whisper* found its imaginative root?

# Intisar Abdel-Fattah

## Four Takes:
### *1. A Street Cart Named Ghabn*[*]

In the 1960s, long before the idea of 'community theatre' was ever heard of in Egypt, a daring young director by the name of Hanaa Abdel-Fattah turned his back on the capital and set off for Dinshwayy – a small village, famous in modern Egyptian history due to a British massacre which claimed the lives of many of its people. He spent six months there, living among the villagers and working with them over Yusef Idris's play *The Cotton King* which was collectively altered and rewritten. The result was a true peasant drama which he staged in a barn. This peasant theatre, however, sadly came to an end when its progenitor left for Poland.

More then twenty years later, his younger brother, director Intisar Abdel-Fattah, came up with an equally dashing idea, if not completely new: a travelling theatre, not unlike the medieval pageant-wagon, or the ancient Greek cart of Thespis, but modelled on the typically Egyptian glass-topped food hand-carts. You can see them at any street corner in the popular areas of Cairo selling a variety of hot meals, particularly the local dish called 'Kushari' (a delicious mixture of rice, macaroni, and black lentils, served with hot sauce and fried onions). The cart would have square openings for puppet-shows on its narrow front and back, while the sides could be lowered, making the cart into a stage, or kept in place and painted or hung up to serve as a back-ground set if the

---

[*] 9 May 1991.

action took place in front of the cart. The box-like underside would of course hold the actors' costumes, equipment and light props. The idea was impressive. This mobile versatile structure would literally carry the theatre into the market-place and the public square; it would be a boon to the theatre-starved population of the poorer quarters of Cairo and the provinces; it would also help revive the tradition of popular street shows which has nearly vanished and would help conserve and inject new life into the fast-fading indigenous popular theatrical forms.

Intisar built his cart with some financial help from the Cultural Palaces Authority (known then as The Mass Culture), christened it the Popular Ghabn Cart (Arabat Ghabn El-Chaabeya) and planned to launch it with a short one-actor comic piece by Alfred Farag, based on a story from the *Arabian Nights* and called *Lazy Buqbuq*. Unfortunately, as often happens in Egypt, the project soon foundered. The artist fell out with The Mass Culture officials (who had, incidentally, delayed the project for two years) over who takes credit for the experiment and to whom it belongs.

They separated, but Intisar, who had conveniently received an invitation to perform in Rome, backed by the Ministry of Culture here, was allowed to keep his beloved cart for a while. He carried it with his few actors to Italy where, together with some Italian artists, he worked out a new and more amplified version of *Buqbuq* in a mixture of Arabic and Italian.

This joint venture was staged in the garden of the Egyptian Academy in Rome and was enthusiastically received from what I heard. That may very well have been the case, but when I saw it on video-tape, I couldn't make much sense of it, nor could I discover any vital connection between the Italian bits, interesting and visually impressive as they were, and the story of the lazy day-dreamer Buqbuq. The combination seemed arbitrary and rather forced. Also, I found it bitterly ironical that what had started as a project for the benefit of the poor and deprived should end up as something of a tourist attraction, designed to impress a leisured audience.

After the Roman trip, the cart was whisked away from Intisar and left to rot in a warehouse somewhere. The indefatigable Intisar, however, built himself a new one with his own money. He tells me that so far he has given six performances with the new cart, five in Ismailia, during some festival, and one in the garden of the Dutch Cultural Centre – hardly a market- place or a public square. Unfortunately, I have not seen any of those performances, but whatever their artistic quality, numerically, they present a very poor record of the cart's public appearances in three years. Whether Intisar's increasing association with the Opera House and its work has anything to do with his relative neglect of his cart is anybody's guess. What I fear is that one day he may wake up to find he is so used to its cool, aristocratic, rarefied atmosphere that he cannot venture out into the open air.

The cart does not figure in Intisar's latest production, but at least the troupe still bears its name El-Araba El-Chaabeya. *Any One To Translate?* is yet another new version of the persistent Buqbuq, this time with a French, rather than Italian, infusion ministered by 'Les fous à réaction' of Ville de Lille. The new version is infinitely better than the last, more well-knit and better integrated. Into the story of Buqbuq, Intisar introduced another very short drama by Alfred Farag, imaginatively interweaving both. The oppressed peasant in the *Straw*

*Circle*, imprisoned in an imaginary circle built out of his own fears and delusions, becomes in the adaptation the son of the destitute Buqbuq who lives in a world of dreams and illusions. What is more, the son is only an imaginary son spun out of Buqbuq's marriage fantasy. In other words, the father in his prison-house of dreams, dreams up a son who is also a prisoner of dreams.

The power of dreams and illusions emerges as the central theme of the play, rather than the possibility of communication as the director claims and the title seems to indicate. Indeed, dreams in the play do not only project an illusory reality; they also suck into their vortex the real tramps and vagrants who surround Buqbuq on the rubbish dump of a market-place at the beginning, transforming them into figures in his dream or figments of his imagination.

The Shakespearean metaphor of life as both a transient performance, spun out of airy nothingness, and a short collective dream 'rounded with sleep' dominates the play; it actually begins with the characters asleep on the rubbish heap and ends with a simulation of the gestures and expressions of waking up. The dream metaphor informs not only the content of the scenes and their visual and auditory composition, but the total design, giving us strange, original and exciting combinations in terms of characters, colours, costumes, sounds and language. And though the show may look at first loose and disconnected, a jumble of discordant elements floating in a vacuum without anchor in place or time, on closer inspection, it reveals an inner coherence not dissimilar to that of a dream or a surrealistic painting.

In this type of structure, the alien French element blended well with the varied Egyptian folk material, forming an integral part of the shape and meaning of the show. Needless to say, the musical side was particularly interesting, but this is always the case in Intisar's productions since he is a professional composer, having composed the much acclaimed film music of *The Collar and The Bracelet*.

With his Franco-Arab experiment yielding such good results, I won't be surprised if we find Buqbuq, yet again, next year fraternizing with the Germans or the British. But this time, let us hope he brings along his much neglected cart and takes it out onto the streets.

## 2. The Book of Outcasts*

For some reason, it seems that director Intisar Abdel Fattah has been wantonly doomed to play the role of impresario at CIFET's inaugural ceremonies. I say doomed because, according to the Festival's regulations, if you are chosen to officiate at this occasion, you are automatically disqualified as contestant. This honour also caries the penalty of allowing you only one performance during the Festival while others may get up to four performance slots on the programme. What is worse, the festive atmosphere of the opening seems to rub off on the work, reducing the level of audience attention and barring any serious critical appreciation. In nine cases out of ten, spectators subconsciously catalogue it as an occasion piece and it is very hard afterwards, however good the show, to shake off the association and see it on its own merit as an independent, viable work of art.

Last year, Intisar's *Tarnima* (Hymn), a beautiful ballet and choral work, suffered such a fate. It played at the Festival's opening, was hugely admired and quickly forgotten. After ten days of theatrical banqueting and surfeiting no one so much as gave it a cursory thought. Curiously it was never revived afterwards. What a great work was here overthrown, as Ophelia would say!

Intisar's present experiment, *The Book of Outcasts*, took months of research, preparation and hard work. The result is extremely rewarding. It seems as if all the director's previous experiments have been drafts or preliminary sketches for it. Sound, in the form of instrumental music, percussion, vocals, chanting and rhythmical verbal delivery, has always

---
* 3 September 1992.

played the leading role in Intisar's work; this is perhaps natural, since he was initially trained as a musician. His musical experience, however, took a sharp, dramatic turn after his stay in Poland. There, he joined some experimental theatre workshops and the influence of those years is unmistakable in his present work. There, he learnt how to make music and theatre out of the simplest sounds, objects and actions of daily life: clapping, hammering, stamping, humming, banging tins, washing tubs or pipes, turning a wheel, the *mu'ezzins* call to prayer, the lamentations for the dead, the yells of joy and the tinkling of cutlery and kitchen-ware.

In his earlier *El-Darabukka* (Egyptian drum – 1986), which had the good fortune of not opening the Festival and, therefore, had a reasonably good run, as runs go in Egypt, this incongruous medley of movements and sounds took on a breath-taking freshness and significance as they were used to explore the questions of identity and belonging and the relation between past and present, myth and daily practices. The work was original in both senses of the word: It was novel and unusual, also deeply rooted in Egyptian soil.

The same is true of *Outcasts*, which is even more complex, more virtuosic and technically smoother than *El-Darabukka*. The theme is the elusiveness of life and the central metaphor, the quest. A traveller, journeying in search of true life, encounters first his shadow who parts from him, then other lost souls and fellow ragged travellers, next a man in white tails and a red bow-tie who proves to be death and, finally, a seductive, tantalizing woman who turns out at once to be life and a siren. When death wins at the end, after a battle-cum-dance, the traveller discovers, ironically, the meaning of his quest. The final scene is yet another variation on the metaphor of the journey which takes here the image of sailing after the images of running, trudging and the train. The traveller stands behind an empty wooden frame with two extra side bars, loose at the bottom. He picks up these and moves them like oars. The linking of death with the image of the boat suggests at once Charon, the ferryman of the dead in Greek mythology and the two night and day boats of the Pharaonic sun-god. As the two images merge, the scene becomes paradoxical, suggesting life and death. And when the traveller suddenly stops rowing and stretches up his arms, shaping with the bars two wings, and freezes he becomes the image of the ancient Egyptian symbol of the soul, the *ba*, i.e., a bird with the head of a man. He also evokes the Egyptian Greek myth of the rising Phoenix and a host of other sacred birds in many mythologies.

Indeed, the whole visual and auditory composition of the show draws heavily on the archetypcal images embedded in myths and what Jung called the collective human unconscious and every detail partakes of the same paradoxical quality of the final image. Take the set for example: two structures of huge twisting and curving pipes flank the stage on both sides from top to bottom and end in big cavernous holes through which Death and Life appear and disappear. The forbidding metallic look of the pipes suggests the harshness and soullessness of the modern industrial world, making it the setting of the conflict; and while the holes suggest the womb, and the whole structure a coiled serpent (two more archetypal images), the idea of rats and sewers is never far off. It is as if every visual detail has been magically transformed into a musical note that resonates in the mind, creating waves of echo after it vanishes.

This brings us to the music which is indeed the moving and shaping spirit of the whole performance. Here oriental and folk singing are stunningly counterpointed with classical soprano vocalise and a variety of original sound-effects and percussion rhythms. Indeed, the soundscape of the performance needs the musical analytical powers of a music expert. But for the non-specialist, like me, it was wonderfully evocative and had a tremendous poetic impact. Moreover, by reworking in a different medium the dominant motifs of alienation and a sense of loss (embodied in Walid Aouni's choreography and the stage design) Intisar Abdel-Fattah was able to expand them into universal experiences and, at the same time, intensify their immediate relevance to his Egyptian audiences. The vocal combat between the male folk singer and the soprano, who intermittently flitted across the scene, gave the central existential conflict a cultural edge: the quest for authentic existence become also a quest for authentic cultural identity.

Other aspects of *Outcasts* deserve to be mentioned: the brilliant choreography, the happy choice of costumes, Samir Abdel Halim's excellent rendering of the traveller's part, Safaa El-Tookhi's will-o'-the-wisp presence as Life, Hanaa Abdel-Fattah's deliberately theatrical impersonation of Death, the ancient, but extremely versatile folk flute-player, the proficiency of the soprano and the folk-singer and the ensemble of outcasts and wandering travellers.

If the Festival must have a contest (and I am personally against it), and if Egypt must take part in it, then Intisar Abdel-Fattah's *Outcasts* should have been chosen to represent it. As it is, the production was irrevocably consigned (by consent or coercion) to the ceremonial opening night at the Big Hall of the Opera.

## 3. Sonata[*]

Intisar Abdel-Fattah's *Sonata* is a sequel to his last year's *Concerto*. Sonata, as the title leads one to expect, relies for its effect on the interaction of music and words. The trio of the father, mother and son is represented by a cello, a piano and a violin. There are also five wind instruments, beside the drums. The work unfolds like a lyrical poem, a swan song, recited by the father against a variegated musical background which includes Tchaikovsky's *Swan Lake* and *Pathetique*, Dvorak's *New World*, and selections from Brahms, Mendelssohn, Debussy and Schumann. The set (designed by Ali Nabil Wahba, the director of the Modern Art Museum), which consists of four sculptures of women, a piano, a round white block and a white transparent cocoon that descends from above to envelop the father and son on the white block, partakes of the same romantic mood and enhances the ethereal effect of the music. Like all of Intisar Abdel-Fattah's work, *Sonata* has proved an eminently rewarding experience.

---

[*] 31 Sugust 1995.

## 4. Lear, A Symphony*

The question of technical polish is an ever-present bugaboo for Egyptian theatre directors. In this respect, *The Symphony of Lear*, directed by Intisar Abdel-Fattah at Al-Ghad Theatre, has great potential except for some rough edges and lack of attention to details. Abdel-Fattah's *Lear* boldly splits Shakespeare's play down the middle, removing the 'Gloucester / Edmund / Edgar' subplot, stripping it down to its original folktale bones, and reducing the play to a straightforward story about a poor old father betrayed by his two eldest daughters and achieving wisdom in the end.

The potential for sentimentality in such a treatment was mitigated by the musical conception of the whole show and its subtle evocation of the Renaissance Masque — that ornate, elaborate theatrical form which reached its height at the English Court at the hands of Ben Jonson and the Italian designer Inigo Jones in the early 17th century. The auditorium of El-Ghad Chamber Theatre was transformed by set-designer Nabil El-Halwagi into a palace hall, decked out in motifs suggesting both Renaissance and Baroque art. Apart from this, the set consisted of a versatile table made of three sections which could be divided and assembled to represent a ship, the stocks, a bier, ... etc. and a wooden throne for the king.

The characters were reduced to Lear, Goneril and Regan (played by the same actress), Cordelia, Albany, Kent and the Fool. But to make up for this severe reduction, four opera signers in formal concert dress were added to double as the main characters, plus live musicians — a

---
* 4 September 1996.

harpist, a drummer and a wind quartet. This superimposed musical structure, with baroque music and arias from diverse operas, infuses variety and richness into the show and eloquently counterpoints the verse. Hassan Abdel-Hamid's *Lear* was unconventional and quite striking; he played the first part very low-key, which made his outburst during the storm all the more moving. Perhaps the only drawbacks in this show are the costumes which needed more attention in terms of design and choice of texture and the poor execution of some of the panels of the set, namely the stained-glass motifs of details from Michelangelo's *The Creation of Adam* in the Sistine Chapel.

# Remembering Allula*

On the evening of 12 March this year Algerian playwright, director and actor, Abdel-Qadir Allula, was gunned down by the Islamic Salvation Front on his way to give a lecture on theatre at the cultural centre of Wahran. Significantly, he was shot in the head: the seat of those enlightened ideas which had long troubled and irked the bigots among his countrymen. He was singled out because, unlike many secular intellectual theatre people, he scorned the safety of the proverbial ivory tower and the protective seclusion of a small theatre and a select, elite audience. His intimate acquaintance with the Western theatre, which he studied in France and Russia, did not alienate him from his Arab and north African roots; if anything, it launched him on an exploratory voyage deep into the heart of the Algerian folk heritage.

He dreamed of a theatre of and for the people; and with him, it was no mere slogan. When he was made director of the Wahran district theatre in 1972, he decided to take theatre to the people in villages and small towns. Those were turbulent times; the agrarian revolution was in full swing and the countryside was in a state of social turmoil. Allula decided that he and his theatre should be part of it. A new play called *El-Ma'ida* (The Table), after the name of an Algerian village where there had been scenes of violence, was collectively written by the company and it toured the countryside on a bus which served the group as living quarters, stage and roadside cafe. It was there, in the villages, among the peasants, that Allula embarked on his long and arduous search for a new form of Arab theatre. With so much truth in him, and

---
* 16 June 1994.

so much popular backing behind him, the only way to silence Allula was to gun him down.

His death was a great loss to Arab theatre, but also a great service. If theatre — which had long been regarded as disposable entertainment, as a marginal phenomenon and a peripheral social activity (not to say a disreputable one) — could cost an artist his life, this makes it a force to be reckoned with. Surely, even the most unscrupulous of commercial entertainers would now begin to respect the profession (if only a little or as a safety measure against the anti-theatre fanatics) and would feel a little twinge of shame if anyone vulgarised it. But alas!

Ironically, on the day the Egyptian theatre decided to honour the name of Allula (together with thirteen other respectable theatre practitioners) there was little sign of such respect. I had hoped that this year, at least, out of respect for Allula and his widow, who was present on the occasion, we would be spared the invariably sloppily trumped up performance that usually accompanies the ceremony. But it seems as if we are doomed to undergo this compulsory annual penance for ever or for as long as the bureaucrats of the state-theatre sector remain in power. This year, however, they outdid themselves, adding insult to injury; not content with the usual, insipid musical hotch-potch they trot out on stage every year, they insolently decided to pad it out with three scenes from Abdel-Rahman El-Sharqawi's *Ma'sat Jamila* (The Tragedy of Jamila — the famous Algerian freedom-fighter caught and tortured by the French before Algeria's independence), his *Watani Akko* (Akko, My Country), and Salah Abdel-Saboor's *Ma'sat El-Hallaj* (available in English as *Death in Baghdad*).

It was outrageous to hear the stirring, limpid, evocative poetry of Saboor, in particular, interrupted every few lines by the feeble-minded doggerel farcically described in the pamphlet of this outlandish spectacle as colloquial verse. But most insulting of all was having these three gracious and deeply serious scenes wrapped in inane dancing (if you can call it that) and singing and packaged in a cloyingly sentimental plot about a couple of goodies looking for their stolen 'birds', meaning children, who were kidnapped by a group of anaemic-looking baddies, dressed in black leotards with Ninja-like head-bands and twisted claw-like fingers. Their leader, however, the archdevil, wore a white silk shirt, ridiculously adorned with a pleated raised collar which looked like an Elizabethan ruff. One did not know whether to laugh or cry whenever the mother (Tayseer Fahmi), in spandex black leggings and a red flannel top, writhed and screamed for her lost *asfour* (bird). And since Samir El-Asfouri, the artistic director of Al-Tali'a theatre, happened to be in the audience, everytime she cried out "Oh, asfouri is lost" there was a wave of suppressed giggling. I learnt afterwards that this travesty of a show had cost the tax-payer two hundred thousand pounds.

Leaving the National where this scandal had taken place I could only think with anguish of the frail-looking Mrs. Allula stepping falteringly onto the stage, with her face half-covered with huge dark glasses, to receive her husband's trophy, little suspecting that, possibly, she was being exploited for a publicity stunt. I also remembered my one meeting with Allula in Tunis in 1991 during the Carthage festival. I could almost hear his voice; for a whole hour, he had spoken passionately, almost despairingly, about the future of theatre in Algeria and the Arab world, frequently lapsing into French. I wondered what he would have made of our evening of festivities.

# III

# Fiction in Action:
# Dramaturges and Storytellers

# 1. From the Page to the Stage[*]

Amina El-Sawi's dramatization of Naguib Mahfouz's novel, *Midaq Alley*, in 1958, started a heated critical controversy about the artistic legitimacy of transferring novels to the stage. It was reductive, some argued, and falsified the novel out of all recognition. Others retorted that, of course, it was different; it had to be in view of the change of genre and medium. Only a fool or an ignoramus would expect to find Mahfouz's novel in its totality, or as s/he knows it, on stage. Making plays out of novels, or films for that matter (Hassan El-Imam's film versions of several Mahfouz novels equally came under heavy fire), entails careful selection, extensive omission, rearrangement of events, curtailment and telescoping the spatio-temporal context. The process involves interpretation as well: the adaptor or dramaturge gives only one of many possible readings of the novel — his or her own — and this reading should be judged independently of the novel in terms of its depth, coherence and formal dramatic integrity.

Indeed, what was wrong with El-Sawi's adaptation, some maintained, was that it stuck too close to the novel and ended up falling between two stools — the narrative and dramatic. Daunted by Mahfouz's literary stature, perhaps, or the enthusiastic critical reception of the novel, led by Taha Hussein no less, El-Sawi, who was thirty-eight and making her debut as a dramaturge after years at the censorship department of the ministry of interior censoring films and publications, did not want to take risks; she strove to be as truthful as possible to the text, cramming as much of the narrative as she could manage within the

---

[*] 11 March, 1999.

conventional time limits of a fifties' performance (roughly three and a half to four hours).

Though it rambled, lacked focus, dramatic tension and complexity (in the view of a number of critics), the play, directed by Kamal Yaseen and presented by the Free Theatre Company which boasted some of the best young acting talents in Egypt at the time (including Sa'd Ardash, Fu'ad El-Muhandis and Abdel Mun'im Madbouly, among others), was a huge success. El-Sawi, who judging by the one play she wrote single-handed (*Marriage Wholesale*, 1959) and an earlier one she wrote with others (*The Struggle of Port-Said*, 1956), had a poor gift for creative writing and a limited artistic imagination, gained her credentials as an adapter of fiction and there was no stopping her after that, whatever the critics thought or said. She went on to adapt three more of Mahfouz's novels for the stage: *Bayn El-Qasrein* (1960), *Qasr El-Shouq*, or *Palace of Desire*, as the English translation is titled (1961) and *The Thief and the Dogs* (1962), as well as Yehya Haqi's *Qnadeel Om Hashim* (*The Holy Lantern*) in 1961, Yusef El-Siba'i's *Land of Hypocrisy* (*Ard Al-Nifaq*) in 1962, and Abdel Rahman El-Sharqawi's *The Land* (*Al-Ard*) the same year.

By the end of 1962, adapting novels for the stage had become an established and respectable practice in the Egyptian theatre and writers were encouraged and even commissioned to dramatize fiction — not that they needed much persuasion: El-Sawi's success was sufficiently alluring. It was regarded by the Ministry of Information and Culture, headed by Abdel Qadir Hatem, as a safe and speedy way of meeting the evergrowing demand for new plays created by the many newly-founded T.V. theatre companies each of which needed at least a new play a month. These companies were designed to provide television with an incessant flow of well-screened, diversified and ideologically sound dramatic material. And towards this end, some of the best and most popular novels written in the sixties, or earlier, made their way to the stage; examples are: Tawfiq El-Hakim's *The Return of the Spirit* (*Aoudat Al-Rooh*), Fathy Ghanem's *The Man Who Lost His Shadow* (*Al-Ragul Allazi Faqada Zillahu*), Abdel Rahman El-Sharqawi's *Back Streets* (*Al-Shawari' Al-Khalfiyyah*), Ihsan Abdel Quddus's *A Stranger in Our House* (*Fi Baytina Rajul*), Mohamed Abdel Halim Abdalla's *For the Sake of My Son* (*Min Ajl Waladi*) and Mohamed El-Tab'y's *When We Fall In Love* (*'Indama Nuhib*).

Foreign novels were left alone; the only exceptions were Dostoyevsky's *Idiot* and *Crime and Punishment* (the latter, like the majority of the Egyptian novels mentioned above, was also made into a movie). The regime's socialist ideology and its anti-Western, pro-Soviet orientation explain this as well as the widespread popularity of Russian literarture and drama at the time. [At the Soviet Bookshop downtown you could for a few pounds buy all the works of Tolstoy, Dostoyevsky, Chekhov, Gorky, and Turgenev]. Foreign plays were also left alone; the long tradition of adapting western plays (particularly French melodrama, comedies, farces, and vaudevilles) which had nourished and sustained the Egyptian theatre for over half a century before the rise of national drama gave way to the new trend of adapting Egyptian novels initiated by El-Sawi. The change was beneficial all round: the theatre companies did not have to scramble any more for scripts, the dramatists were saved from turning into hack writers under the pressure of the companies; the novelists reached a wider audience, becoming more famous and richer; the dramaturges and adaptors stopped being plagiarists and plunderers of foreign drama and became skilled craftsmen who took pride in their work while making a good living; and foreign drama (Shakespeare, Moliere, Sophocles, Lorca, Chekhov, Miller, Brecht, Sartre, Beckett, Ionesco, ... etc.) could tread the boards unbattered.

The dramatization of fiction for the stage, however, did not survive the sixties. Indeed, the final years of that decade had witnessed its waning. In the seventies and most of the eighties – as in the first half of the century – the only narratives to yield plays were the popular epics (*Siras*), some folk tales and the chronicles of history; and with the rise of the private, commercial theatres, there was a marked reversion to the old tradition of purloining foreign plays and Egyptianizing them. Novels continued to be adapted, but for television, as soap operas, and so were some of the famous plays of the sixties, like Nu'man Ashour's *El-Dughry Family* and *Tennery Tower* (*Burg El-Madabegh*).

In the eighties, I could find only five productions based on literary narratives. Samir El-Asfouri's adaptation of Chekhov's *Ward No. 6*, rechristened *The Mad Cell* (*Zinzanat El-Maganeen*) and presented at El-Tali'a in 1980, was a huge success with the critics and the public. In terms of theme, style and atmosphere, it was very much in tune with the mood of the times and its mixture of black humour, barbed political satire, grotesque brutality, farcical absurdity and sensitive portrayal of human suffering made it one of most memorable productions of that decade. A new adaptation of Mahfouz's *Midaq Alley* by Bahgat Qamar, produced by the private United Artists (Al-Fannaneen al-Mutahideen) company, followed in 1984; and three years later, another private theatre company produced an adaptation, also by Bahgat Qamar, of Amin Yusef Ghurab's popular novel *Shabab Imra'a*

(*A Woman in her Prime*), which had been made into a very successful movie in the fifties, directed by Salah Abu Seif and starring Tahiya Carioca in her best role in cinema. (thirty-five years later, another famous oriental dancer, Fifi Abdu, attracted by Carioca's success, attempted the part on stage, in a commercial production directed by Hani Metaweh, but fell dismally short of achieving anything like Carioca's fine and riveting performance).

In the same year, 1987, director Ahmed Isma'il dramatized and produced Fuad Haddad's version of the popular tale of *El-Shatir Hassan* (Hassan, the Clever) which he had written in prison in the 1960s in collaboration with Abdel-Latif Metwalli, giving it a different ideological slant, and recharging it with socialist, progressive ideas. The production was simple but highly imaginative, and though the cast consisted mostly of amateurs and had a small budget, like all Mass Culture productions, it enjoyed a long, successful run at Wikalat Al-Ghuri.

In contrast, Abdel Ghaffar Ouda's production of a stage version of Mahfouz's novel *A Beginning and an End*, or *Bidaya wa Nihaya* (also successfully transferred to the screen by Abu Seif in the early 1960s) was a complete failure. Despite a star-studded cast, including Yusra and Hussein Fahmi, Mahmoud Yaseen, Amina Rizq and Farid Shawki, among others, and the wide publicity it received as a fund-raising project to help repay the national debts of Egypt, it barely survived ten days at the floating theatre in Giza. For a number of years afterwards, Ouda's flash in the pan seemed to have scared fiction off the boards.

It was not until 1994 that fiction found its way back to the stage, guided this time by Sameh Mahran, who is even more of a qualified drama expert than his predecessor, the pioneer in the field, Amina

El-Sawi . El-Sawi had been among the first to join the Acting Institute (later, Theatre Institute) when it opened in 1944, and had studied drama there at the department of criticism and research before graduating in 1947 and embarking on her career as a dramaturge. Mahran, on the other hand, read Hebrew language and literature as an undergraduate, then joined the Institute of Art Criticism at the Academy of Arts for a postgraduate diploma in the arts, followed by an M.A. and a doctorate in drama.

Unlike El-Sawi, who was a faithful disciple of realism, Mahran is thoroughly experimental and his plays and dramatizations display definite feminist sympathies, a predilection for deconstruction, a rebellious rejection of patriarchy, a deep-seated relativism, and a postmodernist frame of mind and sensibility. Predictably, he takes a different attitude to the dramatization of novels, regarding it as a genuinely creative exercise which does not *reproduce* the 'text / novel' in a different genre (an absurd proposition, he thinks), but engages the text, defined as a field of energy capable of generating mutiple readings, in a 'constructive / deconstructive' dialogue which *produces* another field of energy — a script. Influenced by modern Theory (Semiotics, Deconstruction, Feminism, and Reader-Reception theory), Mahran refutes the autonomous authority of the text; but on the issue of 'authorship' he is ambivalent. As a dramatist working with literary texts of known authors, some of them still alive, he is in sympathy with Stanley Fish's idea that the text is a product of the reader and his claim that 'Strictly speaking, getting "back-to-the-text" is not a move one can perform'; they support his conviction that his adaptations are 'productions' and not 'reproductions'. But once the text is produced, he likes to take credit for it as its "Author". In other words, in the process of reading the novels to produce his dramatic script, he tends to go along with Roland Barthes' announcement of 'the death of the author'; but once the process ends and the text is there, he resents being waved aside and pronounced, as an author, dead.

What feeds this ambivalent attitude and, perhaps, generates it in the first place is that dramaturges, as well as literary translators, are never given the credit, respect and financial reward they deserve. They are generally slighted, made light of, ignored, or forgotten. The dramatic script carries the title of the novel it was adapted from, the name of its (the novel's) author, and if the script is good and the production successful, the novelist and director get the credit; if it flops, the adaptor becomes the scapegoat.

Between 1994 and 1997, Mahran (who had already written two original plays before turning his hand to dramatization) produced four experimental scripts based on five experimental novels: *The Child of Sand (Tifl al-Rimal)* in 1994, based on El-Tahir Bin Jalloun's novel of the same title, as well as another novel of his called *Laylat Al-Qadr* (the holy night which occurs in the last week of Ramadan when the gates of heaven are said to open and all prayers are answered); *The Collar and the Bracelet*, in 1996, adapted from Yehya El-Tahir Abdalla's novel of the same title; *The Seven Days of Man (Ayam Al-Insan al-Sab'a)*, in 1997, based on a novel by the late Abdel Hakim Qasim, and *Khafyet Qamar (Lunar Eclipse*, and also the name of a village in the novel) in 1998, adapted from Mohamed Nagui's novel.

When *The Collar and the Bracelet (Al-Tooq wa Al-Iswira)* won Egypt the best director award at the Cairo International Festival for Experimental Theatre in 1996, it encouraged another promising young playwright (Sa'id Haggag) to try his hand at adapting Bahaa Tahir's intriguing novel, *Aunt Safiyya and the Monastery* (*Khalti Saffiya wa al-Deir*). The script was directed by Nasser Abdel Mon'im who had directed three of Mahran's adaptations, including the award-winner, and presented at Al-Hanager on the fringe of CIFET 1998, then transferred to the National where it ran for a month. Unlike Mahran, however, and very much like Amina El-Sawi, Haggag tried to play it safe and ended in disaster. Sticking to the surface of the narrative and its skeletal plot, and ignoring the layers of meaning and deliberate ambiguities generated by the structure, the language, and handling of space and time, he produced a limp, melodramatic script, the latter half of which consists of the ravings of a mad woman, and which can be summed up by the proverbial "hell hath no fury like a woman scorned." Haggag, however, is still young and may do well yet.

Other young theatre artists – usually directors who compose their own scripts in collaboration with the actors and artistic crew have resorted to fiction for material and inspiration; but they seem to favour the short story. In 1991, Tariq Sa'id composed a pungent satirical and exuberant script out of a number of short stories by Yusef Idris, and linked the hilarious, witty, strip cartoon-like episodes with the most famous character in Idris's plays, Farfoor. *Demi-Rebels* was presented during the second Free Theatre Festival in 1991, and voted the best production in the festival at the closing ceremony held at the National.

Foreign short stories attracted another artist, Sarah Enany, who fell in love with Jane Rhys's short stories and created, in close collaboration with Caroline Khalil, an image-based impressionistic script of Rhys's *Vienna*, with certain details and motifs from another two stories in the same collection. The play, directed by Sarah and starring Caroline, was performed at Al-Hanager, in March 1996, with a simple elegant set, real crystal glasses, back projections of certain Klimt paintings, musical motifs from Chopin and the songs of Edith Piaf, and a fresh supply of irises for every performance; it came across as a flow of cinematic images, as fleeting and short-lived as the happiness of the two main characters, and transmitted a poignant sense of the fragility of beauty which rose to a climax when the sheet of glass covering the back screen (on which the Klimt slides and a slide of a big bunch of irises were fitfully projected) suddenly cracked and crashed down in a heap as if of its own accord. The final image was of an empty stage strewn with broken glass and a video projection on the back screen showing close-ups of iris petals falling into the water and floating on the waves.

Two years later, another Sarah (Sarah Nur El-Sherif) put on at the same venue a production of a selection of letters from Abdel Rahman El-Abnoudi's long epistolary narrative, *The Letters of Haraji al-Qutt to his Wife Fatna*, which traces the growing consciousness of a peasant who leaves his village to work at the construction site of the Aswan Dam, and of his wife's who has to learn to cope alone and manage as head of the family. Sarah Nur El-Sherif, who prepared and directed the script, used a dual set, splitting the stage into two locations without a visible barrier. The husband and wife *spoke* their letters to each other across imaginary distances, and the contrast between the physical proximity of the couple on stage and their assumed separation had an ironical effect which started one thinking about the meaning of communication in relation to space and time.

The same year, 1998, Rasha Khayri's daring and lively dramatization of Yusef Idris's famous short story, *Bayt min Lahm* (*A House of Flesh*) was directed by a gifted actress called Riham (her surname I have sadly forgotten) and presented at the AUC Howard theatre. It was a robust production, refreshingly outspoken, unsettling and painfully honest. Idris's story, which centres on the hunger of the flesh (the most iniquitous kind of hunger, as the narrator says) and the desperate, even perverted action it can force the starved to take, features four women – a widow and her three daughters – driven by the hoplessness of their wretched lives and the rigours of extreme physical deprivation and sexual frustration to violate the incest taboo and share one man. The sharing is not planned; when the mother remarries it just happens as a natural, inevitable consequence of the physical situation. All the women know of it, and the widow's second husband, who is blind, first suspects it then is sure of it. Yet, it is never mentioned or discussed. The 'unspeakable' is carefully hidden behind a diligently guarded wall of silence. And, indeed, silence dominates the story verbally, thematically, and structurally. The word occurs thirty-five times in the short narrative which consists of three sequences and moves from the silence imposed by mourning the father, combined with the silence of breathless, hopeful expectation at the beginning, to the guilty conspiracy of silence at the end. The middle sequence which briefly breaks the silence to express hope is cruelly ironical.

There are ways, of course, of projecting such a story on stage with little or no recourse to language, and some viewers missed the silence that envelops Idris's narrative in Khayri's adaptation. But her way is as legitimate as any. She allowed the women to vividly express their rebelliousness and frustration in word and action, violent fights and petty squabbles, and built a convincing, detailed and graphic image of the dismal and arduous daily life of a poor family of working women. The raw realism of the image brought it very close to life while the loud vulgarity of the verbal exchanges betrayed the violent despair underneath and made the gradual creeping of the silence over the characters, one by one, all the more chilling.

Like most of her generation of young adaptors, Khayri is not awed by literary texts or the reputation of their authors. She gave herself the liberty of adding many details to flesh out Idris's shadowy females, individualize them, and bring them to life on stage; and the result was quite rewarding. The AUC production gave Khayri's script uncensored and uncut; and I can still remember the sultry atmosphere and mounting sense of claustrophobia I imaginatively experienced as I watched those tensed up female bodies, bespeaking great mental agony and emotional strain, jerking around in the intentionally cramped performance space created by the director, knocking against each other and the few sticks of furniture.

Every detail of the set – the low, stained, grey walls, suggesting a smelly basement flat, stuffy and humid; the threadbare faded rug; the oppressively tiny window in the back wall behind a humble box-sofa with a thin, discoloured matress; the few pathetic cooking utensils; the grey washing tub; the cheap low table (tabliyya) of unvarnished wood; the old and scratched clothes chest; the women's shabby, frayed dresses and head scarves, made of the cheapest fabrics — everything bore the taint of squalid poverty and hopelessness. Except for one thing: a high, four-poster bed, dressed in clean white sheets and looking invitingly soft and comfortable. That bed, which stood in sharp contrast with its degraded surroundings, became in the course of the performance the focal point of the set and dramatic action.

Gradually, it grew into a multiple, complex and paradoxical sign, signifying at once the escape route from the dreariness of reality, the promise of fulfillment, the longing for warmth and security, the site of bitter conflict, of the craved and forbidden, the lawful bridal bed the daughters dream of, and a hotbed of sin. As the meanings multiplied, the bed seemed to imaginatively expand and occupy the whole performance space — a space that has to be shared by the wretched souls confined in it. Reduced to its two basic actions, Khayri's adaptation, as performed at the Howard, can seem like a grim joke: it begins with the daughters taking turns at sharing the only bed with the mother to get one kind of nourishment, and ends with them taking turns again at sharing it, but this time, with her husband for another kind of nourishment.

Another production of Khayri's adaptation, directed by 'Asim Nagaty, was presented by the Youth Theatre in February, this year, at The House of Zeinab Khatoun. For this production, however, Khayri had to submit her script to censorship. (Any public performance running for more than three days has to be approved by the censor.) Alterations were inevitable: the incest theme had to be watered down and the end changed. In the Zeinab Khatoun production, only one of the three daughters commits the heinous act, and only once, while the blind husband (predictably, perhaps, since he is a sheikh who earns his living reciting the Quran) is absolved of the guilt of colluding in the conspiracy of silence and kept innocent of the knowledge.

In the earlier script, he knows very well what is happening but does not confront the women, using his blindness as a hypocritical excuse to absolve himself of the guilt and shift it squarely onto their shoulders since they can see, as he tells the audience, and he cannot. Any woman who wears his wedding ring he will treat as his lawful wedded wife regardless of her shape or the feel of her skin, he tells us. In the censored script, on the other hand, the Sheikh remonstrates with his wife for taking off her wedding ring when she slept with him earlier that day, feels quite at a loss why she insisted on remaining silent then, and walks out in a huff. The mother is shattered by the discovery that one of her daughters had taken her place in bed and rightly suspects the middle one who has the most vitality and is the most rebellious. When, in the following scene, her eldest daughter asks her to lend her the ring to wear for a day, she refuses (in the story and earlier script she complies) and a violent quarrel ensues. The final scene shows the husband on the large balcony overlooking the courtyard of Zeinab Khatoun where the performance takes place, singing a maudlin song, accompanied by a small oriental band sitting in one corner of the yard, while the four women huddle together on the four-poster bed (carried over from the earlier production) and draw the blanket over their heads.

At Zeinab Khatoun, the flesh and its desires were tamed, the family, judging by the costumes, raised slightly up the socio-economic ladder, the tension and oppressive atmosphere substantially eased, and the physical and mental strain considerably relieved. Instead of a cramped, claustrophobic space underground, we have the spacious, airy courtyard of the old house and its charming architecture. Sitting there, it was difficult to imagine that the life of the characters inhabiting this place could be dull or dreary. There was no hint of squalor, no trace of vulgarity or ugliness anywhere; only pure old-world charm stirring a vague nostalgic feeling. The daughters (played by Intisar, Amani Yusef and Hind Husni) and their mother (Manal Zaki) were beautiful, elegant, and in the bloom of youth; one could hardly imagine them failing to get husbands, unless all men go blind like the Sheikh the mother marries.

The Sheikh, on the other hand, was nothing but a grotesque caricature, and it would require quite a leap of the imagination to think of him as a male or object of desire. This defused the incest bomb: incestuous sex with this travesty of a man would constitute its own punishment. Mustafa Selim's lyrics and Hisham Taha's tunes created a lyrical mood which softened the atmosphere and shifted the accent from sexual to social, economic and general human deprivation. And Hisham Gom'a's design, which kept the props to a minimum, leaving the space free, contributed to the lyrical, romantic mood. When the actresses slid the bed on its wheels around the space in the soft lighting, it seemed like a graceful dance; and when they moved around their individual clothes chests, they looked like excited children delving into their secret treasure-boxes. It was a smooth, inoffensive, charming performance with no claws or fangs.

Just before Idris's unfortunate women were forced out of The House of Zeinab Khatoun by maintenance workers at the end of February, at the nearby Ghuri Cultural Palace, another production adapted from literary narratives opened for a two-week run.

*Fragments of Diamond* was first performed at Al-Ghad hall at the end of 1998, and here, as in his previous productions – *Faust, Passers-by* and *Demi-Rebels* – Director Tariq Sa'id, the founder of the troupe, pursued the same artistic strategy, preferring to construct his text collaboratively with the group from various sources through the method of collage rather than resort to a ready-made one. In his earlier *Demi-Rebels*, voted best production in the second Free Theatre Festival in 1991 by both the public and the critics, he had strung together a number of short stories by Yusef Idris, using Farfour, the memorable hero of Idris's groundbreaking play *El-Farafeer* (The Underlings) as a link, and padding the show with parodies of old movies, political caricature, popular songs and spicy topical allusions. In six short, finely-etched and fast-paced hilarious sketches, the zany Faroor was paraded in many guises and different settings, bringing into sharp satirical focus many of the irking absurdities and contradictions of contemporary Egyptian life.

In *Fragments*, which pointedly refers in the title to its style and mode of construction as if to forewarn the audience and forestall any criticism, theme-and-variation is the dominant structural principle and Anton Chekhov is the narrative source. Sixteen of his short stories are picked out and deftly interwoven with many poems by Salah Jaheen, together with a few songs and bedtime stories, both traditional and original. Like Chekhov and Jaheen who both believed that art should stick close to life and ordinary people, that, as artists, their roles were mainly those of social chroniclers, Sa'id and his group used the stories and poems – their farcical, anecdotal situations, vivid character-sketches and comic and tragic incidents – to write, in the form of an animated, disarmingly simple strip cartoon, a dramatic chronicle of our times from the perspective of the poor and downtrodden. Though never mentioned by name, the benign presence of these two great poets of life is strongly felt throughout as the fragments fall into place and both the characters and their audience are guided, in a subtle progression, towards a maturer, broader and more compassionate awareness of the suffering of ordinary humanity.

The setting is Egypt today and the mode of dramatic representation is openly theatrical. The actors (Magdy El-Siba'i, Ihab Subhi, Shahira Fuad, Haytham Amer, Abdel-Halim Abdel-Hamid, Nora Hemeida, Mina Athenaseus and Amani Samir) use their real names in the initial story-telling situation which is maintained throughout as the general frame of the dramatized episodes. The frame features Shahira Fuad – a young actress with a lovely voice – posing as an aged granny continuously harassed by incessant demands for stories from an insatiable brood of boisterous grandchildren. When she runs out of stock and begins to repeat the same old, fusty tales about sultans and princesses, the children are bored to tears and clamour for something more related to reality and the present. At first, the aged lady who has been bred on fairytales and knows no other feels insulted and goes in a huff. In desperation, the kids try to make up new stories of their own (and this is when Chekhov comes in) or look for others in the memoirs of their dead grandfather (and this is the cue for Salah Jaheen). Slowly and reluctantly, the granny is drawn into the game and learns from the children how to relate to reality and use her imagination. The children too seem to undergo a change and grow wiser and sadder. One notes a gathering somberness halfway through the play, and by the time we reach the end, it has positively deepened into black.

While the granny's silly stories and hackneyed tales are verbally rattled out, the ones taken from Chekhov, regardless of the narrator, are consistently dramatized. As soon as one is launched, members of the group promptly get up to impersonate the characters and act out the narrative with the help of a few simple props. True to the poor theatre style adopted by practically all independent theatre troupes in the spirit of making a virtue of necessity, *Fragments* uses minimal sets and costume changes. The stories and poems flow into each other and gently overlap without hindrance. A woolen cap, a shawl, a chair or an easel is enough to mark a change of character or location. The burden of make-believe falls squarely on the actors as they deftly skip among the fragments, guided by Sa'id's smooth movement patterns, intelligent scene-blocking and sensitive lighting-plan.

Looking at first like a mass of haphazard, jumbled narratives (a calculated effect perhaps), upon reflection *Fragments* reveals its intricate design and the tremendous amount of work that went into it. The vast material collected by the Light core group was carefully sifted and divided into discrete narrative units. Each consists of a number of stories linked by one character, location, or both and so arranged as to spotlight, in a series of takes as it were, one or more of the negative, destructive aspects of life – poverty, greed, oppression, exploitation, callousness, vanity, hypocrisy, deceit, stupidity or mere folly. The narrative blocks are interspersed and punctuated with pithy, humorous or emotionally-charged relevant extracts from Jaheen's poetry either to intensify their impact or herald a narrative transition or a change of mood. This intricate collage is carefully orchestrated to vary the rhythm and achieve a delicate balance between sympathy and satire, irony and compassion, the vulgar and tender, the farcically ridiculous and the painfully serious. Indeed, without this constant shifting of mood, *Fragments*, without a claim to intellectual profundity or dialectical thought, could have easily slipped into sentimentality. The show successfully avoids this trap and the balance it achieves is one both Chekhov and Jaheen would have heartily approved.

## 2. The Brief Summer of Aton*

In these cynical days, one finds it difficult to believe that a popular film and T.V. star, like Nur El-Sherif, could lay aside his busy and lucrative schedule to devote four months of intensive work conducting a theatre-workshop for young amateurs for nothing but the pure love of theatre. But it is true. The sceptical may argue that now that the Egyptian film industry is at a dangerous low ebb and leading roles for middle-aged stars are becoming fewer, many of the film *jeune-premiers* of the past twenty-five years are seeking a new lease of limelight on the boards. And to corroborate their argument, they may refer you to the theatre listings where you will find Adel Imam in *El-Za'im* (The Leader), Hussein Fahmi in *El-Haditha* (The Accident), and Mahmoud Yaseen in *El-Khedive*. Only last year, they may go on to point out, Nur El-Sherif himself was leading the show in the musical comedy *Kunt Feen Ya Ali?* (Where were you Ali?) with his film-star wife Pussy. Granted. But starring in a play for a fat fee is one thing and training and directing amateurs gratis is surely quite another.

The project was no sudden decision and the choice of subject was no fluke. According to Nur, Bahaa Tahir's short story, *The Trial of the Priest* (Muhakamat Al-Kahen), has haunted him for the past nine years (that is three years after his first venture into directing in 1982), and the idea of making it into a play sprouted four years ago. 'Making it into a play', however, is not how Nur El-Sherif prefers to describe what he and playwright Mohsen Misilhi did to the original text. He insists that

---
* 24 March, 1994.

what he had in mind was not a 'dramatization' but a "faithful rendering of the literary text in audio-visual terms using the medium of theatre." I must admit that I found this pronouncement (which he sprang upon me after one of the rehearsals) extremely baffling. I had happened to mention some reservations about the adaptation. Tahir's story, I had said, builds up beautifully through narration to a dialogic climax where Smenkh, the high priest of the reinstated worship of Amon-Ra, confronts his former friend and colleague, and present foe and prisoner, Kai-nen, the high priest of the fallen god Aton.

In the dark cell, the two honest men struggle earnestly with their differences, trying to build bridges of tolerance, understanding and human sympathy across the pit of fire that separates them. Both have been licked by its flames and are only too anxious not to be totally consumed by it. At the end, Smenkh helps his friend escape, soothing him with the prospect that may be one day more people will come round to his god and join the folds of his worshippers. The bigoted zeal of the martyr is distasteful to him and rather silly; he may be too worldly-wise and cynical to accept Kai's romantic religion and his god of light, joy and love; he may see the danger of advocating a happy nature worship without an ethical code and the deterrents of fear and punishment; nevertheless, he is quite willing to tolerate the presence of such romantic fools and dreamers and would even go to great lengths to protect them. His last advice to Kai is to write more poetry, something he himself lacks the talent for. As Kai departs to the realm of beauty and art where he can sing freely to the sun-god Aton, we see Smenkh threading his way back in the dark and pausing for a minute to place a narcissus flower on the solid knee of the dark stone statue of Amon. We last hear him murmuring: "Oh Amon. Why have you made me high priest?" And the words spell out his loneliness, his sense of the terrible burden he bears and his moving stoical resignation.

I put it to Nur El-Sherif that the relationship between Smenkh and Kai could have been used as the basis for a stirring drama; in the story it faintly reminded me of the tragic friendship of Thomas Becket and Henry II of England in Jean Anouilh's *Becket, or l'honneur de Dieu* – a play of which Nur himself is passionately enamoured. On stage, however, it appeared sadly undeveloped, was encumbered by many irrelevant scenes and was often flattened into a dry intellectual debate. If at moments it warmed and throbbed into a semblance of life, it was thanks to the efforts of Ihab Subhi as Kai and Tariq Abdel Fattah as Smenkh.

In response to my remark, Nur El-Sherif trotted out his engimatic claim that he was simply putting the literary text on stage — whatever that means. He even went so far as to declare it from the boards for all the world to hear. In what strikes me as, possibly, a dramatic ruse (and not a very clever one) to forestall any criticism of the dramatic pallidness of the spectacle, the director and his dramaturge replicated themselves on stage in the figures of a fictional director and a fictional playwright in the process of preparing Bahaa Tahir's short story for the stage. Their discussions, arguments, explanations and comments prologue and punctuate the unfolding of the story, allowing the production to underline the topical relevance of the projected events and, perhaps more importantly, providing Nur El-Sherif with ample opportunity to initiate the audience into the mysteries of his creation and explain to the slow, dim-witted critic his artistic purpose and aesthetic design.

After a short, nightmarish opening scene where we glimpse, against a blinding, flashing light, the silhouttes of an ancient Egyptian executioner chasing the director, we are told clearly by the same director that the purpose of the play is to present us, as closely as possible, with Bahaa Tahir's literary text. We are also told that the acting will be naturalistic on the vocal level, stylized on the physical. The movement is designed in imitation of the postures of ancient Egyptian statues and also the figures in mural reliefs. In such flat reliefs, the head is presented in profile, the shoulders and the chest frontally, the lower torso twisted with the naval on the edge of the silhoutte and the feet in profile. Imagine acting in this posture! Naturally, we are told, it takes a lot of arduous training to achieve that. And, indeed, in this direction, the actors proved extremely supple. The only thing they could not manage was presenting the eye frontally while holding the face in profile as in the flat reliefs. But then, you can't have everything. One is only too thankful that there were no women in the show since this would have required the remarkable feat of facing the audience while presenting the breasts in profile.

The queerness of the movement, its statuesque aspect and slow rhythm were effective in that they created the impression of old stone figures slowly coming to life — a purpose openly confessed by the director. The stage-design, too, by Abbas El-Siwifi (who also designed the costumes) had the solid serenity and uncluttered symmetry of ancient Egyptian architecture; on either side, the stage was framed by two pillars followed by two obelisks with golden pyramidal tops; and at the back, a wide stairway led upward to the altar, the hidden sanctuary of the temple with the shrine of the god, which, when open, revealed the shimmering statue of Amon-Re in a pool of blue and golden light.

In the one scene where we see Akhenaton (who was shamefully robbed of his role as the first monotheist in history both in the play and its narrative source and reduced to a mere disciple), a huge white disk occupies the centre of the stage and gradually changes colour from yellow to deep orange, becoming the visible manifestation of the god Amon. For lighting and music, Nur El-Sherif roped in two of the best talents on the market and paid them out of his own pocket. And both proved worth their weight in gold. Ragih Dawood's incidental music rippled softly on the ear like the play of sunlight on water and evoked the feeling of a remotely distant past. And Maher Radi's inspired lighting plan combined with El-Siwifi's mostly historically accurate and elegantly beautiful sets and costumes to make the stage a visual treat. The magical wand of poetry had touched everything, it seemed.

I caught myself at moments longing for all speech to cease that I might surrender completely to the spell of the imagery and the music. The verbal exchanges, since the characters were all one-dimensional, with the exception, perhaps, of Smenkh, frequently lacked the rudiments of dramatic dialogue and often dwindled into declamatory statements, formal debating or insipid yap-yapping. Particularly nettling was the muddled theology which made Kai contradict himself at several points so that one was not quite sure whether he was advocating monotheism, henotheism or a pluriform monotheism. Historically, Akhenaton held all three beliefs in succession, advancing from henotheism to monotheism. In the play, however, Kai seems to hold all three at once. The same confusion infects the political interpretation of the religious struggle in the play. At one point, the director explains to us that Aton's religion abolished the priesthood and freed the people from its tyranny and exploitation. But in the following scene, we hear

Kai complaining bitterly to Smenkh of the persecution, torture and mutilation of Aton's priests!

In the original story, the author does not embroil himself in the political complexities of the historical religious struggle; he uses irony to preserve his detachment and concentrates on the conflict between the poet and the statesman, art and reality, darkness and light. The play, however, sides clearly with Aton and his prophet Kai, portraying him as a Christ-like figure but without the agonizing doubt of Christ at the cross. Consistently he speaks with the passionate certainty of a bigoted zealot and his fierce, intolerant belief makes him quite repellent and even frightening at times. To make matters worse, after presenting the original, tolerant end of Tahir's story on the stage, Nur El-Sherif and Misilhi decide to make their fictional director reject it and replace it with a new one where Kai refuses to escape, opts for martyrdom and is beheaded, in the middle of his frenzied prayers, right in front of us. Was it this perhaps, together with what history tells us of Akhenaton's intolerant creed and the recurrent reference in the play to the "pure faith" of the old fathers in the old city of Oun that made Kai appear to me sometimes as the old prototype of the new religious terrorists and fanatics of today?

Historically, of the two religions, Amon-Ra's seems the more tolerant. Its god may be awful and austere and shrouded in mystery and darkness, but he still allowed other gods to share the heavens with him. Aton, on the other hand, may not dwell in a dark shrine, may be worshipped in the open air in an unroofed sanctuary, but he will brook no rival. There is sufficient historical evidence to suggest that by the 9th year of his reign, Akhenaton's religious fervour intensified, whereupon he pursued an intense persecution of the older gods, especially Amon whose name was excised from many older monuments throughout the land. Something of Akhenaton's fanatical zeal seems to have crept into the show making it a bit disturbing.

Still, there is a lot in the show to make up for its slightly muddled thought: the zest of the young actors, the many flashes of humour and, above all, the enchanting music and scenography and the palpable talent and loving care of its director. Well-done, Nur.

# 3. Schools for Scandal*

Initially, one has to acknowledge the tremendous energy Abdel Ghaffar Ouda has pumped into The Folklore and Music Sector since he became its managing director slightly over a year ago. With over a dozen productions, including the ambitious and much celebrated *Khedive,* his record, in terms of both quantity and quality, leaves the Theatre Sector dragging its feet far behind. Eversince he set foot into the Balloon theatre, his new headquarters — a truly fitting setting for his gigantic bulk – he has been full of new plans — finding new venues, building new annexes, setting up a new experimental unit for young artists (The Theatre of Tomorrow) and another for audiences under 18, restructing the Circus troupe and retraining its artists, renovating the Balloon, fetching new costume-designers for the National Dance Troupe and, on top of everything else, guaranteeing a healthy, nourishing diet for the Circus animals while economising on the budget. Indeed, one feels quite exhausted just thinking of all this man plans to do.

It was not, therefore, at all surprising that Ouda should be the person to undertake reviving the sporadically-attempted but long-neglected project of introducing theatre in education by dramatizing items of the school curricula. Other artists had played with the idea; a few years ago, veteran actress Samiha Ayoub and the late comedian Abdel Mon'im Ibrahim talked of setting up their own private company to offer this lucrative service and, more recently, director Fahmi El-Kholi talked of staging Jane Austin's *Pride and Prejudice.* But

---

* 5 May, 1994.

nothing came of it. It took a man of Ouda's calibre and determination to deliver something tangible.

His first foray into the field was targeted at the third grade pupils of the preparatory stage and was reasonably encouraging. Their geography curriculum was worked out into a musical show figuring four friends travelling through the world and familiarizing themselves with the characteristic aspects of each continent. The chosen formula and subject matter provided ample opportunity for a colourful display of national costumes and dances, interspersed with farcical interludes and hilarious misunderstandings. Of educational stuff, there was fittingly, perhaps, a very light dose, supplied mostly by the children in the auditorium who were frequently called upon to come to the rescue by the delightful May Abdel Nabbi whenever her three clownishly inept companions messed up their geography. But its value as educational aid apart, *Birds' Dreams* (written by Leila Abdel Basit and directed by Hamdi Abul Ela) scored high as theatre, giving the children a taste of its joy and magic.

Unfortunately, the same could not be said of Ouda's second educational venture, a production of Dickens's *Hard Times* for secondary education finalists. The adaptation (by Samir Bishay and Abdallah Hussein) strove to include as many of the novel's characters and events as the space of two hours could hold and the result was a dizzying whirl of torn shreds and broken snatches — impossible to make sense of if you hadn't read the novel and quite bewildering if you had. The confusion was made worse by Samir El-Asfouri's directorial policy which seemed intent on completely disrupting the few strands of conceptual cohesion the adaptation had. Rather than act as a kind of magnet to draw the scattered filings of the story into some sort of order, the two clowns he provided as narrators and presenters, and who kept interrupting the proceedings with their silly jokes and antics, scattered more splinters and slivers. Predictably, the central theme of the novel, about the importance of the imagination, which the adaptation, despite its faults, had tried to keep constantly in sight, was often submerged by this crazy medley of sights and sounds. When it rarely surfaced, it took the form of hollow verbal sounds completely detached from the spectacle on stage.

Still, one would have forgiven the production and its director if the spectacle on stage was anything worth seeing. The single set, with its two raised areas on either side (representing the Gradgrind and Bounderby households) and its painted backdrop of an industrial town skyline swimming in a red haze, was shabby and vulgar. The design was poor and tatty and the fabrics were cheap and dirty. It was the same thing with the costumes. Looking at this eyesore of a spectacle I felt outraged at the memory the children in the auditorium would carry home with them. It was as if they had been invited to feast their eyes on garbage! Worse still was the acting which proved a veritable catastrophe. With the exception of Mohamed El-Dafrawi, as Mr. Gradgrind, and Amina Rizq, as Bounderby's mother, none of the actors took the trouble to learn their lines or believed a word of what they were saying. They sauntered flabbily onto stage, clowned out of place, or contorted their faces into ridiculous grimaces, stumbled on their lines or reeled them off mechanicaly, breaking into giggles occasionally, then wandered off ungracefully. No wonder their impudent indifference infected the children, triggering an outward ripple of visible reaction in the auditorium. Given a lousy example by their peers, the young spectators, in their turn, became insupportably noisy and unruly. The night I was there, poor Ms Rizq had to break off in the middle of a moving speech to admonish them. Rightful as her indignation was, it missed the real offenders — her fellow actors.

The evening was an unmitigated disaster and I wasn't at all surprised when at the end of it I was told that Mr. Ouda had had the good sense of quickly cutting his losses and had craftily palmed the production off on the ministry of education, recovering the stupendous sum he had spent on it. Stupendous sum?! Where had all the money gone then? – was the mind-boggling question. More mind-boggling still is the prospect of having this 'thing' on public display, for the edification of our young, for as long the novel remains on the curriculum of the secondary schools third grade — which is exactly what the ministry of education plans to do! In short, the play could be running for the next three years or more. For the ministry of education, this would be a scandal; for the tax-payer, it would be outrageous robbery; but for the schoolchildren, it would be nothing short of a crime.

# 4. Home-Made Theatre*

To get to the Women and Memory Research Centre through the Muhandiseen maze of small streets, you have only to follow your nose: as you approach, your nostrils will be deliciously tickled by the mouthwatering smell of kebab wafted on clouds of smoke from the *Hati* (grillroom) opposite. Once inside the building (the address is available on application to *The Weekly*), your nostrils begin to itch and twitch: you are greeted by more fumes — this time coming from the poor smokers relegated to the stairwell and landings. Barring a heavily-curtained balcony, the Centre (a small flat on the second floor consisting of two rooms — knocked into one to form a spacious rectangular hall which, at a pinch, can accomodate up to eighty people — a kitchen and a bathroom) is strictly 'no smoking'. But the atmosphere inside is quite genial and informal, and if you are one of those who cannot resist a drag after half an hour of exciting discussion, you are most welcome to let yourself out. You will be surprised how many have succumbed to the same temptation. They stand or sit in small clusters on the stairs and landings furiously puffing and chatting. Inside, you can get up any time and help yourself to the plentiful supply of tea and coffee, *salaisons* and biscuits ranged on a long narrow table on one side of the hall.

My first visit to the Centre about a month ago had been theatrically motivated: the centre was hosting Dalia Basiouny's live presentation of a project to produce Timberlake Wertenbaker's *The Love of the Nightingale* and I went purely to watch her. Soon enough, however, I

---
* 2 July 1998.

realized that far from being a detached observer, I had become an active and deeply involved participant in a broader theatrical performance. The presentation was part of an evening dedicated to the issue of violence against women, and the scenes Basiouny and her partners read from the play, together with all the 'taboo' things that were said before and after, formed a very lively 'dramatic text' — one that cut across the prevailing cultural codes and staged an alternative dialogue which the culture at large discouraged and even condemned.

It was all very theatrical — not in the derogative 'male' sense of the word, but in the feminist definition of theatre as "an engaged dialogue, built on mutuality and intersubjectivity, operating by enactment, not mimesis, and rooted in everyday life." Even the space itself seemed to change character: it was no longer a real room in a research centre run by academics and experts, but an imaginative "empty space", in Peter Brook's sense, where "the personal became the aesthetic" (in Sue-Ellen Case's words), as well as the political. In this space, the women present became a community of 'performing dramatists' (as distinct from 'authorial' playwrights) who collectively created, out of the dialogue between personal experience, the concrete realities of daily living, and art (Wertenbaker's text), an improvised 'performance script' specific to that evening. Unlike traditional 'authorial' dramatic texts, it was not mimetic, aimed at lasting repetition, nor did it claim "a beauty independent of any particular or finite significance;" it was transient, tentative and contingent — what Case would describe as a "dialogue of present time, caught up in the movement of history and development, without the secure fourth wall of formal closure," that is, an ongoing, changing dialogue without final resolution.

What added to the excitement of being caught up in a frtuitous performance unawares was a combined feeling of freedom and secrecy. It was as if we were an underground theatre group giving a performance the censor would never condone. I found myself suddenly remembering the Czechoslovakian playwright Pavel Kohout who (as British playwright Tom Stoppard who dedicated his play, *Cahoot's Macbeth*, to him tell us) was, together with the well-known actor Pavel Landovsky and many writers and actors, prevented from pursuing their careers during the last decade of 'normalization' which followed the fall of Dubcek. According to Stoppard, "it was Landovsky who was driving the car on the fateful day in January 1977 when the police stopped him and his friends (including Kohout) and seized the first known copies of the document that became known as Charter 77." A year later, Kohout wrote to Stoppard announcing the opening of a Living Room Theatre "with nothing smaller than *Macbeth*." He described his LRT as "a call-group. Everybody who wants to have Macbeth at home ... can invite his friends and call us. Five people will come with one suitcase." Two months later, he wrote to Stoppard: "Macbeth is now performed in Prague flats."

It was perhaps the presence of Basiouny which reminded me of Kohout and his Living Room Theatre. A month earlier, around the beginning of May, she had staged a performance at a private flat in downtown Cairo. The owner of the flat, Maher Sabry (a young theatre artist of diverse talents who has just published a collection of poetry) had refitted one of the spacious rooms into a rehearsal space. For nearly a year, he gave Basiouny free use of this space to develop, in collaboration with eight performers (five males and three females), a performance piece called *What Do You Want To Be When You Grow*

*'Down'*? As the punning title indicates, it was a journey through memory (not unlike the ones undertaken by the Women and Memory Centre) — an attempt to uncover and rediscover the world of childhood without the traditional romantic trappings and fictions attached to it. Many activities were used as keys to unlock the gates of memory: doodling and scribbling on the walls (carefully covered with drawing paper by Sabry) was one of them; another was storytelling, done individually or collectively. In one rewarding exercise, Basiouny would start a story and then 'throw' it to one of the performers who would carry it along a bit further before 'throwing' it to another, and so on, until everyone had had a turn at developing the story. The few privileged friends who were allowed to attend the rehearsals found them more exciting than the final product which came across as a collage of movement, mime, music and songs based loosely on the theme of childhood.

*What Do You Want To Be* was performed twice in the same private, domestic space, the rehearsal room in Sabry's flat, which proved capable of accommodating as many as fifty people. The composition of the audience, which consisted mainly of friends, supporters and kindred spirits (the Women and Memory people, Al-Warsha members, and Al-Hanager crowd) could raise for some the problem of elitism and, indeed, the term 'ghetto theatre' did cross the minds of some. But it all depends on what you mean by elitism and ghetto. If by the former you mean social, economic and political privilege, then the question does not arise: this was a very heterogenious audience in socio-economic terms. But if you confine the word to the realm of ideas, liberal attitudes, and shared dreams and ambitions, you would be right in describing it as a 'special' audience. If by ghetto theatre you mean a theatre of a deprived community, not necessarily socially or economically, but mainly in terms of freedom of thought and expression, then, yes, you could put such experiments and events under the rubric 'ghetto theatre'.

Other untraditional spaces explored by Basiouny, Sabry and El-Sabil group included an actual *sabil* (public drinking fountain) recently renovated and reopened in Bayn Al-Qasrain street (in El-Hussein quarter of old Cairo) where they read excerpts from El-Maqrizi's History to the accompaniment of a lute, and a tent at the last International Book Fair with a more developed version of the same performance.

Such performances are usually great fun, even though some of the passers-by in El-Hussein thought El-Sabil group were a bunch of lunatics recently let loose from *El-Abbasiyya* (the Cairo Mad House); but, by dint of their public nature, they cannot afford to be openly provocative in their handling of the heritage; the most they can do is poke fun at it in a genial way without truly criticizing its basic assumptions; the general effect is predominantly one of nostalgia. The same timidity and nostalgic sense characterize the one-woman storytelling performances of selected tales from *The Arabian Nights* which Sherin El-Ansari sporadically gives at various sites, including *Wikalat al-Ghouri*. Despite the substantial dose of parody she injects into her performances through the use of puppets and certain props, and the subversive ironical framing of certain scenes and episodes, she stops short of openly contradicting or even questioning the mysoginistic representation of women in the *Nights* as bitches, witches, vamps and virgins.

Curiously, no questioning of the gender-specific roles and images underpinning *The Nights* was ever attempted in the sixties despite the rage for using folk literature as material for drama and the craze for drawing on popular forms of entertainment to create an indiginous theatrical form. With practically no exceptions, the *Siras*, the popular ballads, *The Nights* and other folk tales, and even the three extant texts of Mohamed Ibn Danial's shadow plays (which date back to the 13th century), were used mainly as safe conductors for political comment, criticism, and propaganda; and while such traditional male images, as the image of the hero, and with it the concept of heroism, were often challenged and revised, the same stereotypes of women persisted. It was not until the late eighties that someone dared strike a blow at the very foundation of the *Nights*, and that someone was (predictably, perhaps?) a woman. In her verse drama, *The Night after the One Thousand and One Nights*, Fatma Qandil redefined the relationship between Shahrayar and Scheherezade in terms of fear and violence, coercion and resistance. A few years later, another woman playwright, Nahid Naguib, took a stab at Scheherezade, redefining her as an epitome of the distorted female bred by patriarchal societies.

It was not until last week that *The Nights* came once more under the scrutiny of feminist eyes. Sumaya Ramadan's retelling of the story which in *The Nights* is meant to explain and justify Shahrayar's extreme and ferocious misogyny was cunningly subversive: it parodied the language and rhythms of the original narrative, sticking to its basic outline, while changing the point of view, bits of the dialogue and some details. Ramadan's *The Tale of King Shahrayar and his Brother: A Different Version Never Published Before* was part of an original evening of storytelling at the Women and Memory Research Centre.

Nine stories were read or, rather, performed by the writers (ten women) with the help of one male, Gasser El-Mogi. All the stories, the fruit of a two-month workshop at the centre on the rewriting of folk tales from a feminist point of view, were either new versions of old tales (culled mostly from the *Folklore Magazine* published by GEBO) — such as Mona Ibrahim's *The Mistress of Wisdom and Perfection*, or Amal Omar's *A Woman-Made Man* — or original writing inspired by them — like Munira Suliman's *The Beginning* or Iman Ghazala's *Mahasin and Ihab*. The reworkings of old texts were preceded by a reading of the original, and the constrast between the old and new versions was often hilarious and extremely dramatic. At one point, we got three versions of the same story, each from a different perspective: the tale of *Sit El-Hosn wa al-Gamal* (The Mistress of Beauty and Propriety) *and Her Seven Brothers* was read in the original by Omayma Abu Bakr, then given in a new version by Hoda El-Sadda (read by her with Amal Omar and Gasser El-Mogy), then projected in a further version by Ranya Abdel Rahman from the point of view of the evil *ghoula* (ogress) who emerges in the new narrative very much like the untouchables of India.

At another point, a summary of the original of *The Tale of Na'am and Ni'ma* was read by Hala Sami, then followed by two new versions of the story, the first by Hala Kamal and the second by Sahar El-Mogi and Dalia Basiouny. The effect of being exposed to three different versions of the same story in quick succession was startling, stunning and extremely theatrical. We were in the presence of genuine theatre, ghetto or otherwise: competent performers who acted the stories rather than read them, and used many of the ploys and affective techniques of the old, popular storyteller; a genuinely dialectical, dialogic text made up of many stories, clashing voices and shifting points of view; an intelligent, responsive and critical audience; a meeting place and a set duration. Of course, El-Sadda and her partners never intended their evening of storytelling as a theatrical performance; they meant it as a presentation and discussion of the results of their workshop. But once the process was set in motion, they intuitively realised that oral storytelling was inherently theatrical and instinctively behaved as performers. Without knowing it, they had used storytelling — the live presentation of personal views and feelings in fictional terms — as a point of intersection between feminism and theatre. Hopefully, The Women and Memory Research Centre will continue to cultivate and explore this fruitful meeting point and will eventually venture into more public spaces and address a wider audience. But if and when they do, will they have to make concessions ? Ay, there is the rub.

# 5. In Memory of a Vanished Place: Anecdotes and Vignettes*

As I stepped into the small (Salah Abdel Sabour) hall of Al-Tali'a theatre, I experienced a vivid, overpowering feeling of having been transported, physically, as it were, in time and space. The inside of the hall had been carefully dressed to evoke the interior and atmosphere one traditionally associates with old rural or provincial cafes where storytellers and *Sira* singers were once a permanent feature. The transformation was impressively thorough and meticulously detailed, extending even to the lighting cabin which was cunningly camouflaged. The two walls framing the audience seats and benches were coated with a thin wash of pale blue paint, with a decorative, crisscross frieze, in dark blue, running round them in the middle, and were hung with wickerwork baskets and earthenware water jugs; the windows, real or imaginary, were covered with straw mats or latticework, and the wooden floor with coarse woollen rugs.

The storyteller's capacious seat, dominating the centre of the performance space facing us, was of rough, unpainted wood and spread with a plaited, patchwork rug. Beside it, on the floor, was a water jug and a wicker tray holding a reed flute and a large checked handkerchief for the singer to mop up his sweat. The space behind him, occupied by a chorus of six singers (half male and half female), lead by a versatile soloist (Hala El-Sabbagh) and six musicians (violin, flute, accordion, *duff*, *riqq*, and percussion), and lead by composer Imad

---

* 7 June 2001.

El-Rashidi on the lute, had the look of an open courtyard, with a rough stone wall at the back and a trellised canopy on top, piled high with palm leaves, and supported on thick tree branches. One could also glimpse a bit of embroidered, gaily coloured tentcloth in a corner at the back, suggesting an invisible extension of the space in the form of a traditional marquee. Were it not for the notable absence of the usual traditional drinks and anything faintly resembling a *shisha* (water-pipe), the illusion would have been complete.

Those of us who had seen last year's smash-hit, *The Black Rabbit*, at the same venue, starring the formidable, almost legendary nonagenarian Amina Rizq in a splendid comeback after many years absence from the stage, did not need the play's programme to tell them that the spectacle they were about to see was the work of director Isam El-Sayed and stage-designer Mustafa Imam who had also collaborated on the Rizq play; it was palpable in the directorial conception and quite visible in the set. Both productions strive to create a powerful sense of the physical reality, the concrete, active presence of the place where the action happens, and achieve it by uniting the performance and audience spaces through a set which monopolizes the whole interior of the hall.

The intimate, gripping, and, sometimes tense, atmosphere generated by this restructuring of theatrical space into a total, enveloping environment, invariably inspires a sense of deep involvement which can be manipulated in different ways, according to the play and the kind of impact the production aims for. In the case of *The Black Rabbit*, a harrowing psychological drama where the initial realism gradually gives way to symbolism and gains figurative energy, the intimacy was disturbing, almost distressing, triggering a claustrophobic sense of entrapment. I remember feeling the darkness physically pressing on me and the lurid shadows on the walls, cast by the dim kerosene lamp, about to jump at my throat; I could not wait to get away and out into the fresh air the first time I saw it. And though I went a second time, like one hypnotically drawn by a siren (the siren being Rizq, of course), I could not shake off that feeling of nervous terror or the urgent impulse to flee.

In the *Tales of Mahrous Farm*, however, the atmosphere was festive, jubilant, relaxed and I reveled in the pervasive spirit of camaraderie, of infectious mirth, and, surprisingly, in the extreme physical proximity of my fellow human beings, despite the heat; and, at one time, the spirit of the place overpowered me and I found myself sitting crossed-legged on my seat and swaying to and fro to the rhythm of the music. No menacing shadows here, thank God, but strong, brilliant lights and a string of winking coloured bulbs; no eerie, scary music to rattle the nerves, chill the heart and make the skin break out in goose pimples; instead, bright, humorous singers and musicians who often interrupt the storyteller, playfully teasing and contradicting him, or break out in unexpected and enormously funny solo asides, or engage the audience, the narrator, or each other in comic musical dialogue and witty repartee. But, luckiest of all, no dreary, murky soul-searching, or delving into the dark and turbid recesses of a tortured mind; only stories, hilarious anecdotes and delicious caricatures of the people who once lived in Mahrous village. They belong to a vanished time and a vanished place, are unabashedly romantic and disarmingly redolent with nostalgia.

For once, the traditional *Hakawati*, popular bard or storyteller, does not speak of ancient or legendary heroes – of Antara or Abu Zeid El-Hilali, extolling their heroic deeds and exploits or singing of their loves and sorrows. Like Wordsworth's exemplary poet, who is "a man speaking to men," Sa'id El-Faramawi's bard is a simple man who sings of the lives of ordinary, and less than ordinary people – the underprivileged and marginalized, the silent majority, who go through life unnoticed and ignored, and are soon forgotten when dead. Like a Fisher King, he casts his verbal net into the dark waters of oblivion to save as many memories as he can. And as he shares his catch with us in the *Tales*, he conjures up a cherished place, a way of life, the people who made it and passed away, taking it with them; and, in the process, out of the scattered memories and the floating spots of time, he reconstructs his own personal history and defines himself.

In the programme, El-Faramawi describes his text as "an autobiography of a time as lived through and manifested in a place." The time it records, indeed recreates, are the early years of the July revolution – the years of innocence and glorious hopes – seen through the eyes of the bard as a child and recollected, across a gap of almost half a century, by the same person, but as a wiser and infinitely sadder man. Likewise, the place, Mahrous farm, is projected in two contrasting versions, past and present. Curiously, it turns out not to be a farm after all, but a street which lay on the outskirts of the city of Toukh in the 1950s, 35 kilometers from the centre of Cairo. Now, with the city expanding in all directions and eating up the countryside around, it lies pathetically squashed and smothered in the city centre, hemmed in on all sides by a maze of streets and alleyways and tall buildings.

But farm or not, the geography of the palce is accurately described and its shape and contours sensitively and lovingly dwelt on. What brings it to life though and charges it with poignant personal feelings are the people El-Faramawi reproduces in the funny cartoons he executes on the spot or in lively verbal sketches, projects in old photographs on a side screen, or impersonates by voice and body language. For in case you have not heard of him before, El-Faramawi is a richly gifted, all round artist who is at once a poet, a fiction writer, a cartoonist and painter, a competent singer and flue-player, a fascinating storyteller and inspired performer. But here, he acts no part, wears no mask or costume. He represents himself, and the stories he tells are as much about himself as the people of Mahrous village. Through them he recovers his childhood and early youth and momentarily recaptures, for himself as well as the audience, something of the splendour in the grass and the glory in the flower. But for him, unlike Wordsworth, there is no comfort in the things that remain.

A note of gentle grief, of tender sorrow creeps in at the end, clouding what has gone before, the funny descriptions, witty comments, ridiculous caricatures, risible follies and droll actions, with a mist of wistful despondency. A lover of biographies, which I find much more amusing and exciting than fiction, I could not but fall in love with this live autobiography, the first of its kind in Egypt, and one of the most moving, entertaining and rewarding shows I have seen in years.

# 6. A Secret History*

Mohamed Mustagab's *The Secret History of No'man Abdel Hafiz* is a curious work of fiction, at once bewildering, fascinating, repulsive and outrageously funny. Published in the mid 1970s, a period of social upheaval and ideological turmoil, it reflects the profound scepticism and great confusion of values which marked those turbulent years. Technically, it continues the modernist critique of traditional mimetic art, launched in the sixties, but in a spirit of blatant cynicism, and, using the narrative strategies characteristic of a lot of postmodernist fiction, it recklessly carries the essential ironic nature of the novel as a genre to its extreme outward limits, threatening to destroy it altogether.

The content of the novel, the purported secret history of the eponymous hero, as far as one can extricate it from the baffling narrative (with its deliberate entangling of myth with history, its many digressions and asides to the reader, and constant accretion of unrelated data), is, to say the least, ludicrous and banal. It traces, with obsessive (yet, ridiculously fruitless and obfuscating) attention to detail, historical veracity, and accurate documentation, the story of the humble birth, dubious genealogy and impecunious progress through life of a wild, beggarly vagabond until his marriage, in his late teens, to a modestly well-off country young woman, with a pronounced speech defect, which (the lisp, not the betrothal) much chagrins his mother. Unless one considers as remarkable feats such deeds as stealing into farms and fields, under cover of night, to purloin fruit and poultry, climbing palm trees, jumping small canals, haring over fields and meadows, working

---
* 5 July 2001.

for an undertaker and sleeping in graveyard, wearing no underwear and sneaking furtive looks at bare female limbs left inadvertently uncovered, or acquiescing to a belated (and, as it turned out, appallingly bungled, horrifically painful, and nearly lethal) circumcision, there is nothing that remotely qualifies as heroic in No'man's life. And, there is nothing secret either, except, perhaps, for the final part of the one night he spent, at the age of nine, in the opulent bedroom and lascivious presence of a rich, elderly female paedophile, who had tricked his widowed, penurious mother into bringing him to her lair with the promise of adopting and raising him in the lap of luxury.

The stolid, pompous narrator, a scholar and academic historian who ponderously annotates his text at every step with tedious, irrelevant footnotes, inconsiderately breaks off his narrative of what happened that night at the most suspenseful point, just before the climax. He reports how the "great, venerable lady" had stripped naked, indulged in a wild, orgiastic dance, kissed, with unbridled passion, every inch of No'man's ritualistically bathed body, and frenziedly sobbed at his feet, while rolling her head on the ground. But, just as she is about to place the bare, diligently fondled body of her, by now, dazed and frantically excited child-paramour on the white, quivering flesh of her unclad, luxuriant lap, he falls silent. What happened to make the child, in the next paragraph, hare off, stark naked, out of the house and into the village alleyways, screaming in terror and pursued by howling dogs, remains a teasing mystery; and, in view of No'man's obstinate silence on the subject, the absence of other reports, reliable or otherwise, or further data, the scrupulous narrator volunteers no explanation, not even a conjecture.

The shock-effect of the episode is exacerbated by this sudden, frustrating rupture in the narrative which tantalises the imagination, opening the gates for lurid, even macabre and cannibalistic suggestions, and becomes all the more disorienting on account of the absolutely detached attitude and utterly dispassionate tone adopted by the narrator. The weird, grotesque actions of the demonic lady are related in a horrifyingly objective, matter-of-fact style, like ordinary, quotidian occurrences, or natural phenomena, released from any ethical anchorage. The narrative seems to unfold in a moral vacuum where all attempts at explanation, justification or evaluation on the basis of good and bad, right and wrong seem futile, redundant and quite absurd. Mustagab's irony is morally nihilistic, devastating and thorough, levelling everything on its way. Paradoxically, however, the absence of the traditional moral coordinates of human existence does not always result in the reduction of the characters to a subhuman species. Just as the obviously fictive and apparently factual can easily combine, figure simultaneously or become interchangeable or indistinguishable from each other if we are suddenly jolted out of our accustomed way of perceiving the world, as often happens in this work, the characters portrayed from this radically different and amoral perspective can easily transcend the level of ordinary humanity and acquire superhuman or mythical proportions.

Take the sketch of "the venerable and equally beautiful lady" who wanted to adopt No'man in the chapter the narrator dedicates to her, as its title announces. The lady in question "consists of one nose, two lips, two eyes, two eyebrows, two cheeks and a neck, followed by a chest, two breasts, a navel and two thighs – formations which rarely exist together, unimpaired in the women of the village." However, "it is believed that a number of men, not many, have met with arbitrary ends soon after discovering the difference between the composition of the honourable lady's body and that of other women." But Fawqiya, who prefers to relax in a bath tub full of milk, sleeps naked in the sun on her belly, frequents graveyards after dark and dances to the tunes of a gypsy *rababa*-player (who, for some unknown reason, has aged prematurely and suffers from a crippling mysterious disease in his "lower half"), has other assets besides beauty. Generous, erudite and fond of company, she entertains the local intellectuals in her literary salon and regales them with learned talk, erotic anecdotes, salacious witticisms, the choicest of victuals and the best *arak* in the province. "She lost her father in a much publicised murder, then her second husband, then her third, who kicked the bucket while nestling between the thighs of a demented woman. No definite news of her first spouse – only rumours. Some say he was struck dumb at the sight of some scandalous deeds under his roof and became a recluse; others, that he was murdered by his wife's third husband, or, according to another tale, became a wandering dervish who travels around in sackcloth."

Other characters and events are similarly mythologised, particularly, No'man's father who has a chapter all to himself, and is alternately presented as a holy man, a chicken thief, a profligate idler and home-deserter, and the episode of No'man's own circumcision which develops into a grotesque, mock-pilgrimage between holy shrines, nearly triggering a civil war between two villages and ending with the mutilated, bleeding male organ swelling between its owner's legs out of all credible human proportions. Like the ghastly experience in Fawqiya's den, this harrowing episode is carefully described (sparing no gory details), but with the same curious detachment of a scientific observer. In no other way could we, as readers, tolerate it. The fact that we do, and even manage to laugh at the slapstick brawling of the two barber-surgeons of the rival villages over who should have the honour of circumcising No'man and at other absurd details, is a tribute to the craft of the author.

The cunning, dramatic method of narration he has contrived, and realized through the fictional figure of a scholarly narrator, who delivers the story in the form of an academic thesis, researching the history of a popular hero, acted as a buffer between the reader and the senseless, sordid, brutal and chaotic pageant that passes for reality in the novel. But the devices which distance the readers from Mustagab's mock-hero and his world do not bring them any closer to his narrator. Indeed, he is often experienced as an irritating, intrusive presence – a pedantic, muddleheaded, loquacious professor, thoroughly incompetent at his job. Not only is he prone to frequent short circuits and sudden power failures, but he displays a pathological predilection for dwelling on irrelevancies and seems unwittingly intent on driving the reader to distraction, trying to pick up and tie the loose ends he blithely leaves trailing behind him.

In the final analysis, it is the narrator and his miserable failure to deliver a coherent reading of history, despite his scrupulous research, rather than the mock-*Sira* hero, No'man, and his elusive history, that are the focus of the novel and the butt of its trouncing satire. Mustagab's message is simply a negation, a drastic refutation of the old big narratives, the fictitious ideological constructs that claimed to make sense of reality and possess the truth, and the smugly confident worldview which generated them. In the topsy-turvydom of values, experienced by Mustagab's generation, reality has become relative, obscure and uncertain – a hazy, tentative text which raises and foregrounds the question of authorship, exposes its conventions in the act of using them and incorporates a multiplicity of alternative narrative lines, all equally valid or invalid, with no possibility of ranking them in any order of value or authenticity. Like Ionesco's dumb orator in *The Chairs*, who is hired by the aged protagonist to tell his tale to the world and deliver his message after his death, Mustagab's narrator, though glib of tongue, has no tale to tell and no message to deliver.

With a novel like that, where the very act of narration is the subject and the form is the meaning, indeed, the be-all and end-all of the work, it seems sheer, suicidal folly to think of transferring it to the stage. But who could restrain Bahig Isma'il once he had taken the idea into his head? He was obviously haunted by the novel and, being a gifted playwright, wanted to exorcise it the only way he knew how. The result was not a dramatisation, but a parallel text which attempts to reconstruct the secret history of No'man through a different, simpler and, perhaps, wiser narrator – in this case, a popular story-teller, with the experience of all the *Siras* behind him. The new narrator, firmly planted in the present, expanded the temporal framework of the narrative well beyond its original scope, which ended just before the 1956 Suez war. No'man's history becomes that of Egypt, viewed from the ideological perspective of the poor and downtrodden through the ages, and his bleeding wound, which Isma'il insists is still open and has not healed, is blazoned as a symbol of the continuous bleeding by the rich (the old feudal lords under the monarchy or the new ones under the republic) of the poor.

In this new, thoroughly committed reading, the characters, particularly No'man's long-suffering mother and the legendary Lady Fawqiya, are intensely charged with political implications until they light up as bright symbols – the former of Egypt, the motherland, and the latter, of her ruthless exploiters and oppressors, whatever their guises. One must admit that the material of the original text, divorced from its form, lends itself to such simplistic, straightforward interpretation. After all, the childless, sexually voracious Fawqiya, who attempts to steal and devour No'man, belongs to the landed gentry and can pull strings in the upper echelons of power, and when, early in the novel, No'man's mother carries him to the government hospital, in the nearby town, to seek a cure for his mysterious ailment, she is rudely shooed away by the porter and denied admittance on account of her humble status and shabby appearance.

One can therefore forgive such alterations, particularly as Isma'il infused his script with a healthy dose of earthy jokes and bawdy humour, obliquely hinted at Fawqiya's morbid passion for the child No'man (which is all anyone could do given the watchful eye of the censor), and built up No'man's courting of his prospective, lisping bride into a delicious sequence of comical, rough-and-tumble flirtation, country-style. What I could not forgive, however, could barely stand, though I am not the least bit squeamish, was the sight of No'man's white *galabiya*, richly stained with the blood supposed to be streaming from his genitals. Meant to inspire our sympathy and indignation at his undeserved suffering, it was, instead, grotesque and embarrassing. Bleeding wound of Egypt or no bleeding wound of Egypt, this was simply too much. The verbal analogy, literally translated into visual fact, was strained to breaking point and turned into parody.

"Out, damned spot! Out, I say!" I kept intoning. "What, will that galabiya ne'er be clean?" I wondered. But the spot obstinately stayed for the rest of the show, overshadowing and souring everything – the endearingly naïve set on the makeshift stage, pitched in the open courtyard of Manf hall and flanked by two real, majestic trees, the gay country airs and festive dances, the unaffected exuberance of the chorus of young peasant girls, the narrator's sturdy presence and humorous crossing in and out of the past, and Magda Munir's powerful and sympathetic performance as No'man's mother. But, all the good acting in the world could not make me forget that bloody stain or wash it clean from my sight.

# 7. Faces in the Mirror:
## Images of Sheherazade on the Egyptian Stage*

In never ceases to amaze me how the popular mind in the Arab world can condone the most atrocious crimes committed by males against females and how lying and wiliness are extolled as feminine virtues and trotted out under the rubric of wisdom. In a seminar at the AUC last winter, after a lecture by Iraqi scholar Feryal Ghazouli about Sheherezade, Mona Ibrahim, a young assistant professor at Cairo university, wondered aloud about the validity of the image of Sheherezade propagated by *The Nights*. The reforming of the rake theme, familiar in European fiction and drama in the 18$^{th}$ and 19$^{th}$ Centuries, was here stretched beyond the bounds of credibility. Far from an ordinary rake, Shahrayar was a downright brutal murderer. "How could a woman tolerate being nightly raped by such a man and then treat him like a baby, sending him to sleep with bedtime stories?" Ibrahim validly asked. The answer was 'fear' and the survival instinct. Sheherezade had to spin out the web of her days with yarns, Ghazouli said.

Though the stories of *The Arabian Nights* have inspired many writers and provided material for scores of films and plays, their narrator took sometime to arrive on the scene. The first person to air Sheherezade on the Egyptian stage, as far as I can discover, was Sayed Darwish in a four-act comic operetta that carried her name and for which the pioneering colloquial verse writer, Biram El-Tonsi, wrote the

---

\* July 2003 (based on an article published in *Al-Ahram Weekly* on 19 January, 1995).

lyrics. It was performed by Darwish's own company in 1919 and was later revived, according to an extant theatre bill, in 1926, under the direction of the first acknowledged Egyptian theatre director, Aziz Eid, with comedian Bishara Wakim (whose lively comic performances are preserved in old movies) and Alia Fawzi in the leading parts.

Long before the theme of the good ruler being corrupted by his evil entourage became rampant in the drama of the 1960s, after Nasser's accession to power, El-Tonsi and Darwish presented us with a startling image of Sheherazade as a dissolute queen, spoilt by her vicious, power-grabbing court, and turned into a ruthless autocrat. Rather than spend her nights taming Shahrayar (here conspicuous by his absence) and ridding him of his ferocious blood lust, she amuses herself with chasing after prospective handsome lovers, even as the country faces the threat of foreign invasion. Fortunately, however, Za'bulla, a valiant, virile officer, comes to the rescue, arriving timely on the scene to subject her to a long and tempestuous process of edification which steers the play to a happy end.

Za'boulla, the hero, a simple, upright man of peasant origins, is a budding symbol of the national hero (modelled perhaps on Saad Zaghloul – remember 1919 was the year of the famous national popular uprising against the British) and he is deeply in love with one of the queen's ladies-in-waiting, also originally a peasant. When the flighty, selfish and pleasure-loving Sheherezade (a clear symbol of the ruling royal family then) falls in love with him and tries to seduce him with promises of wealth and power, he resists and remains steadfast. Eventually, after many trials and ordeals, he manages to knock some sense into her and she promises to reform, dismiss her villainous stooges and become a good queen. Salah Abdel-Sabour was to return, years later, to the same skeletal plot-frame in his verse drama *A Princess Waiting* (1971).

In 1934 Tawfiq El-Hakim dragged Sheherezade onto the stage once more and made her into an emblem of the mystery of life. She was projected purely through Shahrayar's eyes and became the focus of his agonized philosophical-cum-existential quest for the truth and reflections on the paradoxes of appearance and reality. In El-Hakim's hands, the tangible reality of the woman and her solid presence seemed to dissolve into thin air, making her into a diaphanous symbol of the inscrutability of life and the unknowability of the truth. The "battle of the sexes" theme, which frames her relationship with Shahrayar, both in the *Nights* and in the popular mind, was here waived aside or, rather, transmuted into a juxtaposition of subject and object, of meaning and experience, of reality and representation in the creative mind and subjective consciousness of Shahrayar as El-Hakim's surrogate. A profound theme indeed, but quite unwieldy stage-wise. This may explain why El-Hakim's *Sheherazade* had to wait until 1966 to make its way to the boards. And even then, when the climate was more tolerant of new theatrical forms and experiments, and despite a good cast headed by Sanaa Gamil and Mohamed El-Sab', and with the brilliant Karam Mutaweh (fresh from his studies abroad) in the director's seat, the play proved baffling and attracted few audiences.

In this respect, Sheherazade fared better with Ali Ahmed Bakathir (a prolific and unfairly ignored dramatist). In *The Secret of Sheherazade*, performed with great success at the old Opera House in 1953, with Amina Rizq in the title role, the heroine of *The Arabian Nights* occupies the centre of interest and recovers her traditional image as the ideal female who tames with kindness and stoops to conquer. Besides her beauty, wisdom, moral uprightness, eloquence, artistic and literary accomplishments and many seductive arts, she is also a bit of a psychiatrist. Not only does she cure Shahrayar of his sexual impotence (triggered by his wife's adultery and the root cause of his murderous misogyny in the play), she also manages to rid him of his obsessive sense of guilt and to save his soul.

Bakathir, however was essentially a romantic moralist in an Islamic vein and the psychological perspective of the play remains superficial. The real message, as summed up in the Qur'anic epigraph to the printed text, is simply that it only takes a good woman to reform the worst rake. But even if one swallows this stupendous fallacy, there remains the intractable fact that the rake in question is a homicidal maniac who has nearly decimated the female population of his kingdom. The reader is asked to accept: firstly, that a depraved fiend like Shahrayar is capable of love and repentance and, secondly, that a young woman, let alone an intelligent female whom he drags into his den and rapes, could actually love him. Bakathir obviously worked from the premise that madness in great men forgives all crimes, especially when the victims are women, and that maleness *per se* excuses everything.

As hero, Shahrayar literally gets away with murder. Bakathir, however, craftily camouflaged the monstrous side of Shahrayar under the mantle of sexual impotence, confident that his audience, predominantly male with occasionally a sprinkling of brain-washed females, would view it sympathetically as a perfectly acceptable motive for the worst atrocities. Indeed, the play's concentration on sexual impotence and healing largely accounts for its popular success at the time, particularly since the author took all possible precautions not to cause offence or challenge any deep-seated assumptions. It was at once excitingly daring in theme and thoroughly conventional in mental outlook and moral attitude. Not surprisingly, despite many erotic, purple patches and a strong streak of sexual titillation, *The Secret of Sheherazade* maintains a didactic, preachy tone and abounds in moral sentiments.

More irking still is the insistent harping of the text on the blackness of the slave with whom Shahrayar's first wife is suspected of having committed adultery. It brings out all the traditional negative associations of blackness and slavery and seems intended to make the wife's offence appear more heinous than if she had committed it with a free, non-black man. It is tempting and could be worthwhile to ponder the streak of racism strongly discernible in the *Nights* and see if it could be linked with the shameful involvement of Arab merchants in Africa in the slave trade in the 19$^{th}$ Century or even before; but this is not the place for it. It is, however, a point to be heeded by future deconstructivists of *The Nights*. One wishes Bakathir had paid even scant attention to this and other issues, or had not swallowed the conventional attitudes embedded in *The Nights* and in his patriarchal culture in such a wholesale manner, without the slightest degree of critical scrutiny. As it seems, he did neither. In *The Secret of Sheherazade*, it did not seem to matter to him how many innocent women Shahrayar had killed. The main thing was to pamper and cure the insane ruler and then everything would be alright.

Worse still, in 1955, Aziz Abaza, a redoubtable poet, wrote a verse drama called *Shahrayar* in which that butcher of a king became the object of desire fought over by both Shaherezade and her sister, Doniazade. Once more, Sheherazade was reduced to a symbol, this time of superior knowledge, while her sister became the embodiment of carnal pleasure. As if a woman could not combine both! And why should women always be condemned by writers to the status of symbols?! The battle between the two sisters over the hoggish sultan results in the conversion of Shahrayar to a near mystic and ascetic moralist. It was once more a case of using Sheherezade as a prop on which to project the dilemmas of Arab males and their deeply-divided, fascination-revulsion attitude towards women.

In the 1970s, Sheherezade popped up again in a musical comedy at the Balloon theatre, written by Rashad Rushdi, directed by Galal El-Sharqawi, and starring Libliba. Rushdi was the first dramatist to invest her with a positive political dimension as the symbol of Egypt. Refreshingly, she escapes the palace of Shahrayar (the corrupt ruler and symbol of Nasser's autocratic regime) and teams up with the popular hero, El-Shatir Hassan (played by comedian Mohamed Awad) to expose the corruption of the state. The production had a distinct Egyptian flavour and atmosphere and was rife with theatrical, topical allusions. It felt as if Sheherazade had suddenly been transposed from Haroun El-Rashid's opulent court in $8^{th}$ Century Baghdad to a popular quarter in present-day Cairo and reborn as a typical Egyptian *bint balad*.

In the 1980s, Sheherazade not only kept her political dimension, but acquired a definite feminist one. In a verse drama staged at the Youth theatre, Sheherazade finally rebelled and decided, at the hands of playwright and poet, Fatma Qandil, to cast off her long-inherited robes and appear as a real woman and a revolutionary. Qandil's play made her into a thorough rebel who denounces both her husband's male chauvinism and his despotic rule. Rather than indulge Shahrayar's whims or bewitch him with her tales, she conspires against him and leads a revolution that eventually destroys him. Predictably, this new image of the legendary charmer did not meet with favour. The heroine of the *Nights* was projected here as an outspoken feminist who reads *against* the text of *The Nights* in order to undermine the image imposed upon her by its successive authors, or by the popular mind in general. In Qandil's hands, the tales were clearly interpreted as a political ruse, a manoeuver to hoodwink the tyrant Shahrayar and lull him into a false sense of security. Once more Sheherazade was allowed to escape his iron grip and redefine herself as a social and ideological rebel.

No one however has gone as far as Nahid-Na'ila Naguib in ideologically deconstructing the frame-story of *The Nights*. Naguib takes up the character of Sheherazade and gives it a new, startling interpretation. She begins with the premise that mental and physical coercion cannot breed sane characters. Imagine a woman living for years in total oppression, under fear of death, and having to succumb daily to sexual and mental abuse. What can you expect ? In the *Harem*, leading a life of idle luxury and sensual indulgence, under fear of death for disobedience, women can only rot, Naguib argues. How can you expect wisdom out of such fetid, paltry stuff. Naguib presents us with a Sheherazade who, after years of imprisonment in the court of Shahrayar, of impotent inaction, churning out silly tales, has become thoroughly corrupted. She is projected as scheming, lustful, greedy and morally degenerate. This new image, however repellent, has a lot to justify it in terms of realistic psychology. It is only logical to assume that a life of isolation, bored indolence and cloying sensuality can eventually erode the toughest mind. Needless to say, Naguib's message did not prove palatable to the censor who refused permission for the text to be publicly performed. When the writer asked for an explanation, she was told she had tampered with the national heritage, distorting one of its hallowed symbols. Indeed, it is doubtful that any play by a man or a woman which dares controvert the traditional image of Sheherazade will see the limelight or be sympathetically viewed if it does.

Ezzat El-Amir's *The Reign of Sheherezade* (also of the seventies, but staged at the National in December, 1994) attempted to be bold without being outrageous, steering a middle course between the traditional view of the character and the political interpretation she received in the 1970s and 1980s. It presents us with a Sheherazade who is at once a freedom fighter and a typical slave girl, a rebel, spear-heading a revolution against a despotic tyrant, and a faithful, loving wife to that same deeply hated and universally resented and damned tyrant. The compromise does not work and the old formula of the conflict between love and duty which the author calls to his aid fails to reconcile the two faces of the heroine.

Indeed, in her performance of the title role (her third stage appearance), film star, Raghda, seemed to be hopping between two different texts all the time, while Ahmed Maher's sudden plunges, as Shahrayar, from light-hearted comedy into the depths of melodrama were quite disconcerting. They were at their best in the battle-of-wits scenes, or engaged in sexual bantering. For the rest, their performances seemed belaboured and artificial. But one could hardly blame them; the text itself is more like a debate than a drama and, as such, could only sustain the interest of the audience for half an hour. Instead, it was stretched over two hours and embroidered with many songs and dances which served only to repeat the play's already obvious and banal political message. Slides were used too, as well as a short puppet show and, at one point, director Mahmoud El-Alfi drowned the stage in smoke – all in the interest of visual vivacity; but nothing – not even Raghda's voluptuous beauty and Ahmed Maher's vivid ranting – could relieve the boredom as the minutes ticked away. At the heart of the play one sensed an absence. It was not simply that Sheherazade was split down the middle, she had also been made into a mere mechanical and most unconvincing mouth-piece for the author's somewhat stale political ideas and reduced to a lifeless symbol of the nation and the guardian-angel of Shahrayar, the ruler.

In February, 1995, within two months of El-Amir's play, Sheherazade surfaced again at Al-Hanager Centre in Abu El-Ela El-Salamouni's *Diwan Al-Baqar* (The Chronicle of Cows). This time, however, she appeared incognito, as Norhan, the Europe-educated, intellectual daughter of an honest, enlightened vizier in some imaginary country. Like Sheherazade, the westernized Norhan, played by actress Nahid Rushdi, tries to use her wits and narrative powers to knock some sense into the head of the sultan who had fallen under the spell of a Tartuffe-like sanctimonious rogue who had virtually usurped his powers, assumed his authority, and turned his people, through his wiles and frenzied preaching, into a herd of cows. In Karam Metaweh's production, her efforts land her in deep waters. She ends up on the stake, condemned to death by fire. In the original text, however, she is saved when, in a desperate, last bid for survival, she defies the charalatan's hypocritical, fanatical sermons by appealing to the people's inherent love of dancing. She urges a former *ghaziyyah* (a kind of gypsy dancer) to tear off the veil she had been forced to wear and display her banned art. The *ghaziyyah* obliges and all is saved. As an antidote to bigotry and fanaticism, her dancing proves more effective than all Norhan's stories. Talk of the power of the body![*]

Three months later, in May the same year, and at the same venue, French-trained actor and director Gamil Rateb staged a revival of Tawfiq El-Hakim's 1935 *Sheherazade*. The production was a repeat of an earlier one Rateb did in Paris with French actors and bore the marks of the French classical tradition – the cool, elegant surface, the intense passion, the simple, austere design and the resonant vocalization. In it, El-Hakim's seemingly dry, intellectual drama came alive and gained in urgency and tragic stature. The rigidly schematic conflict between the male and female principles, the mind and the body, essence and transient manifestation was charged with visual poetry and intense emotion. Rateb distilled the two major extended metaphors in the text – the Circle and the Mirror – and reproduced them visually on stage in the set design, the lighting and the movement.[**]

In October 2002, Abdallah El-Toukhi's *The One Thousand and Two Nights* opened at the same venue (Al-Hanager) and offered a political reading of the frame-story of *The Arabian Nights* strongly

---

[*] For a full description and analysis of the text and this production, see my book *The Egyptian Theatre: Plays and Playwrights*, Cairo, The General Egyptian Book Organization, 2003, pp. 349-355.

[**] See my full review of this production in my *The Egyptian Theatre: Plays and Playwrights*, ibid, pp. 27-31.

reminiscent of Fatma Qandil's above-mentioned play. Time-wise El-Toukhi's play, written during his last illness (he died in 2001), begins where *The Nights* end; hence the title. It opens on the morning after Sheherazade has won her bet with Shahrayar: they had wagered that if she could persuade him to keep her alive for one thousand and one nights he would set her free. Foolishly, she never doubts he will keep his promise; but just as she prepares to leave the palace, changing her traditional Harem costume for jeans and sneakers, as befits a modern Sheherazade, Shahrayar storms in, announcing he could never let her go. He professes love and need for her while secretly resenting the idea of her freedom and sense of independence. When she insists on leaving, a battle of wills ensues and sensing that she would rather die than give in, he resorts to trickery. With the help of his villainous prime minister, he initiates a war with a neighbouring country and pleads with her to mind the kingdom while he goes to battle. She soon discovers that she is no more than a titular ruler and that the corrupt prime minister is the one really in charge. When the returning soldiers begin to spread the truth about the reason for the war, they are herded into lunatic asylums and when Sheherazade has a showdown with Shahrayar he throws her into a dungeon.

One fine morning, Shahrayar discovers that he is a king without subjects. The whole population of the kingdom has gone underground to join Sheherazade and prepare for a revolution to overthrow the monarchy. The prime minister who covets the throne is quick to send his spies and agents to infiltrate their ranks and cause sedition. His plan succeeds and a fierce power struggle erupts in which both the true and fake revolutionaries prove as despotic and greedy as Shahrayar. Finding herself a prisoner for the second time and, worse still, a pawn in a game of political power, with each of the rivalling parties claiming her as leader and committing atrocities in her name, the desperate, disillusioned Sheherazade seeks the help of Om El-Kheir (literally, mother of goodness), an ancient wise woman who shows her the way out through a secret tunnel.

In the final sequence, the prime minister's plans fall through and his camp is defeated, the officers who took part in the disastrous war and were straitjacketed when they told the truth assume power, Shahrayar is deposed and allowed to go free because, like the Egyptian 1952 military coup d'etat, "this is a white revolution" (as the new ruler robustly declares) and Sheherazade is left despondently wondering with Om Ek-Kheir about the future of this purportedly democratic new regime. As you can see from this somewhat lengthy summary of the action (if one can call it that, since most of it is reported rather than seen), the play is a transparent parable of recent Egyptian political history which palpably reflects the author's divided feelings about the political upheaval of 1952, his initial hopeful optimism, growing scepticism and eventual disillusionment. In terms of conception and technique, it fails to measure up to the human depth and complexity or taut structure of his best work, such as **Black Rabbit.**

In July, the following year (2003), also at Al-Hanager, Effat Yehya and Nehad Abul-Enein staged a play-reading of a new venture into the magical realm of Sheherezade. *Once Upon a Time*, written collaboratively by Yehya and Tunisian actress Amel Fadji, a member of Fadil Gu'aibi's prestigious *Familia* company, features an imaginary meeting between the Arabian princess and her Greek, oppositional counterpart, Antigone. The project germinated in an international symposium on Greek Drama and *The Arabian Night*, held in Marakesh, in the year 2000. At the end of the two-week grueling lecture-sessions, as Effat tells me, the participants were given four days to prepare an intercultural dialogue, in dramatic form, and asked to team up with one or two members of the group to produce something that related to the event. In the early 1990s, Yehya had built a play, *Desertscape*, round the first act of Caryl Churchill's *Top Girls*. The idea of women from different ages and diverse geographical and cultural backgrounds meeting outside the ordinary geo-temporal frame had intrigued her and resulted in an intelligent adaptation which brought together Churchill's Pope Joan (a brilliant scholar who passed herself off as a man, was appointed Pope and killed when she became pregnant) side by side with Sheherazade's docile and lovely "Anis El-Galis," the perfect embodiment of the ideal odalisque. No wonder Yehya jumped at the proposition: to stage an encounter in the after life between Sheherazade and a Greek character was irresistible.

The first draft of the dramatic project, according to Yehya, did not focus on the stories of either Sheherazade or Antigone. Rather, it sought to distill the essence of both, and combine the image of the female rebel with the theme of taming a powerful, possessive male in a third fictional figure drawn from *Kalilah wa Dimnah*, a book of fables by the 8$^{th}$ Century Abbasid Persian writer, Ibn Al-Muqaffa'. It told the story of a Moorish princess who had mystical longings and succeeded in taming the king who fell in love with her. Rather than join his *Harem* to entertain him with her feminine charms or stories, she managed to persuade him to allow her to go her own way and remain alone in the desert, dancing under the stars, singing to the moon and conversing with the deity. This initial draft of the project found favour with the sponsors of the workshop and in July, 2002, Yehyia was allowed one week in Paris with Fadji to develop it further. The two women worked closely for that space of time and the result was a highly poetic text in terms of construction and verbal texture, but somewhat puzzling in its ideological underpinnings.

With exquisite costumes and a few carefully chosen props and accessories / a dainty teapot, burning incense in an antique dish, enveloping the gallery at Al-Hanager in a grayish-blue aromatic haze, and traditional Turkish music playing softly in the background – Effat and Nehad read or recited their parts, emphasizing the points of contact and juxtaposition between the two legendary figures. The stories of both women – Antigone, the woman who never said 'yes', and Sheherazade, the woman who never said 'no', are foregrounded; and though they differ in course, detail and direction, they ultimately constitute two variations on the theme of the oppressed woman. Paradoxically, by the end of the dialogue and intersecting monologues, both Antigone's 'no' and Sheherazade's 'yes' become ambivalent. Antigone never said 'yes' but failed to get her way; Sheherazade never said 'no' and yet achieved what she set out to do. Both women, however, are losers. Though sexually surfeited, Sheherazade died just as unfulfilled as the virgin Antigone. Both lived in the shadow of death, which forms a major point of intersection between the two stories.

It was to save her father, her sister and herself from death that Sheherazade threw herself into Shahrayar's arms, and her cryptic allusion to her brutal rape at his hands on their first night together – in the form of a few splintered verbal images – is quite painful. More shattering still is the fact that when he raised his sword at dawn to murder her, she clung to him desperately to arouse him sexually once more though she was, as she admits, in great pain. The stories came later, she confides to Antigone, and, ironically, what freed her finally from her bondage and the fear of death was the sight of her father lying dead. Antigone, on the other hand, had to bear the burden of the curse put upon her parents and all the deaths it entailed until it was finally her turn. Despite her long acquaintance with death and her heroic, rebellious confrontation with Creon, the text vividly portrays her panic when she finds herself entombed alive.

What *Once Upon a Time* ultimately seems to suggest is that, in the context of a patriarchal culture, whether a woman says 'yes' as a rule and succumbs to the dictates of the status quo or opts for clear, straightforward opposition, she is doomed. Both women were deprived of the joy of life early on in youth. Antigone never got to enjoy Haemon's love and Yehya's Sheherazade had to give up Qamar El-Zaman, the man she really loved. By way of vicarious compensation, she wove him into her stories and slept with him in her imagination, using the body of Shahrayar as a surrogate. When Antigone asks her if in time she came to love the tyrant, she simply says: "I loved his body." Equally, Shahrayar, as she admits, never really knew her. He slept with a different woman every night, all fictional fabrications.

But enchanting and occasionally gently humorous as this imaginary encounter was, I could not at the time help feeling a bit uneasy about the two women's obsession with their fathers and their total, oblivious disregard of their mothers. It felt as if, like the mythical goddess, Athena, reportedly conceived in the thigh of Zeus, both women were engendered exclusively by men. And yet, at one point, Yehya's Sheherazade tells Antigone that when her father died she felt the load of fear lift off her shoulders. She went to Shahrayar and boldly told him that from now on there would be no more stories. She wasn't afraid then, nothing seemed to matter; she didn't even feel angry; anger seemed such a useless luxury, she says. When Shahrayar begs her for one last story after which he will set her free, she tells her own and he falls silent. I remembered Tunisian actress, Jalila Baccar, telling us during a meeting of creative Arab women in theatre, held in Susa some years ago, that she could never really come into her own as an actress and feel free with her body on stage while her father was alive. I think Effat's Sheherazade was freed in a similar way. When Antigone asks her to forgive as she has forgiven all who have wronged her, the woman who never said 'no' stoutly declares that she will never, ever forgive. To do so would mean unlearning the lesson and going back into bondage.

# PART IV

Behind the Scenes:
Critics and Managers

# Tonight We Improvise:
## *Ali El-Ra'i**

> *It was thanks to Ali El-Ra'i's passionate belief that theatre was performance, a multilanguage medium, that a generation of theatre critics and reviewers escaped the tyranny of the text, and learned that theatre is, as its Latin name denotes, above everything, a place to see. To this El-Ra'i added that it was a communal celebration ... and joyful entertainment.*

The first time you meet Ali El-Ra'i you are likely to wonder how a man with such a dauntingly severe exterior can have anything to do with comedy, let alone broad street comedy and the art of the motley crowd. It is only upon closer acquaintance with the man and his work that you realise how much appearance belies the reality. As soon as you learn to catch that sudden impish twinkle in the eye, the unexpected, barely audible tinkle of laughter in an inflection of the voice and that elusive, fleeting smile of his, barely perceptible in a slight upward curve of one side of the mouth, you begin to get an inkling of the natural warmth of the man which he keeps carefully hidden behind a rigid mask.

It is only an inkling though, for I doubt if Ali El-Ra'i ever completely drops his mask except, perhaps, among his family and his closest circle of intimate friends. In social transactions he is polite and

---

\* 30 June, 1994.

courteous, but in a cool, formal manner — almost aloof, at a safe distance, as if surrounded by an invisible barrier. This could be explained as natural reserve, shyness or a deeply and painfully sensitive nature. Still, one cannot help suspecting that his childhood had something to do with it.

Unlike artists, theatre critics, scholars and theoreticians (the philosophers and historians of theatre) are neither expected nor ever called upon to indulge in childhood recollections. In his most recent book, however, *Personal Cares and Theatre Matters* (Dar El-Hilal, 1994), Ali El-Ra'i alludes briefly to his earliest experiences of the art of performance and in the process unwittingly drops a few remarks which provide us with an insight into what his childhood was like. He remembers the "loud calls of a hawking clown at the door of a circus tent pitched in front of our house — the circus of Ibn Ammar — inviting me to step into that magical world I had heard about from my street playmates; but I could not scrape together the one and a half piasters to gain admittance. I had to make do with listening to the reports of those who were luckier than myself and could afford to enjoy for themselves the feats of the jumpers and acrobats and the spectacle of performing animals."

One only realises the sense of deprivation buried in those words when, 220 pages later and forty years on, an older El-Ra'i dwells lovingly on a night spent at the National Circus, which he had helped establish and develop. Significantly, he winds up his eulogy of the circus artists with a brief shot from real life: "One morning, I was walking down the street, deep in thought, when suddenly I overheard this dialogue between a child and his father. The child was begging to be taken to the circus and the father was promising to do so. Something in the father's tone however left the child unreassured, so he went on pestering, "the Circus, let us go to the circus," until the father finally submitted: "All right, we shall go to the circus."

El-Ra'i's father could hardly afford to take him to the circus; indeed, his monthly pension of a little over ten pounds was barely sufficient to keep his family decently, let alone provide his children with proper education. Humbly, El-Ra'i tells us of the endless applications with which his father bombarded the officials of Wizaret Al-Ma'aref (the Ministry of Education) to convince them of his straitened financial circumstances and plead for exemption from school fees for his children.

A precociously serious attitude towards life, an early sense of responsibility, possibly a protective shield of studied aloofness were the results of those early years. El-Ra'i had to work extremely hard to preserve his right to a free education and he never forgot where the money came from. It came from the people and he promised himself that one day he would pay it all back in service. And that is what he has done. He describes the feeling of indebtedness as "a fire that always scorched me on."

His university studies in the English department seemed to take him far away from the jugglers, the street-shows, the fair-ground and the circus arena. He was now deep in the classics, reading Shakespeare, Blake and Byron and becoming acquainted with Greek, Italian, French and German literatures. He had also developed a passion for Taha Hussein and Tawfiq El-Hakim. Like them, he wanted to bestride the world, planting one foot firmly in the East, in Arabic literature, and one in the West. Ever since, he has remained one of the most enlightened and staunchest believers in the value and necessity of inter-cultural dialogue. Indeed, in all his writing one detects a determination to open out onto other cultures and familiarise himself with 'the other' — be that other Indian, Japanese, European or American.

One of the most interesting and intriguing aspects of the recently published volume *Masrah Al-Sha'ab* (The People's Theatre), which includes the three seminal books he published in the late sixties: *Al-Komedia Al-Murtagala* (Improvised Comedy), *Funoon Al-Komedia* (The Arts of Comedy) and *Masrah Al-Damm-w-Al- Dumu'* (Theatre of Blood and Tears), is this constant trafficking between different cultures. And he makes himself at home wherever he wanders, physically or in the imagination. He is at home in Shakespeare's Globe, in Joan Littlewood's Theatre Workshop, in the Arts Lab down Drury Lane, with Judith Malina and Julian Beck and their Living Theatre in New York, in the Noh and Kabuki theatres of Japan, on the streets of Rome and down the alleys of Venice, where you can almost see him hobnobbing with Arlecchino, Colombina, Pantalone and other Commèdia dell'arte characters. He is equally at home with Moliere, Schiller's *Die Rauber*, French melodrama and vaudeville. Indeed, on every page of *The People's Theatre*, El-Ra'i surprises and impresses the reader with the depth and breadth of his knowledge of world drama.

This comes as less of a surprise when one learns that he read for his Ph.D. at Birmingham University under the redoubtable Allardyce Nicoll. He finished his thesis on the theatre of George Bernard Shaw in two and a half years and spent the remainder of his four year grant (from 1951 to 1955) devouring the books in the university library and frequenting the theatres of London, Stratford-upon-Avon and the active Birmingham Repertory Company. But however far El-Ra'i travelled and however much he saw, he remained faithful to his childhood friends: the street jugglers and dancers, the circus clowns and acrobats, the strolling actors, puppeteers and story-tellers. He carried them around in his heart, comparing them with other popular artists, seeking for parallels and common roots. He traced their kinship with the *Commedia dell'arte* players, with Shakespeare's theatre, with Brecht's *Mr Puntila and his Servant Matti* and found in Joan Littlewood's ideas about "a theatre for the people," and in her collective method of work at the Theatre Workshop, the strongest vindication of his love for and belief in them.

The years El-Ra'i spent studying English in Cairo and in Britain were truly formative, not because of the amount of knowledge and experience he gained, but because they helped clarify for him his own understanding of theatre and his political thought and leanings. His belief in socialism merged harmoniously with his belief in a theatre of and for the people — a theatre actively committed to art and human freedom and progress.

El-Ra'i, however, did not articulate these ideas in writing at once. He had no time. When he came back to Cairo in 1955, it felt like coming back to "a brave new world." This is how he describes it: "When I went back to Cairo in July 1955, I found 'a bliss, a realm magnificent.'" The July Revolution had released the energies of this glorious nation and opened the gates wide before its creative people. The revolution offered us intellectual nourishment, and a glowing moment in the life of our country, the moment when all the barriers crashed down... It was a moment at a crossroads and raised many questions. Whenever such a moment has happened, it has always proved to be a life elixir for the theatre; it was behind the rise of theatre in ancient Athens, in the European Renaissance and, in modern times, in the late 19th century" (*Personal Cares*).

Armed with a doctorate, El-Ra'i could have easily found himself a post on the teaching staff of the university and joined the ranks of the academics. But not for him the shady, secluded academic halls. The clowns and performers he had carried around inside him since his childhood days were now clamouring to be let out and given a respectable place in the world. The stage was now set and the moment ripe. A special department for the arts had been set up under the auspices of the Ministry of National Guidance in 1955 and it was followed in 1958 by a fully-fledged Ministry of Culture, all to itself — the eighth of its kind in the whole world. El-Ra'i soon found himself mingling with the biggest intellectual guns in the country, sitting next to Tawfiq El-Hakim and Mohamed Zaki Abdel-Qader on a committee assigned to look into the condition of the Egyptian theatre, and in 1958 he found himself at the top of the first State Establishment for Theatre and Music — a post he held for eight years.

Those were the golden days of the Egyptian theatre in terms both of drama and the art of performance. Among theatre artists — writers, directors and actors — El-Ra'i's ideas and his campaign for 'a theatre for the people' found fertile soil. Indeed, some artists had already found their own way there, driven by the wind of national pride and a quest for identity. They had already begun to till this soil. Others were quickly following suit. It is difficult now, over a gap or more than thirty years, to assign a pioneering role to any one individual, to decide who said or advocated what first; and perhaps it was difficult even at the time. Such ideas were in the air here, and had been around in Europe since William Butler Yeats and his Balinese dancers, Antonin Artaud and his theatre of cruelty and Brecht and his epic theatre. The call to return to the popular roots of theatre was certainly no man's property.

Ali El-Ra'i's major contribution in this respect, apart form his many practical services to the cause in those years, lay in the field of scholarly research and theatre criticism. This valuable, pioneering work, however, did not start until he left his post as head of the theatre establishment in 1966, then resigned governmental service altogether in 1967. This was the period of the big 'clean-up', when all leftist intellectuals and artists — branded as communists — were kicked out or coerced by the defeated regime. Many of them were forced into 'voluntary' exile — Sa'd Ardash, Karam Metaweh, Galal El-Sharqawi and Ahmed Abdel-Halim, to name but a few. Out too, in 1972, went El-Ra'i, when he set off for Kuwait where he stayed for nine years.

Far from the madding crowd, and the sickening intrigues and counter-intrigues, El-Ra'i was once more master of his time. He produced three feats of scholarly achievement and original insight in rapid succession, *Improvised Comedy*, *The Arts of Comedy* and *Theatre of Blood and Tears*, now published in one volume, *Masrah Al-Sha'ab* (Theatre of the People), by Dar Sharqiyat. They were also labours of love, and this comes across not only in the obviously meticulous and painstaking care of the author, but also in the vivid, lively and warm style of the writing. The history of Egyptian theatre since Mameluke times was scoured, researched and carefully sifted for manuscripts, documents and the names of long forgotten artists and plays. Some valuable manuscripts were printed for the first time. Each one was prefaced by extended essays defining the genre, detailing its history and progress (and sometimes demise) and comparing it with parallel practices, current and old, at home and abroad.

But apart from the plethora of information, the insights, the many anecdotes and the warm affection with which all three works are imbued, what unites them and makes them seminal works in the history of Egyptian theatre scholarship and criticism is their view of theatre as primarily performance, rather than verbal text delivered from the boards. At the time, in the heyday of Egyptian dramatic literature, when Egypt was revelling in its unprecedented crop of talented playwrights, such a view was unusual. In those days, theatre reviews centred on the text itself, giving the scantiest and most perfunctory attention to the the other elements of the performance, including the actor. Read the collected reviews of Mohamed Mandour or Louis Awad or the majority of those published in the 1960s *Theatre Magazine* and you get a strange image of a theatre where nothing happens but words. It was as if the reviewers listened with their eyes closed and even ignored the music. It was thanks to Ali El-Ra'i's passionate belief that theatre was performance, a multi-language medium, that the following generations of theatre critics and reviewers learned that the Latin word for theatre means "a place where you see." And what a revelation that was. To this El-Ra'i also added that it was a communal celebration — as Yusef Idris had earlier affirmed — and joyful entertainment. This, coming from a committed socialist, was a vigorous and healthy antidote to the narrow ideological theatre criticms rampant in those days.

# Rescue Operations:
## 1. Sami Khashaba:
### *Interview**

In the course of a two-day symposium held by the British Council in 1991 at the small hall of the Opera House (under the title "The British Theatre: Egyptian Perspectives"), the issues of funding, sponsorship, subsidies, censorship and state control in both countries were raised and extensively discussed. Actor and director Karam Metaweh, then head of the Egyptian state theatre establishment, was present in his official capacity. He had only had the job for a year, or maybe less, but it had been enough time for him to become thoroughly disillusioned. He bitterly complained that the governmental body in his charge was bureaucracy-ridden, infested with swarms of idle, petty officials who were eating up its budget. Any new initiative was bound to run into such a thick tangle of rules, laws and regulations and endless paperwork that it could hardly survive. He finished by comparing the state theatre organisation to an old, decayed, ramshackle building, long overdue for demolition.

Metaweh may have been an inept administrator, as some people described him at the time — after all, few great artists really succeed as administrators. But the performance of his successor, Sayed Radi (Metaweh resigned in March 1992), led even the most fervent supporters of the state-run theatre to doubt its viability in its present form. Change was indicated, and not simply of leaders. A new formula or mode of operation were badly needed.

---
\* 14 December 1995.

At one time, even the minister of culture himself seemed to have given up on the state theatre establishment. At the Journalists Union, last June, when taken to task over its poor performance in recent years, he stoutly declared (disturbingly echoing Metaweh's earlier pronouncement at the Opera House) that he had come to look upon it as an old, rotten and decaying tree that could neither be revived nor uprooted. It would eventually collapse of its own accord, he said with enviable equanimity; and until such time, he would concentrate on cultivating new theatrical ground. For the future, he said, he was pinning his hopes on the young free theatre troupes whose productions he was planning to sponsor through the Cultural Development Fund.

But much as the minister of culture may have wished to shut out the sight of the 'decaying tree', he was forced in the subsequent months to give it long and serious thought. In July, Sayed Radi reached the age of retirement, and although it was decided that he should stay on, at the top of the 'tree', so to speak, until the end of the Cairo International Festival for Experimental Theatre, the need to find a new, and hopefully more competent, head was pressing.

For two months, the Egyptian theatrical and media circles buzzed with news and rumours. Names were bandied about, engaging people in mild or heated controversy. There was even some betting. But throughout, and from the moment it first began to float around, Sami Khashaba's name proved a clear favourite.

As a young man, Khashaba arrived on the cultural scene armed with substantial credentials. Not only was he the son of the famous Dereeni Khashaba – a distinguished literary critic and translator and one of the pioneering figures in the field of theatre studies in Egypt, he had also spent four years in prison from 1960 to 1964 for political dissent. At a time when the Egyptian intelligentsia was predominantly of the Left and constantly engaged in a tug-of-war with the nominally socialist military regime, this painful and harrowing experience (deeply etched in Sami Khashaba's mind and vividly remembered in all its details, down to the smell of dung in Al-Hadrah prison's animal farm) was regarded as an impressive rite of passage into intellectual circles. Professionally, however, it was something of a handicap. For a number of years, Khashaba, with a B.A. in journalism from Cairo University (1960), held no permanent job, but worked as a freelance journalist, translator and critic, contributing theatre and literary reviews to magazines and newspapers and publishing several translations of seminal English books on theatre. In all this, he seemed to be strictly following in his father's footsteps, proving himself worthy of the name of the man who had introduced him to Homer and Ibn Khaldoun at a very tender age, inspired him with a passionate love for dramatic literature and culture in general, and died at the age of 59, shortly after his son was released from prison in 1964.

In my talk with Khashaba Junior (it was more of a friendly conversation than an interview), I asked him if he regarded himself as an extension of his father. "Rather, I am his faithful student," he replied. Of his two sons (he is married to film critic Khayreya El-Bashlawi), only the younger, Haytham, who studies French literature at Cairo University, is likely to pursue a similar career. The older, Hashem, has opted for a career as a computer programmer. Of the difference between the three generations of intellectuals in the family, he said : "Of course I have more and easier access to knowledge than my father ever had. I can use the Internet at the office of the

Universities Higher Council whenever I need to, and all the English newspapers and the latest books reach me at my office in *Al-Ahram*. I try to keep up-to-date with the developments in thought and culture. My son, I expect, will find it easier than I do. He is already reading Foucault and he is still an undergraduate. I only discovered Foucault a few years ago."

From 1964 onward, Khashaba managed to build a solid reputation as a well-informed, serious-minded cultural figure. Apart from his many translations, he published three books (*Issues of Contemporary Theatre*, *Issues of Modern Egyptian Theatre* and *Figures from the Literature of The Resistance*) where literature, drama and theatre were consistently viewed in the wider context of culture and politics. His *magnum opus*, however, a dictionary of modern literary, cultural and philosophical terms (of which one volume has already been published) and a related and complementary "who's who" of contemporary thinkers and philosophers, owes its genesis to his work as foreign and cultural editor at *Al-Ahram*. He joined the paper as a permanent member of staff in 1978 and his deep involvement in the cultural section and heavy responsibilities as sub-editor-in-chief and editor of the weekly Friday cultural page resulted in a gradual physical (and, perhaps, mental) withdrawal from the bustling life of theatre.

As drama faded away as a central preoccupation, his writing began to reflect a keen and absorbing interest in history, sociology, philosophy, and literary and critical theory. Gradually, without ever suspecting it, the modest, affable, good-natured, unaffectedly affectioante Sami Khashaba was slowly sprouting the forbidding halo of the aloof, inaccessible thinker. Among the members of the thespian tribe, particularly the young, his name inspired respect and even awe; but it remained a name, unattached to a physical presence. Over the years, Khashaba's visits to the theatre had become few and far between. Upon hearing that he had been entrusted with the running of the state theatre sector, many theatre people, particularly those who had never met him and knew nothing about his intense involvement in theatre in the sixties and seventies, wondered how he would cope with the practical side of the job. But that was not their only worry. Immediately after Khashaba's appointment, some of the things he said in the press were misinterpreted, and he was sometimes misquoted with the result that many got the impression that he meant to take the theatre back to the sixties, or even further back, to the age of classical tragedy. The prospect of being treated to endless declamations in one turgid and pedantic drama after another seemed very depressing.

Khashaba was neither surprised nor the least bit offended when I told him what many thought. In fact, he seemed rather tickled. Leaning back in his chair and smiling broadly, he said: "I think you critics are responsible for this rumour. I am not a grim and gloomy person, and I have kept in touch with what has been happening in the theatre. I am aware that deep, serious tragedy has gone out of favour and that black comedy is in. But there will always be a place for the classics in the repertoire – a system and tradition I am determined to revive. The heritage of Egyptian drama too will have its place, but some of the very old texts will have to be re-worked or handled experimentally to bring them up to date and make them relevant. As for contemporary drama, there is no shortage of texts. The problem is that most playwrights nowadays need to work with a director or dramaturge to make their literary texts fit for the stage, and some of them don't like that, though it is widely practiced in the West. Arabic drama will have a niche as well, and we will try to keep up with the latest in world theatre."

To do all this, money is needed and, also, wise planning, good management, a competent administrative apparatus and adequate venues — things the state theatre system singularly lacks. How will he manage it? With disarming frankness, Khashaba admitted that it wasn't going to be easy. But it wasn't impossible. With great lucidity, conviction, and sound practical sense, he proceeded to explain the course of action he had mapped out with the minister to get the state theatre out of its doldrums. It is a realistic course, based on sound economic thinking.

He was fully aware, he admitted, that he has inherited a vast, rambling, and almost derelict organisation. Over half the budget, he said, went into salaries, incentives, over-time payments plus other items (maintenance, cleaning, transport, etc.). At any one time, half of the work force are really idle, an unnecessary financial burden. And few as they are, he said, the state theatres are generally poorly equipped and in a bad state of repair. Some urgently need extensive restoration, others need to be pulled down and rebuilt. All the artists and technicians working for the state theatre companies, he continued, have become stagnant and needed intensive retraining to improve their standard of performance.

As he went on calmly and methodically enumerating all the problems and tasks facing him, I kept marvelling in my mind why, in heaven's name, he had accepted the job? But to every problem, Khashaba proposed a logical, practical answer, and all the solutions displayed keen business acumen. Whoever said this man had his head in the clouds?!

The infrastructure (buildings and equipment) takes priority in Khashaba's plans. With the help of loans and donations from banks, private businesses and other financial institutions, as well as foreign aid from Japan, France, Britain and other countries, theatres like the National, El-Tali'a, El-Salaam, the Puppet theatre and Sayed Darwish in Alexandria, will be refurbished and have their technical facilities overhauled and new equiopment added. The floating theatre in Giza will be roofed in and renovated; but not a single tree, plant or blade of grass, Khashaba emphatically said, will suffer in the process. Other theatres, like Metropol, Mohamed Farid and Masr, which were declared unsafe after the 1992 earthquate, will be pulled down and rebuilt as commercial-cum-entertainment complexes. The commercial area of each building, when sold, will bring in enough cash to cover the costs for a theatre hall, a concert hall and a library in the upper storeys.

New venues are also contemplated, particularly in the provinces. Khashaba has already taken permission from the governor of Gharbiyah to renovate and use the theatre in Tanta, and shortly will negotiate a similar arrangement for theatres in Mansoura and Assyut. Plans for a number of small, portable theatres are also being hatched: the tents and seats will be bought locally, but the technical equipment will have to be imported. Also, the theatrical spaces available at El-Mahka (near the Citadel), the Manesterly palace, in Manyal, and El-Hod El-Marsoud garden, in Sayyeda Zeinab, will be fitted out and extensively used.

What about the human elements? The artists, technicians and army of civil servants?

For the artists and technicians, he is already arranging with Dr. Huda Wasfi, the director of Al-Hanager and the National, several training programmes, workshops and refresher-courses here and abroad. Cultural contact and exposure to new and different artistic experience, he believes, are essential for developing the skills of the artist and stimulating his or her imagination and creativity. Khashaba also believes in financial incentives. To attract more actors to the state theatre productions and persuade those on the monthly payrolls of his theatres to pull their weight and not play truant, he has laid down new financial regulations that allow attractive remunerations over and above the salaries. Another project, in the pipelines, is a resident theatre company in Alexandria, based at Sayed Darwish theatre. It will provide the city with a much needed cultural service and create work for many artists, particularly those who come from Alexandria.

Moving to the subject of the army of civil servants under his command, Khashaba acknowledges that some sections of the organisation have far too many employees than needed. "The salaries they get are more like redundancy payments." Since he cannot sack them (and would not want to in any case for humane reasons), he has come up with the practical idea of retraining and redeploying the supernumeraries. Some sections, particularly those that require special technical skills, like the puppet theatre, have a shortage of workers. Retraining the existing manpower works out cheaper than contracting outsiders. Another way of saving money is to insist that you get real work and real service for the money you pay. "I shall continue to pay my employees the incentives they have come to regularly expect and depend on for making ends meet. But I shall insist that they do real work in return. The same goes for the private companies who are contracted to do the maintenance and cleaning of the buildings. If they don't do the job properly, I'm not paying."

Still on the theme of money, Khashaba said that for the next few seasons, the accent would be on popular productions that bring in good box-office returns. "A lot of money is needed for the projects of the infrastructure. This does not mean that we are going commercial," he hastened to add. "The state theatre will always remain a cultural service. That is why I am not putting up ticket prices. In fact, to draw more young people to the theatre, we are thinking of allowing all university students into our theatres for a nominal fee of two pounds. The real money will come from marketing the product on a wide scale on video tape, or else selling the broadcasting rights. That is why we need marketing experts and a careful plan."

Khashaba talked of other dreams and plans — joint theatrical ventures with prestigious private companies; productions going on tour in the provinces and the Arab world; a network of small theatres stretching over the country from north to south ...

"And the abolition of censorship, perhaps?" I interrupted.

"It will be a very very long time before we can do that — Ours is an orthodox society. In ethics and ideology, we, both Muslims and Christians, are traditionalists. We cling to our heritage and are loath to change. Whether we like it or not, we tend to conform with the established and accepted standards in everything. That is why it will take our society a long time to get rid of censorship and learn to respect the conscience and moral judgement of the individual."

"Would you describe yourself as a religious person?"
"Well, I am a believer, but not a practicing Muslim".

"Would you describe yourself as a modernist, postmodernist, free thinker, or what ?"

"I like the free-thinker category. But I am wary of labels that have definite Western shading. I deeply believe in cultural specificity; but I also believe in the value of cultural contact and even accultration. As a man of this age I cannot escape the influence of its philosophies and schools of thought. For a long time I have been trying to interpret modernism and postmodernism in purely Egyptian terms, to find their equivalent in Egyptian thought."

"You still edit the weekly cultural page. With your new responsibilities, how do you find time?"

"I sleep six or seven hours, wake up early, read for three hours and then am out all day. There is plenty of time."

Before parting, I couldn't help asking:

"You said it will be a long time before we can shake off censorship. How long do you think the state-run theatre will survive?"

"Politically, ideologically and economically, the country is gradually moving in the direction of liberalism. As part of society, theatre will reflect this change. Eventually, the major part of theatrical activity will be free. Nevertheless, a state theatrical institution of some kind will remain. The government will sponsor and support it but will not interfere with its work or seek to control it ideologically."

# Rescue Operation 2:
## Huda Wasfi:
### *Interview**

Of the five newly appointed managers of the state theatre companies, Hoda Wasfi stands out as a particularly happy choice. She combines deep theoretical knowledge with valuable practical experience and commands wide respect in theatrical circles. With her boundless energy and infectious enthusiasm, she will be a staunch and invaluable ally for Khashaba. Though an academic by training and profession, a serious theatre scholar and an unbendingly objective and straightforward person (too straightforward sometimes for the liking of some), she has the passionate temperament of an artist and the furious rhythm of a dynamo.

Her adventurous spirit, intellectual vitality, dedication and utter indifference to all the paraphernalia of office and outward shows of power have given Al-Hanager, which she has run for the past four years, its unique informal, zingy and thoroughly unbureaucratic atmosphere. She runs this active, highly productive, bustling place with only a handful of technicians and assistants. To reach her, you do not have to go through the usual, long, official rigmarole: if she is there, you just walk in and see her; and she has the rare talent of being able to attend to four or five people at once. She can sound sharp and peremptory at times, but only when she is faced with blatant negligence or inefficiency, and I have seen her sometimes driven to fury by some stupid law or bureaucratic regulation.

---
\* 14 December 1995.

Sometimes Wasfi strikes me as one of those people who are never destined to lose their innocence or develop the slightest degree of cynicism. With two grown children, one married and one at university, she is still shockable and can handle neither malice nor deceit. It comes, I suppose, from being brought up to speak her mind frankly and from her long years in the cloisters of academia. Paradoxically, however, she does not lack worldly wisdom and has a very clear grasp of the mechanisms of cultural work in Egypt and its socio-political and ideological context.

Speaking of her plans to revive the National (an institution which over the years has sunk under the weight of its own history and stately reputation, as she described it) she said: "You cannot hope to disrupt the old, ossified institutions in a radical way quite suddenly. It has to be a gradual and subtle process. Take the Hanager, for example; it was originally conceived as part of this process. Its position on the fringe of the state-theatre institution is supposed to give it substantial freedom of movement; but the freedom is subtly controlled, since the centre has no independent budget and has constantly to appeal to the ministry for funds with every new project. One reads a kind of contradiction here, a hesitation, a reluctance to be pinned down to a definite course of action. Nevetheless, in time, this policy, timid and wary as it is, works. The gain in freedom, however slight, creates tremours that shake the foundations and, in time, they produce wider reverberations. What is sadly missing now is the power of direct confrontation. It is actually missing all over the world — perhaps because of the climate of postmodernism which does not encourage faith or certainty or direct conflict. Does not postmodernism, in one sense, mean living with contraditions and ambivalences and working through them? This is what I am trying to do. It is difficult, exhausting and time consuming, but what can you do? I hope to do something at the National and have plans; but I realize I shall have to go about them carefully, in a round-about way, because there is a lot of resistance to change — the resistance of the dominant ideology, system of work, and private interests."

Some of Wasfi's plans for bringing about gradual change without fruitless and counter-productive confrontations sound quite exciting. They include an honest reappraisal and sifting of the dramatic heritage of the National by giving public play-readings of all the texts in its repertory, followed by discussions with the audience to gauge their reactions; the ones that win favour will be entrusted to young directors to see what they make of them. The productions that result, plus the audience response, will help to determine, at least for this age, the value, viability and relevance of those texts. Even the plays of the hallowed sixties will be put on trial. Already a young female director, Iffat Yehya, is working on Saadeddin Wahba's famous *Sikkat as-Salama* (*The Road to Safety*). In fact, out of the seven productions Wasfi plans for the National this year, five will come from the theatre's cupboards. They will be done on a limited budget by young directors and address matinée audiences. The other two will be *grand* productions, targeting an older and more conservative audience. Eventually, Wasfi hopes that the National will appear on the tourist attractions list and that some of her productions will be fit to play in foreign international festivals. "It's a shame," she says, "that over five years the National has not produced a single production fit to represent us at such festivals."

Another of Wasfi's plans to attack the thick, dead tissue that has formed round the National over the years and pump new blood into it is cultural contact and exposure. Not one to let the grass grow under her feet, she has already arranged an all-the-year-round programme of cooperation with the Higher Institute of Theatre Technique in Avignon, and already three experts from the institute have arrived at the National and are conducting a lighting and sound workshop with the theatre's technical staff. She is also currently shopping around for an international director of great standing for a production of one of Moliere's plays. This is her way of nudging awake the pantheon of veteran actors she has inherited with the National.

"These people," she says, "will never accept to do a workshop. But if I invite a well-known international director every year to direct them in a play, they will feel challenged and flattered and want to work with him. It will not change the method of acting they have been brought up in and used for years, but it will definitely refine it and make it more sophisticated. It is a kind of cross fertilization which, I am sure, will have positive results. The talented artist — and most of these people are really talented, however old and set in their ways — cannot resist a chance to develop his or her skills and discover new rhythms. And mind you, these people have their audiences too, who like their traditional method of acting and I intend to cater for them, and even for the lovers of melodrama. It is still a very popular form as I argued in one of my papers."

Wasfi's association with Al-Hanager and the Experimental Theatre Festival (whose director she was for many years) has given her a false reputation for favouring only the new and experimental in art. In fact, she does enjoy all forms of theatre so long as they are well done. On the question of technical skills and new modes in performance, she says: "I do not want the Egyptian theatre to fall into the trap of extreme formalism as the Tunisians have done. Nor do I want it to remain imprisoned in the old formulas. We have to find a middle way."

The middle way may come about through another contemplated cross-fertilization process between Al-Hanager and the National on the model of the Comedie Française and the Vieux Colombier theatres. Jacques Lassalle established the latter when he took over the leadership of the former to serve as a base for experimenting with new ideas. The association proved highly fruitful and Wasfi intends to try it; but neither establishment will lose its autonomy.

The French model in theatre and cultural matters in general haunts Wasfi's mind. She admires the way the French manage and promote their culture. "The French take their culture very seriously and treat it as a *figure de marque*, as an ambassador abroad," she says. "Their ministry of culture works in close association with their ministry of foreign affairs which has a special department called the *Association Française d'Action Artistique* (AFAA)." The whole world, indeed, she continues, has finally woken up to the vital importance of cultural development, as the U.N. Decade for Cultural Development project testiofies. Through festivals, the French have managed to make obscure cities like Avignon and Nantes internationally famous, and very prosperous in the process. The British did the same for Glasgow, replacing its old grim image with an attractive, exciting one and creating jobs for thousands of people. Culture, she firmly believes, is as important as bread, and the returns of investment in culture are enormous both on the economic and human levels.

"When you hold an annual festival like *Les Allumés* over six years in an old city like Nantes – it is really an old port – and expose its conservative community to different modes of art from all over the world, you are actually teaching that community all about cultural plurality and difference, the need for tolerance, for accepting the otherness of the other, and reveling in it, and for respecting cultural specificity."

In citing the French and other European cultural models, Wasfi is not advocating slavish imitation, but, rather, seeking inspiration as well as confirmation of what she deeply believes in. Besides, she is one of those people who have a dialectical cast of mind and can only think through comparisons. She also has a habit of illustrating and corroborating her ideas with examples; it is as if she feels a need for anchoring all ideas and abstract concepts in a tangible reality that gives them validation. That is why when she tries to understand and define the National theatre in its present condition, she tends to view it in relation to the Comedie Française on which it was originally modelled. And when she tries to understand what is wrong with her society, she finds it fruitful to compare it with others in specific, concrete terms, through examples. With her, meaning can only emerge through this dialectical process which entails a close investigation of lived experience – hers and others'. A woman like Wasfi can only succeed at the National. But even if the system proves too much for her, she will give a good fight before she concedes defeat.

# Rescue Operation 3:
## *The National Theatre Conference**

Well, it finally happened, Or has it really? After many delays and a lot of footling about to decide upon a date, the National Theatre Conference was held last week at three sites simultaneously — the National, El-Tali'a and the Puppet theatres. The organisers – the members of the theatre committee of the Supreme Council for Culture – had supposedly spent almost a year and a half preparing for this momentous event, doing research and collecting data, and had meant it, as they repeatedly announced, as an occasion for a public, democratic debate on the future of the Egyptian theatre. Within a few hours of the official opening, however, it became apparent that the committee's months of deliberation had yielded nothing but a boring and diffuse rehash of old slogans and outdated views, and that the thrust of the conference was not towards the future but, rather, in the direction of the past.

Alfred Farag, the head of the theatre committee and the conference, set the tone in his keynote speech: he conjured up a golden vision of the sixties and his rousing rhetoric was redolent with nostalgia. Incredulously, I listened to him making an impassioned plea for more control, more committees and more bureaucracy. Oblivious of all historical, political and economic changes, he argued for stricter state control of the theatre through 'specialised committees' manned by his generation. As if we did not have enough of those! He and his

---
* 17 July 1997.

generation, he seemed to be saying, had produced 'good, serious' theatre in the sixties and could do it again if they were put in power. The drift of the argument was that salvation lay not in dismantling the old and ailing state-theatre structure and looking for alternative modes of state support and a freer, more open system of work, but in preserving the status quo (with a few minor alterations) and providing it with better administration (more strictures?) to improve its efficiency.

No wonder the young theatre people in the audience were enraged. Farag's speech seemed like a calculated attempt to channel the conference from the start into one specific ideological direction and preempt the expression of any different views. The deeply-entrenched ideological bias of the committee and its hierarchical, discriminatory view of theatre were clearly pronounced in the allocation of sites to the different subcommittees. Whereas the subcommittee dealing with the state-theatre organisation enjoyed the coolness and red plush seats of the National, the one devoted to regional and amateur theatre was banished to the Puppet, there to roast in sweltering heat.

During the first day (the conference lasted for three) I kept moving around among the different sites, hoping for something fresh. Playwright Saadeddin Wahba presided over the first session of the state-theatre committee at the big hall of the National and clamped down on all opposition. An exciting and challenging paper submitted by playwright Mohamed Salmawi proposing new ways of funding theatre away from the government was greeted with scathing sarcasm from Mr. Wahba and was peremptorily dismissed. It was the same story at the Puppet, but more lively, with more shouting and screaming. The audience there were predominantly young and fiery, and given the suffocating heat and the chairman's insistence that no subjects other than those on the official agenda of the conference be discussed, no wonder tempers ran high. More incensing still was the fact that the young people present were not allowed to suggest solutions to their own problems other than those put forward by the organisers, and were merely asked to unquestioningly endorse the recommendations of their 'elders and betters'. On the other hand, the invited representatives of the so-called 'private theatre sector' proved much wiser. They were conspicuous by their absence. I suppose they had better things to do.

Anyone even remotely connected with the Egyptian theatre nowadays knows that things are not what they should be and that something urgently needs to be done if theatre is to survive, let alone thrive. The sad thing is that the problems are well-known, and so are the solutions, if only people would open their eyes and clear their heads of the Sixties clutter. Space and the freedom to make theatre and raise funds untrammelled by restrictive laws and regulations are all that is required. The manifesto of the 1$^{st}$ Free Theatre Festival made this point seven years ago and unfortunately it is still valid today. The National Theatre Conference would have been well-advised to start from there. As it was, it yielded nothing but a long list of recriminations, an even longer list of useless recommendations, gallons of tea and coffee and mounds of cake.

# Noblesse Oblige:
## *Rashida Taymour*[*]

Like many nations, the Arabs have had a long tradition of artistic, literary and cultural patronage. It was not uniformly enlightened, and while it often proved a blessing, in some significant cases it was a curse disguised. Indeed, one could justifiably argue that the history of Arabic poetry for instance, to pick a telling example, is in a sense the history of the uneasy relationship between poet and patron, between the rebellious but penniless, dependent creative talent and the wealthy, aristocratic and powerful benefactor.

In recent history, private patronage has given way to patronage of the state and the change, in many cases, has been only nominal — exchanging gifts and donations for grants and subsidies. There were some spells, however, when the change proved definitely to be one for the worse, and the new faceless patron proved downright vicious. The strings attached to the money in the case of private patronage did not evaporate when the state took over; they were simply disguised, becoming, in their new invisibility, far more menacing, crippling and difficult to defy.

Private patronage of the arts, however, is making a comeback in Egypt, and the state (which has recently decided to remove its socialist mask and shed many of the roles that went with it, including its responsibility for the arts) is quite willing for it do so. This became abundantly clear when the Minister of Culture, Farouk Hosni, went to

---

[*] 12 May, 1994.

Al-Hanager in full force, flanked on either side by his top officials, to give his blessing to the individual initiative of a wealthy aristocrat and preside over the ceremony of the privately-established Mohamed Teymour awards.

Behind the occasion and the awards, established in 1991, is the grand-daughter of the playwright Mohamed Teymour, Rashida Teymour. The photographs of Teymour show an extremely handsome young man, of pronounced Parisian elegance. Fortunately for him, perhaps, but most unfortunately for Egyptian theatre, this talented young artist did not live to experience the ravages of time or to have his fine features sicklied over with the wrinkled cast of old age. The fact that he died young (he was born in 1892 and died in 1921) may account for one of the competition's rules which limits the age of the contestants to thirty-five. And while the young winners may not hope for fat financial rewards (the first prize-winner receives LE 3,000, the second LE 1,500 and the third LE 750), they are guaranteed a respectable panel of judges, a reasonable amount of publicity, a handshake from the Minister of Culture and, most importantly, get their plays into print through the presses of the General Egyptian Book Organisation.

(Another instance of the state cooperating with private patronage).

This year, however, Rashida Teymour went a step further, adding a new bonus. From now on, the winner will not only get the chance to see his script in print, but will also experience the wonderful thrill of seeing it coming to life on stage. For this purpose, Rashida Teymour approached the dynamic director of Al-Hanager, Hoda Wasfi, and it was arranged that Al-Hanager would undertake to stage the production within a budget allocated by Teymour.

The result of this joint effort was a good production of last year's winning play: *A Special Party in Honour of the Family*, by the young and promising Sa'id Hagag. Unfortunately, however, and presumably for financial reasons, it ran for only three nights. Still, it was better than nothing and a good way to celebrate a budding talent. The problem was that however hard one tried to shove aside the problematic ideological underpinnings of the occasion, the play seemed intent on shoving them back under one's nose. It set out, as the ironic title indicates, to attack and discredit the bourgeois idea of the 'family' — very much in the savage vein of August Strindberg — but ended up dismissing today's 'fathers' in favour of yesterday's 'grandfathers'. The anger, sometimes embarrassingly raw and melodramatic, turned out to be targeted not against the patriarchal concept of the family but, paradoxically, against its disintegration and the gradual erosion of the values it supports in modern times.

The ideological message put across forcefully from the stage seemed, despite the thin guise of rebellion, startlingly conservative and too close for comfort to the sentiments of the specially-invited audience. It was as if the author had taken Eugene Ionesco's satirical dig at the bourgeois family in his *Jacques or the Future is in Eggs* (a play on which Hagag draws heavily) and turned its premise upside down. When the set collapses on the stage at the end of Ionesco's play, it signifies the inevitable (and much desired) collapse of bourgeois values; in *A Special Party* it signified the opposite, sounding a resounding plea to save such values and their supporting nuclear structure in the family ideal.

For director Hanaa Abdel-Fattah, who undertook the burden of production, ideology was not the only problem. The text has crucial weaknesses and is heavily derivative in places, sounding sometimes like many foreign plays jumpled together and rendered into Arabic. The classical Arabic medium and the expressionistic dramatic style chosen by the author may have been partly responsible for this, making the dialogue occasionally sound like a parody of translated foreign plays. In the neutral setting, an unspecified desert and wind-swept wasteland, the typically Egyptian, and, hopefully, transient phenomenon of selling daughters to oil-rich Arabs under the guise of marriage, lost its topical relevance and urgency. With more experience, the author could have, perhaps, built it up into a symbol of universal significance, but here it fell completely flat.

Given these serious shortcomings, it was a wonder the show turned out the way it did. Director Hanaa Abdel-Fattah is no fool and he must have been fully aware of what he was up against. He put his long experience and his talent into the service of the play and chose his production staff well. Nabil El-Halwagi's set and Kamal Othman's lighting-design were inspired, providing a figurative, bewitching smoke-screen which enveloped the text. Through it, the movement of the young actors, their pauses and expressions became suggestive and highly evocative, hinting at some other mysterious, subterranean text, lying somewhere beneath the vapid verbal surface. But the real delight and high-light of the evening were the young actors, all amateurs. They merged well into the atmosphere of the stage image and gave good, disciplined and sensitive performances. Thanks to them and to the production staff, what could have been a prosaic disaster turned into a theatrical poem.

# A Rainbow After the Deluge:
## *Nadia El-Shabouri and Husam Atta**

I am a great lover of Assyut, its ancient monastaries, rugged landscapes and warm, proud people. Behind their rough exterior and air of aloofness, there is genuine courtesy and true gallantry. I have had personal proof of this when many years ago, travelling alone to cover the National theatre's visit there with Lenin El-Ramli's *Ahlan Ya Bakawat*, my train stopped at Beni Hussein, some 20 kilometres away from the city. There would be an indefinite delay, we were told, due to some problem with the rails ahead. It was getting dark, and in those days, Assyut and its outlying villages had won a fearful reputation as hotbeds of fundamentalism and terrorist activities. The *Bakawat*'s visit, like the earlier Adel Imam's *El-Wad Sayed El-Shaghal*, had come in the wake of a violent attack on a small regional company there; and since the authorities then were taking a non-confrontational line, opting for a policy of pacification, a bigoted, militant minority was left free to intimidate not only actors, but the body of students and teachers at Assyut university and large sections of the governorate's population.

As the passengers trickled away to melt into the gathering dusk outside, my anxiety grew. The prospect of spending the night alone on the train did not seem very enticing and I frantically debated in my mind whether to risk walking or thumbing a lift on the highway — a choice of two evils! All the while I cursed myself for wearing high heels and not bringing along a scarf by way of a veil. My ordeal, however, did not last for long; I was rescued from my dilemma by a group of young

---

* 8 December, 1994.

Assyuti men (in typical 'Sa'idi', that is to say Upper-Egyptian, get-up) who were not fooled by my external Cairene coolness. They firmly told me, as they were leaving the train, that it was not safe to stay, and asked (almost ordered) me to join them. In pitch darkness, they shepherded me across the rails to the motorway, stopped a car, and two of them escorted me to safety. At the gate of the armed forces rest-house, where the *Bakawat*'s tribe was lodged, they dropped me with a curt greeting and drove away before I could believe what had happened. It pains me still that I never thanked them and mistrusted them all the way, and how I wish I had invited them to see the *Bakawat* the following evening.

Since the deluge, Assyut has been a lot in my thoughts – the crowd of friends I have made there over many theatrical trips in the past ten years, the places I visited, and poor, sad Drunka, that peaceful village of huddled mud houses and a single minaret you pass on the way to the enchanting Monastery of the Virgin up in the nearby mountains. Nothing is left of it now but a few charred brick walls and the minaret, standing alone like a lost soul. I longed to go there and see for myself what happened, but I never thought the occasion would be a theatrical performance. Indeed, with such a heavy death toll and so many families in mourning, it seemed to me that any form of entertainment or celebration, including the feverishly publicised *Aida* or the previous Luxor festivities, were in very bad taste if not downright indecent. Granted that the return of tourists is a consummation devoutly to be wished; but the feelings of the Upper Egyptians have to be respected, especially when they have to bear their sorrows in draughty tents, sometimes with poor (or without) sanitary facilities, and with few blankets to share in the bitter cold of Upper Egypt's winter nights.

Last week, however, the telephone rang; Assyut was on the line. My caller was Nadia El-Shabouri – a woman of great courage and boundless energy, and a formidable cultural agitator. A native of Alexandria, and a graduate of its faculty of fine arts, she moved with her husband to Assyut twenty years ago and went on to establish one of the finest children's cultural centres in the country, then to win the much-coveted post of cultural director of the governorate of Assyut — an unprecedented achievement for a woman in Upper Egypt. Since getting the job, which was only recently, she has already established three new cultural centres in Manfalut, Abu Teeg, and El-Ghanayem – places one has come to associate with religious bigotry and fanatical violence.

Despite her fitful flights of fancy and some crazily ambitious dreams, El-Shabouri had always seemed to me a woman of solid common sense and great sympathy. On this occasion, however, she stunned me by proposing that I come to the city of Assyut to watch a play. "But isn't it too soon after the disaster?" I incredulously asked. As if reading my thoughts, she replied: "But this is for children. When they asked me to start adult cultural activities at the camps, I told them the people would beat me up and I wouldn't blame them. Give them bread and blankets first and then maybe we can give them some hope. But with children, it is different. They desperately need it. Besides, our play is all about learning to say no, and we shall soon tour with it." Dangling an irresistible final carrot, she added: "It is adapted from Brecht and directed by Husam Atta."

She knew how much I admired and respected the work of that serious young director who, two years ago, won first prize at the

Bordeaux festival for children's theatre with his brilliant *The Magic Well*. A native of Assyut, he frequented El-Shabouri's centre as a child and got his first taste of theatre there. After moving to Cairo, he remained faithful to the centre, visiting it often and directing its most successful productions.

The secret of Atta's success with children is that he never adopts a condescending attitude towards them and never makes any concessions when directing for them. Treating them as peers, he never accepts a text that does not delight him personally, and once he starts, he plunges into the game with childish glee, splashing colours everywhere, filling the stage with zingy movement, vibrant sounds, zany wigs, clownish costumes and vigorous masks. He prefers to work with large numbers of actors to recreate the circus atmosphere, and he enjoys shuffling them like a dexterous card-player. But however large the number, his sets (usually bright, simple and exaggerated like children's drawings) never look crowded or messy. Sometimes, when the plan is too ambitious or includes dancing (as in his latest show) he uses the help of a choreographer, but the distribution of the shapes and colours on the canvas remains firmly his own. And though he works exclusively with adult actors (his exacting dramaturgy requires strenuous training and he hates putting children under any strain), he never fails to integrate his young audiences into the action at some point.

In his adaptation of Sa'dallah Wannus's *El-Feel Ya Malik El-Zaman* (The Elephant, O King of All Time), he has children from the audience come up on stage at the end to speak to the fearsome king when the hapless villagers who went to complain to him about his ferocious pet are struck dumb with fear in his presence. In *The Magic*

*Well*, the children are frequently called upon to assist the heroine with her tasks, and in his production of Aristophanes's *Peace*, they help the characters define the meaning of war and peace at the end.

Atta's current production, *The Compulsory Journey*, follows in the same tradition. Once more, it is an adaptation – this time of Brecht's two short school operas *Der Jasager* and *Der Neinsager* (*He Who Says Yes* and *He Who Says No*). The latter play, which is a repetition of the former but with a different end, is here acted in the farcical style of the old silent movies at a 'fast forward' pace, and the children in the audience are frequently treated by 'the teacher' in the play as an extension of his body of students, then are finally encouraged to voice their opinions and say no. Hopefully, more of them will do the same and will recognize with Brecht's sick boy – the 'neinsager' – "the need for a new custom which must be established now, at once: the custom of thinking afresh in every new situation." It is a lesson all Egyptians, especially in Upper Egypt, need to learn. Then, maybe, we won't have bigots and bureaucrats or another Drunka.

# Appendices

Appendices

# Appendix 1

## Down Memory Lane:
### *Abeer El-Sharqawi Recreats the Splendour that Was Once Fatma Rushdi* \*

The wave of nostalgia for the twenties which has recently engulfed most Egyptian T.V. drama (denoting a mood of disenchantment with the present?) seems to be spilling over into the theatre. Fortunately, its first manifestation came in the form of a moving tribute to the legendary actress Fatma Rushdi who died on 23 January two years ago. At the time I wrote for *The Weekly* a mini-story entitled *Down Sunset Boulevard* which I had meant to be an 'objective', 'neutral' account of the dramatic rise and fall of a star. It turned out to be nothing of the sort. In my hectic and feverish casting around for reliable historical data – dates, names, places and events – I felt sometimes, indeed quite often, as if I was losing sight of the woman I was supposed to be writing about.

Reconstructing the facts of the past, let alone trying to recapture something, even a shadow, of the feel of what it was like to be there, is a horrendous nightmare that most researchers in Egyptian history know quite well. What saved me finally from sinking into a lethal quagmire of flimsy impressions, opinionated judgements, vertiginously contradictory statements and dizzying historical lapses was the fact that, one month before she died, I had had the fabulous luck of seeing Rushdi herself and hearing her talk for three hours at the initiative of

---

\* 15 January 1998.

Mahmoud El-Hidini, the head of the National Centre for Egyptian Theatre, to whom I shall be eternally indebted.

Listening to her felt like experiencing a series of epiphanies at a breath-taking pace. She made everything cohere and make sense; her charismatic presence (which long years of poverty, public neglect and self-imposed solitude had not diminished in the least), her infectious *joie de vivre* and overriding sense of humour made me realise intuitively and, literally, physically, the kind of impact she must have made on her audiences so many years ago. What was finally written, and was dedicated to her, was, from first to last, inspired by her.

It is funny how people whom you have seen only once can become much more real to you than people you have known all your life. But isn't this part of the magic of theatre?

And talking of the magic of theatre, allow me to insert a parenthetical paragraph and inform you of my suffering during this holy month of Ramadan from the dearth of any theatrical experience, magical or dreadfully mundane. What we get during this holy month, as evidenced by the high pile of invitations on my desk, is a jumble of indiscriminate *spectacles*, bundled under the rubric of 'folklore', and solely intended to numb the spectator's intelligence and senses, presumably to ease the process of digestion in preparation for the midnight (Sohoor) meal. I was foolish enough to accept one of these invitations, lured by the irresistible architectural charm of Wikalat Al-Ghouri, the site of the performance. Thank God the Wikala is open to the sky: I spent most of the time stuffing tissue paper into my ears and watching the soft clouds pass gently over the face of the moon. I envied the indifference of nature to all the silly drumming and babbling of humanity.

When I got the invitation for *Walla Zaman Ya Fatma* (*It's been so long Fatma*), my heart sank, or, to be absolutely honest, I got an intestinal cramp. How can anyone impersonate the great Sarah Bernhardt of the east? Abeer El-Sharqawi, though talented and with strong features that project well from the stage and a solid training at the AUC Performance Arts Department, was still too young, I thought, to comprehend the tangled web of emotions and loyalties that made Fatma Rushdi the artist she was. The chosen performance space too, the recently restored and redecorated Yusef Idris hall, seemed, size-wise, too cramped — too preposterously small to accommodate a figure of the magnitude of Rushdi. I made my way to the theatre feeling thoroughly cynical, and to console myself, I stopped by the *Fuul* and *Ta'miya* shop opposite the theatre to get a sandwich and washed it down with a strong glass of tea.

Ten minutes into the performance, I realized my folly. This is a performance so filling and satisfying it should be received on an empty stomach. Everything about the performance had a kind of poignant transparency that extended from the tragic pallor of Abeer's makeup-free face and the bewildered, vague and distant look in her eyes (like someone gazing into an existential abyss or traversing the vast spaces between past and present, between what is and all the possibilities of being) to the white gauze curtains that fringed the four metre square performance area. Inside the square which occupied the centre of the long, rectangular hall, with the audience ranged on both sides, was a black, revolving disc, also fringed with white gauze drapes. This extremely simple, but visually eloquent set (by Salwa El-Urabi) was stunningly in tune with Fu'ad Hajaj's text which, rather than attempt a chronological narrative, opted for a structure based on counterpointing significant moments.

The chosen moments which highlighted her relationship with her mentor, director, and husband, Aziz Eid, in its various stages, her triumphs and moments of glory and also her tragic degredation during the last years of her life (and which tactfully glossed over her affair with Ilia Adru'i which forced Eid to divorce her when it became public knowledge) were so beautifully organized by director Hussam El-Din Salah into a subtle pattern that made the spectator feel as if the successive moments were synchronic, though temporally spaced, and the movement of the gauze curtains were crucial in producing that effect.

Equally crucial for the success of this production and for the realization of what I would like to call its 'double-exposure' effect is the live musical performance of Ahmed Khalaf. Impersonating Sayed Darwish, who first discovered the theatrical talent of Rushdi, and accompanying the actors on his lute, translating their moods and states of mind into rhythm and melody, and occasionally treating us to the best of Sayed Darwish, he acted like the precious string on which the chosen moments of Rushdi's life were strung.

But what if we were to write the life of Fatma Rushdi from the vantage point of Aziz Eid? It would seem from the text of the production that Fu'ad Hajaj flirted with the idea; but he left it half realized. Actor Mohamed Abdel Raziq, however, carried the nascent possibility to it actual fulfillment. I do not think Abeer El-Sharqawi could have given us that wonderful performance without the support of Abdel Raziq and the bunch of fine actors who included Lubna Mahmoud, Hamid Marzouk, Mohamed Abdeen and Mustafa Hussein.

# Appendix 2

## Age Cannot Wither Her:
### *Amina Rizq*[*]

On a mild night in late September, two months ago, I went to see *The Black Rabbit* at El-Tali'a. After the show I was too excited to leave at once and hung around for a while in the courtyard of the theatre sipping tea and chatting with friends about the play. They shared my excitement; though written in 1967, Abdalla El-Toukhi's text does not date. The symbolic quest for an illusive black rabbit on which a crippled, selfish, cantankerous old woman arbitrarily sends her daughter — an affectionate, meek and guileless soul — one night, with nothing to light her way but a spluttering kerosine lamp, exposing her to the danger of snake bites or a sudden seizure, induced by her fear of darkness and terror of ghosts, would have had a political meaning in the sixties when the regime used the same hard-and-soft technique, the same tactics of coaxing and intimidation the mother uses to wear out the resistance of her daughter and completely dominate her.

But in 1999, the play comes across as a symbolic psychological drama about the insidious power-game which underlies family relationships sometimes, about the ruthlessness of old age feeding on young lives, and about the frustration, hidden resentment and guilt-ridden feelings of daughters torn between their duty to care for their aged and senile parents and their natural youthful longings. The

---

[*] 11 November, 1999.

daughter's journey through the dark, rambling, rundown country house becomes a voyage into the dark recesses of the mind, a dive into the unconscious to discover the root of the suffering and find the way to liberation. To bolster this interpretation, the original muted end was replaced by a violent confrontation between mother and daughter, spelling out the ugly reality of their relationship and the daughter's rebellion and decision to leave; and though she comes back when the mother collapses, she does it of her own free will.

Another of the show's assets, we agreed, was Mustafa Imam's stage-design which opted for realism and magically transformed the whole interior of the Salah Abdel Sabour hall into a typical, old country house of a once well-off rural family. The transformation was so thorough it extended to the brick ledges and wooden seats and benches on which we sat, on different levels, around the hall. But the most riveting aspect of the play, however, was the acting. The casting of Amina Rizq and Sanaa Yunis as the termagent mother and timid daughter was ingenious and refreshingly bold. Although Rizq has a vast repertoire of mother roles, ranging from tragedy to comedy, melodrama and farce, one would not normally associate her with vicious, domineering mothers. Nor would one normally think of a versatile and very funny comedian like Sanaa Yunis as a possible candidate for the daughter's part. But director Isam El-Sayed did, and has reaped the rewards.

The parts were a challenge to both actresses and they defiantly accepted them. Every night they give a thrilling acting match, played with great dexterity and immaculate timing; and day after day, they prove that Yunis can take on serious and complex parts and handle a wide range of emotions with masterful ease, and that the fluffy, frail Rizq can transform herself by the demoniac fire of genius into a rapacious, malicious, and loathsome old hag. And though Rizq sits all the time and never changes her place, her eyes seem to draw the whole place into their orbits, and even when the area she occupies is darkened, her presence continues to be eerly felt, becoming even more sinister because shrouded in darkness.

We had talked for half an hour, and just as I was preparing to leave, I caught sight of the great Rizq emerging from the darkened entrance of the hall and advancing towards the steps leading down to the courtyard. She walked slowly, with difficulty, limping and leaning heavily on the arm of the young assistant director. I gazed at her in wonder, trying to reconcile this small, fragile figure, in a homely black dress and turban, with the overpowering presence I had experienced during the show. Sanaa Yunis crossed my line of vision momentarily as she rushed up the steps towards her, and her earthy, twangy voice rose above the distant din of the Ataba Square traffic and the loud medley of garish noises issuing from the crazy carnival of tradesmen in the street outside. She was coaxing Rizq to stay on for a while with the promise of a sweet and juicy watermelon – something she could never resist. After a feeble demurral, Rizq allowed herself to be led to an armchair and lowered herself into it gingerly.

I smiled as I remembered her reputation for thrift, which the uncharitable sometimes describe as a miserly streak, and her renowned lusty appetite and passion for food. My hairdresser who once accompanied her to Libya on a trip, in his professional capacity of course, describes her proudly as a hearty eater with a wonderful digestion who is capable of consuming four big meals a day, then asking for a light snack of cheese, bread, fruit, and yogurt before she went to bed. Was it a kind of compensation? I wondered – a substitute for another need? – a yearning to fill a different kind of emptiness? When people are deprived of one pleasure they usually over-indulge another; and this woman, as far as is known, has never married, had children, a steady boyfriend, love affairs, or even the odd romantic escapade. While every step of her career is well documented, her private life, apart from a sketchy description of her family background and strict, harsh upbringing (whose reliability rests solely on her), remains shrouded in mystery. It is not that she is reluctant to give interviews or talk about herself in public; she does both as often as any other actress, and even more liberally. It is that everytime she would have us believe that her public and private life are one and the same thing — that "having married the theatre" early in her life, as she is fond of saying, she "never had any other life outside it." Can a woman dissolve so completely into her art that it becomes her sole reality?

"Yes," I remembered her saying in a long interview to the Cairo *Theatre* magazine in 1995. "I was besotted, infatuated with acting and loved my art with my whole being," she said. "It completely possessed me," she went on; "I acted the whole time, even as I walked in the street and when the play was over, I would act it all over again to myself, at home, in front of the mirror." She could still recite from memory whole plays and not just the parts she had acted, she proudly declared, adding, "I used to kneel in the wings and watch the actors on stage through a small slit in the curtain until my cue arrived. This meant experiencing the play as a whole and learning all the parts by heart. I could, therefore, stand in for any part at a moment's notice." Citing *The*

*Confession Seat* as an example she said: "I started in it as an extra, then played the attendant, then the heroine, then the mother. The only part I didn't do was the Cardinal, and Yusef Wahbi who played it used to kid me about it and say that one day he will give it to me."

The image of Yusef Wahbi sent my thoughts on a different track. I remembered all I had read about his life-long close friendship with Rizq, their long successful artistic partnership in dozens of plays and films, her passionate loyalty and candid acknowledgement of her debt and gratitude to him during his life and after his death (in 1982), and her single-minded dedication to his Ramses company which she joined at the age of thirteen soon after it was formed in 1923 and stuck to it through many vicissitudes until it was finally dissolved in 1944. When Wahbi tried to revive the company afterwards – in '47, '57, '60, '69, and '70 – every time only managing a short season, Rizq, though she had joined the National theatre company in 1944, was always there, supporting her 'teacher', 'mentor', and 'maker' and often acting her old parts. And when in 1960 Wahbi recorded for television twenty-three plays from the Ramses repertoire, Rizq was by his side in many of them.

In the light of all this, would it be too wildly far-fetched to suspect a kind of romantic attachment in the Wahbi/Rizq relationship, whether mutual or just on her side, and to suggest that this perhaps was the real reason why she never married? Conjectures along this line were tentatively made in the past but could neither be proved or disproved, and the nature of this rare relationship remains as enigmatic as ever. When questioned directly about it (in a commemorative book issued by the Cultural Places Organisation in 1998 on the centenary of Wahbi's birth), Rizq dismissed it as ridiculous and totally unfounded. "I was only a child when I joined the company," she protested, "and Yusef Bey (as she always calls him) treated me as such and used to put me on his knee and play finger games with me." Wahbi continued to regard her as a child, and so did all his wives who were never jealous of her, she assured her interviewer, adding, "but the public tend to confuse life with art, and the love scenes on the stage or screen with reality."

I was nudged out of my musings by a friend urging me to join the group who had clustered round her, and were lapping up her reminiscences and anecdotes. It was a rare treat; for at ninety, Rizq rarely stays up late and prefers to rush home and to bed directly after the show. She was explaining, in her rich, melodious voice, one of her major assets, about her knee which she had hurt when she stumbled over a high kerb; hence the limp. She could not understand why they made them so high and neither could anyone. She spoke of a health-farm abroad suggested to her by a fellow actress who went there for beauty treatment. "She tells me it's quite cheap," she assured herself rather than us; "but would they cure my knee?" she wondered.

"Health farm my foot," grunted Sanaa Yunis in disgust. Personally, she was going to London when the play stopped to "have a break, see a play or two and do some shopping;" she invited Rizq to join her, assuring her that it would do her a lot more good than any "newfangled health-farm" and that she could also have her knee checked there. "After all, weren't farms supposed to be for animals?" she asked, looking impishly at her. It was obvious that Yunis had no great liking for the actress who frequented the health-farm and Rizq laughed. But already her mind was busy calculating costs. When Yunis mentioned a nice little hotel which gives her substantial discounts, Rizq said, as if thinking aloud, "I could always stay with my niece who studies there; no need to spend money on a hotel."

London awakened memories of a distant holiday she spent there once, all by herself. After an impatient "where is that watermelon you mentioned?" directed at Yunis, she said in a dreamy voice that after years of continuous exhausting work with the Ramses company, performing in Cairo in winter and touring the provinces in summer, she decided to give herself a holiday and spend it in Europe. She had visited Europe before with the company, as well as Syria, Lebanon, Turkey, North Africa and Latin America; but that had been hard work as well, even harder, since they always travelled third class by boat or train, had to put up with cheap accommodation, sleeping five to a room, look after their own luggage, costumes and accessories throughout the trip, and perform in make-shift theatres, in primitive conditions. And on top of that, they had to pay for their own meals out of their regular salaries since they were not given travelling expenses.

As she spoke, she seemed to shed off years and her voice and features softened and acquired a strange liveliness. In the dim light, the fine wrinkles disappeared and her complexion looked pale and translucent while her big blue eyes gleamed like two fresh puddles in the moonlight. I suddenly thought how beautiful she must have been when young.

"I had given myself three months and decided to start with London, go on to Paris and end up with Italy," her voice nudged me. She rented a comfortable small flat in Notting Hill Gate overlooking the Park and soon discovered in the same building a Greek grocery store which stocked all the ingredients used in Egyptian cooking. Instead of three weeks as she had planned, she spent the whole three-months holiday there, blissfully cooking and consuming her favourite dishes and looking at the Park. "It was wonderful and very cheap," she wound up, and I did not know whether she meant the flat or the whole holiday.

It is not the kind of holiday I would relish, but she made it sound so idyllic and, somehow, deeply touching. It suddenly struck me that the bustle and glitter of the theatrical world meant little for this woman, that what really interested her in the whole pageant was the work she did there. I also felt that she was perfectly honest when she said in the '95 interview that she had lived her real life on the stage and enjoyed the whole gamut of human feelings and experiences, including love, marriage and motherhood, through her parts and therefore did not feel she had missed anything and regretted nothing. Having waded through so many violent tragedies, sentimental comedies, turbulent melodramas, light veaudevilles and social satires on stage, it is no wonder that once in London, "far from the madding crowd" of actors, fans and admirers, and from the patriarchal sway of the dictatorial, domineering Wahbi who controlled her life, all she wanted was peace and quiet, solitude and, of course, the comfort of plenty of good food.

"I can't wait any longer for that watermelon," she said as she heaved herself up in her chair, leaning on the arms. Yunis rose to help her, saying: "You'd better take it home with you. Everyone is leaving." Rizq was delighted, but like a polite child tried to demur; Yunis duly pressed her and she nodded, asking her with a shy smile to have it put in the car of the young woman who had offered to take her home. She waved to us through the window as the car left.

I sat looking at her empty chair for some time afterwards, trying to remember all she had said — her sardonic remarks on today's spoilt, spineless actors, on the deplorable lack of discipline and good management in the state-theatre companies, on the paucity of productions and their depressing artistic quality, her genuine sorrow at the disappearance of the repertoire system, her brisk and wry dismissal of the sisterhood of veiled, repentant actresses as having unwittingly done us all a favour and helped to clean up the artistic scene, her funny anecdotes about fellow Ramses actors and actresses, her ardent pride in the history of the company, and her solid, unwavering faith in the art to which she had given her life.

I finally left, thinking of all those brave female pioneers of the Egyptian theatre who, young and vulnerable as they were, without money or education and heavily trammelled with backward ideas and taboos, had defied their families, society and traditions and ventures forth on the treacherous theatrical seas, alone and unaided, except for the lucky patronage of a Wahbi, as in Rizq's case, or an Aziz Eid, as in that of Fatma Rushdi, Rose El-Yusef and Zeinab Sidqi. What pluck, what stamina, what determination to embrace such a dangerous, stigmatised profession as acting was at the time, even in the case of men, and mount the boards unveiled, living in the public eye, when most women were content to stay behind bars and thick veils, in the safe cloisters of their homes. With infinite faith, such pioneers as Amina Rizq had fought the waves, tamed them, and soared on their crests to the stars.

# Appendix 3

# A Taste of Vintage*

Three years ago, director Isam El-Sayed pulled off a feat that many had previously attempted without success. He managed to lure Amina Rizq back to the stage after an estrangement that had lasted almost twenty-five years. The bait was Abdalla El-Toukhi's one-act play, *The Black Rabbit* – a harrowing psychological drama, in the mode of symbolic realism, about a destructive, love-hate relationship between an aged, crippled, bloodsucking mother and her kind, gullible, weak-willed daughter.

Though written in the 1960s, it had never been produced before, perhaps on account of its nasty image of the mother as a malicious autocrat and spiteful bully. It was the first time an Egyptian dramatist had dared contradict or suggest an alternative to the traditionally idealized and hallowed mother-figure, prick the bubble of selfless, unconditional filial duty, and incite the audience to rebel against any form of pernicious parental authority. The play was deemed too shocking and somehow out of tune with the predominantly political theatre of that period. Political tyrants rather than tyrannical parents were the most immediate threat that theatre needed urgently to confront, so it was believed; private life, personal and family relationships could wait till after the dawn of freedom – they have been waiting since.

When asked sometime before *The Black Rabbit* why she deserted the stage though she continued to act in cinema and television, Ms. Rizq

---
* 24 October, 2002.

explained that though she pined for it, she didn't like what she was offered. There were few decent plays around, she remarked, and still fewer decent parts for old actresses. When offered the role of the viciously mean and selfish mother, she accepted it at once, even though it was subsidiary to that of the daughter (played by Sanaa Yunis) and considerably smaller. Before rehearsals started, she fell off a pavement while doing her shopping in Zamalek, where she lives, and suffered a serious leg injury. It would take a long time to heal, she was told, and has unfortunately impaired her walking since. Rest was strictly advised, which seemed to put paid to all hopes of a comeback. But contrary to all expectations, she stubbornly went along with the project, punctually attending rehearsals, as her mentor, Yusef Wahbi, a rigid disciplinarian had taught her in her youth, in the golden days of the Ramses company back in the 1920s, and performing her part sitting down in one position throughout. And rather than impair her acting, her forced immobility made it all the more powerful and hypnotic, concentrating all her energy in her eyes and voice.

In her hands, the stereotype of the selfish, domineering mother subtly grew into a sinister, menacing presence, like that of the wicked witches of myth and folk tales, inspiring irrational fear, despite her frail, ordinary appearance and mundane surroundings. The audience held their breath in awe as they watched her, and even when she was silent and seemed to doze off in her seat, their eyes obsessively gravitated towards her in mounting suspense and resentful fascination. In the hushed small hall of El-Tali'a theatre, one could feel the floodgates of secret memories, forbidden thoughts, unacknowledged grievances and guilty feelings opening involuntarily and giving their owners welcome catharsis. Ugly and deeply unsettling as the revelations were, for most of the audience, particularly the female members, who are always the ones landed with sick, senile, fretful parents and relatives and asked to cheerfully give up their own lives and dreams in the name of filial duty, they felt painfully honest and you could overhear many of them saying as much at the end of the show.

Now, three years after *Black Rabbit*, Ms. Rizq is physically much weaker and can hardly walk without support. Her talent and spirit, however, are unquenchable. I had thought then I had seen her last stage appearance ever, that the part of the termagant mother was her theatrical swan song; to my joy and delight, she has proven my wrong. When I reviewed *Black Rabbit* in 1999, I chose for a title "Age cannot wither her", and O, my prophetic soul, it has not. She is back on stage, with the same director, in a play by the same author, but this time at Al-Hanger rather than El-Tali'a. And though Abdalla El-Toukhi is no longer with us (he died last year), his daughter, Safaa, is there, side by side with Ms. Rizq, presenting with her a new political reading of the frame-story of *The Arabian Nights* (or *The One Thousand and One Nights*) and the fates the legendary Scheherazade and Shahrayar.

As Om El-Kheir (literally, mother of goodness), the ancient, wise storyteller who assists this new Sheherazade to outwit Shahrayar and escape from the underground cell where he imprisoned her, Ms. Rizq was everywhere in terms of the total theatrical experience and its impact on the audience. She was the one who laid the scene, introduced the characters, explained their thoughts and motives, bridged the gaps between the scenes, commented on the course of events and drew the final moral. And she did all this sitting on a chair, inside an enormous, emptied-out, revolving tree trunk, on one side of the stage, which turned to reveal her when she spoke and to hide her when she had finished. Regardless of what she was given to say, which was mostly in monologue form, or what one ultimate thought of the story she told, one could not help falling under her spell, thrilling to every modulation of her husky, spirited voice, every flicker of her eyes, every movement of her lips, every gesture of her hands. She seemed so natural, so refreshingly spontaneous, and yet behind it all was a massive arsenal of techniques developed over 78 years of intensive stage experience.

It is Ms. Rizq above all – her titanic talent, exuberant theatrical sense, infectious excitement, enormous stamina, charisma, and vintage charm which make **The One Thousand and Two Nights** such a memorable experience whatever the faults of the text or direction. And for bringing her back to the stage, Isam El-Sayed and his sponsor, Huda Wasfi, the artistic manager of Al-Hanager, have earned a place in the hearts of all Rizq's fans, as well as the eternal gratitude of theatre lovers and all the audiences who flock nightly to Al-Hanager to bask in her inimitable, heart-warming, incandescent presence.

رقم الإيداع ١٣٨٧١ / ٢٠٠٤
I.S.B.N. 977- 01-9185- X

مطابع الهيئة المصرية للكتاب

# INDEX

Abaza, Aziz
   *Shahrayar* — 24, 217-8
Abdallah, Mohamed Abdel Halim
   *For the Sake of My Son* — 163
Abdallah, Yeha El-Tahir — 167
Abdeen, Mohamed — 274
Abdel-Aziz, Aida — 98
Abdel-Fattah, Hana — 143, 151, 262
Abdel-Fattah, Inistar — 143
   *Any One to Translate* — 145-7
   *The Book of Outcasts* — 148-51
   *El-Darabukka (Egyptian Drum)* — 149
   *Sonata* — 152
   *The Symphony of Lear* — 153
   *Tarnima (Hymn)* — 148
Abdel-Hakim, Shawqi — 68
Abdel-Halim, Ahmed — 237
Abdel-Hamid, Abdel-Halim — 176
Abdel-Hamid, Hisham — 136, 139, 154
Abdel-Hamid, Sami — 137
Abdel-Qader, Mohamed Zaki — 236
Abdel-Saboor, Salah
   *Ma'sat El-Hallaj*
     *(Death in Baghdad)* — 156-7
   *A Princess Waiting* — 213-4
Abdou, Fifi — 90, 94, 99-100
Abdu, Fifi — 165

| | |
|---|---|
| Abdul-Enein, Nehad | 224 |
| Abdul-Fattah, Intisar | 21 |
| Adawiya, Ahmed | 99 |
| Adru'I, Eli | 14, 16, 274 |
| Aeschylus | |
|   *Agamemnon* | 68 |
| Ahmed, Abbas | 72 |
| Al-Asadi, Jawad | 132 |
| Al-Atrash, Farid | 41, 139 |
| Ali, Nagat | 168-9 |
| Ali, Sayed | 126 |
| Allula, Abdel-Qadir | 155-7 |
|   *El-Ma'ida (The Table)* | 155 |
| Al-Muqaffa, Ibn | 225 |
| Al-Yusef, Rose | 13 |
| Amer, Haytham | 176 |
| Amin, Hohair | 134 |
| Ammar, Ibn | 232 |
| Anouilh, Jean | |
|   *Becket* | 181 |
| Aouini, Walid | 103-29, 151 |
|   *Coma* | 106, 113 |
|   *The Desert of Shadi Abdel Salam* | 112 |
|   *Excavations of Agatha* | 106, 112 |
|   *The Fall of Icarus* | 117 |
|   *The Last Interview* | 105-10, 113 |
|   *Mahmoud Mokhtar and the Khamaseen Winds* | 122-4 |
|   *Tanakodat (Contradictions)* | 103-4 |

| | |
|---|---|
| *Underground* | 119-20 |
| *The Wardrobe* | 126-9 |
| Arafa, Sharif | 47 |
| Ardash, Sa'd | 21-2, 75-81, 132, 162, 237 |
| Ari, Ahmed Abdel | 26 |
| Ashour, No'man | |
|   *The El-Dughry Family* | 164 |
|   *The Female Sex* | 30 |
|   *The People Upstairs* | 30 |
|   *Tennery Tower* | |
|     *(Burg El-Madabegh)* | 164 |
| Atallah, Armin | 15 |
| Athenaseus, Mina | 176 |
| Atta, Husam | 265-7 |
| Awad, Louis | 52, 78, 238 |
| Awad, Mohamed | 218 |
| Ayoub, Samila | 32, 58, 77, 187 |
| Aziz, Mohammed Abdel | 76 |
| Baccar, Jalila | 228 |
| Badawi, Adel Rahman | 77 |
| Bahgat, Nihad | 47, 92, 94 |
| Bakathir, Ali Ahmed | |
|   *The Secret of Sheherazade* | 24, 215-7 |
| Bakheet, Gamal | 98 |
| Bakr, Abu | 197 |
| Barthes, Roland | 167 |
| Basiouny, Dalia | 191-5, 197 |
|   *What Do You Want to Be* | |

| | |
|---|---|
| *When You Grow Down?* | 193-4 |
| Basit, Leila Abdel | |
|    *Birds' Dreams* | 188 |
| Basyouni, Nada | 135 |
| Beckett, Samuel | |
|    *Endgame* | 76 |
| Bernard, Kenneth | |
|    *Dr. Magico* | 84 |
| Bidair, Karima | 126 |
| Bishay, Samir | 188 |
| Brecht, Bertolt | 75-81 |
|    *Drums in the Night* | 77 |
|    *The Caucasian Chalk Circle* | 80 |
|    *The Exception and the Rule* | 75-6 |
|    *The Good Soul of Setzuan* | 77-8 |
|    *Mother Courage and Her Children* | 80 |
|    *The Threepenny Opera* | 58 |
|    *The Yasayer, The Naysayer* | 267 |
| Carioca, Tahiya | 165 |
| Case, Sue-Ellen | 192 |
| Chekhov, Anton | 86, 164, 175-7 |
|    *The Cherry Orchard* | 24, 68 |
| Churchill, Caryl | |
|    *Top Girls* | 225 |
| Darwish, Sayed | 15, 213-4, 274 |
| Dawood, Ragih | 183 |
| Dawwara, Amr | 59, 61 |
| Diab, Mahmud | |
|    *Bab Al-Futuh (Conquerors' Gate)* | 78 |

| | |
|---|---|
| Dickens, Charles | |
|    *Hard Times* | 188-9 |
| Dostoevsky, Fyodor | 163 |
| Dürrenmatt, Friedrich | |
|    *The Visit* | 31-2 |
| 'Eid, Aziz | 13-7, 214, 273-4, 283 |
| Eid, Kamal | 77 |
| Ela, Hamdi Abdul | 188 |
| El-Alfi, Mahmoud | 221 |
| El-Amir, Izzat | 31 |
|    *The Reign of Sheherezade* | 220 |
| El-Ansari, Sherin | 195 |
| El-Asfouri, Samir | 83-102, 157, 188 |
|    *The Cell* | 86, 164 |
|    *Hazimni Ya . . .* | 90-4, 100 |
|    *Honey is Honey and Onions are Onions* | 83-5 |
|    *Kida OK* | 100-2 |
|    *The House of Spinsters* | 86-9 |
| El-Assal, Fatheyn | 35 |
| El-Beheiri, Mokhles | 61, 134, 138 |
| El-Dafrawi, Mohamed | 189 |
| El-Dimirdash, Farouk | 75-6 |
| El-Faramawi, Sa'id | 202-3 |
| El-Haj, Fadya | 110 |
| El-Hakim, Tawfiq | 233, 236 |
|    *The Fate of a Cockroach* | 30 |
|    *Isis* | 24 |
|    *The Return of the Spirit* | 163 |

| | |
|---|---|
| *Shams El-Nehar* | 30 |
| *Sheherazade* | 30, 215, 222 |
| *The Tree Climber* | 21-2, 28 |
| El-Halwagi, Nabil | 153, 262 |
| El-Hedini, Mahmoud | 22, 171 |
| El-Hifnawi, Karima | 61 |
| El-Kholi, Fahmi | 187 |
| El-Meligi, Mohmoud | 17 |
| El-Mogy, Gasser | 197 |
| El-Muhandis, Fuad | 33-4, 162 |
| El-Murshidi, Sohair | 69 |
| El-Naggar, Yasmin | 134 |
| El-Ra'I, Eli | 231-8 |
| El-Ramli, Lenin | |
|   *Ahlan Ya Bakawat* | 263 |
| El-Rashidi, Imad | 199-200 |
| El-Rihani, Naguib | 15, 138 |
|   *Salama Fi Kheir (Salam is Well and Thirving)* | 48 |
| El-Sab', Mohamed | 215 |
| El-Sabbagh, Hala | 199 |
| El-Sa'dani, Salah | 52 |
| El-Sadda, Hoda | 197-8 |
| El-Salamouni, Abu El-Ela | |
|   *Diwan Al-Baqar (Chronicle of Cows)* | 221-2 |
| El-Saqqa, Ahmed | 101 |
| El-Sawi, Amina | 161, 166 |
|   *Marriage Wholesale* | 162 |

| | |
|---|---|
| *Midaq Alley* | 161 |
| El-Sayed, Isam | 23, 200, 276, 285, 288 |
| El-Shabouri, Nadia | 265 |
| El-Sharnoubi, Farouk | 94 |
| El-Sharqawi, Abdel-Rahman | 162 |
|   *Back Streets* | 163 |
|   *Ma'sat Jamila (Tragedy of Jamila)* | 156 |
|   *Watani Akko (Akko, My country)* | 156 |
| El-Shakqawi, Abeer | 273-4 |
| El-Sharqawi, Galal | 132, 218, 237 |
| El-Sherif, Sarah Nur | 135, 169, 179-85 |
|   *The Letters of Hraji al-Qutt* | 169 |
| El-Siba'I, Magdy | 176 |
| El-Siba'I, Yusef | 162 |
| El-Siwifi, Abbas | 182-3 |
| El-Tab'y, Mohamed | |
|   *When We Fall in love* | 163 |
| El-Toukhi, Abdalla | 287 |
|   *The Black Rabbit* | 23, 28, 275-7, 285-7 |
|   *The One Thousand and Second Night* | 28, 222-3 |
| El-Tookhi, Safaa | 151 |
| El-Tunsi, Bayram | 84, 213 |
| El-Urabi, Salwa | 273 |
| El-Yusef, Rose | 283 |
| Enany, Sarah | |
|   *Vienna* | 168-9 |
| Euripides | |
|   *Electra* | 58 |

| | |
|---|---|
| *Everyman* | 133-4 |
| Fadji, Amel | 224-5 |
| Fahmi, Aida | 57-61 |
| Fahmi, Farida | 37-45 |
| Fahmi, Hussein | 165, 179 |
| Fahmi, Tayseer | 157 |
| Fahmi, Yusra | 165 |
| Farag, Alfred | 79, 255 |
|    *The Fall of a Pharaoh* | 30 |
|    *Lady Buqbuq* | 144-5 |
|    *The Straw Circle* | 146 |
|    *Suliman Al-Halabi* | 78 |
| Fattah, Tariq Abdel | 181 |
| Fayed, Heba | 126 |
| Fawzi, Alia | 214 |
| Fish, Stanley | 166-7 |
| Fo'ad, Shahira | 176 |
| Fukeih, Fadi | 59 |
| Gad, Layla | 77 |
| Gad, Nehad | 29 |
| Gamil, Sanaa | 29-36, 215 |
| Geith, Hamdi | 30 |
| Ghanem, Fathy | |
|    *The Man Who Lost His Shadow* | 164 |
| Ghazala, Iman | |
|    *Mahasin and Ihab* | 197 |
| Ghazouli, Feryal | 213 |
| Ghurab, Amin Yusef | 164 |
| Goldoni, Carlo | |

| | |
|---|---|
| *The Servant of Two Masters* | 68 |
| Gom'a, Hisham | 174 |
| Grace, Louis | 33 |
| Gu'aibi, Fadil | 224 |
| Haddad, fuad | |
|    *El-Shatir Hassan (Hassan the Clever)* | 165 |
| Haggag, Sa'id | |
|    *Aunt Sftiyya and the Monastery* | 168 |
|    *A Special Party in Honor of the Family* | 261 |
| Hajaj, Fouad | 72 |
|    *Walla Zaman Ya Fatma (It's been So Long, Fatma)* | 273-4 |
| Halim, Samir Abdel | 151 |
| Halim, Tahiya | 105-10, 122 |
| Haqi, Yeha | 162 |
| Haroun, Mustapha | 123-4 |
| Hassan, Salama | 71-4 |
| Hatem, Abdel Qadir | 162 |
| Hemeida, Nora | 176 |
| Hijab. Reem Sayed | 109-10 |
| Hineidi, Mohamed | 93 |
| Hosni, Farouk | 259 |
| Husni, Hasan | 93 |
| Husni, Hind | 173 |
| Hussein, Abdullah | 188 |
| Hussein, Mustafa | 274 |
| Hussein, Taha | 161, 233 |

| | |
|---|---|
| Ibn Daniyal, Mohamed | 196 |
| Ibrahim, Abdel Mon'im | 187 |
| Ibrahim, Mona | 213 |
|    *The Mistress of Wisdom* | 197 |
| Idris, Yusef | 168, 170-1, 173-4, 238 |
|    *The Cotton King* | 143 |
|    *Al-Farafeer (The Underlings)* | 67, 175 |
|    *El-Mukhatateen* | 79 |
|    *Terrestrial Farce* | 31 |
| Imam, Adel | 45-50, 179 |
|    *El-Wad Sayed El-Shaghal* | 263 |
| Imam, Moudi | 47 |
| Imam, Mustafa | 200, 276 |
| Intisar | 173 |
| Ionesco, Eugene | |
|    *Amédée* | 84-5 |
|    *The Chairs* | 76 |
|    *Jacques* | 261 |
|    *Macbett* | 83 |
| Isma'il, Ahmed | 165 |
| Isma'il, Bahig | 210 |
| Izzadin, Reem | 134 |
| Jahin, Salah | 77, 175-7 |
| Jalloun, El-Tahir Bin | 167 |
| Kahfagi, Samir | 4 |
| Kamal, Hala | 197 |
| Karim, Awatef Abdel | 77 |
| Khalaf, Ahmed | 274 |
| Khalil, Caroline | 168-9 |

| | |
|---|---|
| Khashaba, Sami | 240-9 |
| Khayri, Mohamed | 51-6 |
| Khayri, Rasha | |
|   *Bayt min Lahm* | 170-2 |
| Kohout, Pavel | 193 |
| Kulthum, Umm | 123-4 |
| Landovsky, Pavel | 193 |
| Lerchenberg-tony, Eva-Maria | 132 |
| Libliba | 218 |
| Littlewood, Joan | 234-5 |
| Lorca, Frederico Garcia | |
|   *The House of Bernarda Alba* | 24 |
| Madbouli, Abdel Moneim | 34, 152 |
| Mafouz, Naguib | 113, 161, 164-5 |
| Maher, Ahmed | 220-1 |
| Mahmoud, Hani | 123 |
| Mahmoud, Lubna | 274 |
| Mahran, Sameh | 165-7 |
|   *The Child of Sand (Tifl al-Rimal)* | 167 |
|   *The Collar and the Bracelet* | 167 |
|   *Khafyet Qamar (Lanar Eclipse)* | 167 |
|   *Laylat Al-Qadar* | 167 |
|   *The Seven Days of Man* | 167 |
| Madour, Mohamed | 238 |
| Mansour, Anis | |
|   *The Neighborhood* | 30 |
| Marzouk, Hamid | 274 |
| Mas'oud, Mahmoud | 61 |
| Mekkawi, Abdel Ghaffar | 75 |

| | |
|---|---|
| Mekkawi, Sayed | 77 |
| Metaweh, Hani | 132-41, 165 |
|    *The Last Whisper* | 136-41 |
|    *The Lone Traveler* | 140 |
|    *Ya Misafer Wahduk* | 133-5 |
| Metaweh, Karam | 18, 63-9, 78, 215, 221, 237, 239-40 |
| Metwalli, Abdel-Latif | 165 |
| Mishilhi, Mohsen | |
|    *The Trial of the Priest* | 179-85 |
| Mokhtar, Mahmoud | 122-4 |
| Molière | |
|    *The Affected Ladies* | 30 |
|    *The Imaginary Invalid* | 30 |
|    *The Miser* | 30 |
| Mon'im, Nasser Abdel | 168 |
| Mostafa, M. | 126 |
| Munir, Magda | 212 |
| Munir, Sherif | 93, 101 |
| Mustafa, Raouf | 89 |
| Mustagab, Mohamed | |
|    *The Secret History of No'man Abdel Hafiz* | 205-12 |
| Nabbi, May Abdel | 188 |
| Nagaty, 'Asim | 172 |
| Nagui, Mohamed | 167 |
| Naguib, Nahid-Ma'ila | 196, 219 |
| Nait, Karima | 127 |
| Nasser, Abdel-Ghani | 89 |

| | |
|---|---|
| Nasser, Zein | 134 |
| Nijm, Omar | 87 |
| Nunn, Trevor | 86 |
| Omar, Amal | 197 |
|   *A Woman-Made Man* | 197 |
| Othman, Kamal | 262 |
| Ouda, Abdel Ghaffar | 165, 187-90 |
| Pirandello, Luigi | 78 |
| Previn, André | 86 |
| Qamar, Bhagat | |
|   *Midaq Alley* | 164 |
|   *Shabab Imra'a (A Woman in her Prime)* | 164-5 |
| Qandil, Fatma | |
|   *The Night After the One Thousand And One Nights* | 196, 218-9, 223-4 |
| Qasim, Abdel Hakim | 167 |
| Quddu, Ihsan Abdel | |
|   *A Stranger in Our House* | 163 |
| Rabi', Sawsan | 89 |
| Radi, Maher | 183 |
| Radi, Sayed | 34, 239-40 |
| Ra'fat, Asim | 55 |
| Raghda | 220-1 |
| Rahman, Nagwa Abdel | 55-6, 197 |
| Rateb, Ahmed | 50 |
| Rateb, Gamil | 222 |
| Ramadan, Sumaya | |
|   *The Tale of King Shahrayar and* | |

| | |
|---|---|
| *His Brother* | 196-7 |
| Ramzi, Hani | 101 |
| Raziq, Mohamed Abdel | 274 |
| Rehim, Sha'ban Abdel | 101 |
| Rhys, Jane | 168-9 |
| Rida, Ali | 40 |
| Rida, Mahmoud | 40-3 |
| Rizq, Amina | 13-4, 17, 21-8, 34, 165, 189-90, 200-1, 215, 275-83, 285-88 |
| Roman, Mikhail | |
|   *Smoke* | 30, 51-6 |
| Rushdi, Fatma | 13-9, 24, 271-2, 283 |
| Rushdi, Rashad | 218 |
|   *The Light of Darkness* | 31 |
| Sabri, Farouk | |
|   *The Leader* | 47-50, 179 |
| Sabry, Maher | 193-5 |
| Sa'd, Ali | 98 |
| Saeid, Samah | 126 |
| Sa'id, Tariq | |
|   *Demi-Rebels* | 168, 174 |
|   *Fragments of Diamond* | 174-7 |
| Salam, Shadi Abdel | 111-4 |
| Salama, Amir | |
|   *Optical Illusion* | 59-61 |
| Saleh, Midhat | 93 |
| Salwami, Mohamed | 256 |
| Sami, Hala | 197 |

| | |
|---|---|
| Samir, Amani | 176 |
| Seif, Salah Abu | 164-5 |
| Selim, Kamal | 17 |
| Selim, Maher | 168 |
| Selim, Mustafa | 174 |
| Shafiq, Fuad | 97 |
| Shafiq, Mohamed | 114 |
| Shakespeare, William | 133 |
|    *King Lear* | 153-4 |
|    *Macbeth* | 30, 193 |
|    *Othello* | 24 |
|    *Romeo and Juliette* | 24 |
| Sharara, Tarek | 127 |
| Sha'rawi, Huda | 124 |
| Shawqi, Ahmed | |
|    *The Death of Cleopatra* | 19, 24 |
|    *El-Sit Huda (Madame Huda)* | 95-8 |
| Shawqi, Emil | 168 |
| Shawki, Farid | 165 |
| Sidqu, Zaynab | 14, 283 |
| Sjana, Jozef | 132 |
| Soliman, Hanan | 168-9 |
| Sophocles | |
|    *Antigone* | 78 |
| Sorour, Naguib | 68 |
|    *Yasin and Baheya* | 78 |
| Stoppard, Tom | |
|    *Every Good Boy Deserves Favour* | 86-9 |
| Strindberg, August | |

| | |
|---|---|
| *The Dance of Death* | 31 |
| Subhi, Ihab | 176, 181 |
| Subhi, Mohamed | 31 |
| Suliman, Munira | |
| *The Beginning* | 197 |
| Synge, J.M. | |
| *Riders to the Sea* | 58 |
| Taha, Hisham | 124 |
| Tahir, Bahaa | 168, 179-82 |
| Teymour, Rashida | 260 |
| Tonsy, Nancy | 109-10 |
| Tulaymat, Zaki | 32 |
| Tulba, Ashraf | 61 |
| Wahab, Farouk Abdel | 77-8 |
| Wahba, Ali Nabil | 152 |
| Wahba, Saadeddin | 256 |
| *Sikkat as-Salama (Road to Safety)* | 251 |
| Wahbi, Yussef | 13-4, 25-8, 39, 279-80, 283, 286, 288 |
| Wakim, Bishara | 214 |
| Wannus, Sa'dalla | |
| *Al Malik huwa Al-Malik (the King Is the King)* | 48 |
| *El-Feel Ya Malik El-Zaman (The Elephant, O King of all Time)* | 266 |
| Wasfi, Huda | 131, 246, 249-54, 260 |
| Wertenbaker, Timberlake | |
| *The Love of the Nightingale* | 191-2 |

| | |
|---|---|
| Williams, Tennessee | |
|    *The Rose Tattoo* | 30 |
| Wilson, Munir Makram | 134 |
| Yaseen, Mahmoud | 165, 179 |
| Yaseen, Kamal | 52, 162 |
| Yehya, Effat | 224-6 |
|    *Desertscape* | 225-8 |
|    *Once Upon a Time* | 224-5 |
| Yusef, Amani | 173 |
| Yunis, Sanaa | 23, 276, 280-2, 286 |
| Zaghloul, Saad | 123-4 |
| Zaki, Manal | 173 |
| Zaki, Mona | 101 |
| Zeid, Ahmed Abou | 126 |
| Zein, Mostafa | 12 |

# ERRATA

*The corrections below refer to the first edition of <u>Perspectives</u>, by Nehad Selaiha, originally published b GEBO General Egyptian Book Organization, Cairo, Egypt, 2004. The scans of the original pages were created by the Martin E. Segal Theatre Center in the spring of 2020 with the kind permission of the estate of Nehad Selaiha.*

p. 7, l. 18: for "Floggin" read "Flogging"

p. 8, l. 6: for "Innocen" read "Innocence"

p. 108, l. 22: for "matresses" read "mattresses"

p. 242, l. 26: for "affectioante" read "affectionate"

p. 289, l. 10: for "my" read "me"

p. 294, l. 19: for "Thirving" read "Thriving"

p. 303, l. 12: for "Juliette" read "Juliet"

# The Egyptian Theatre
## Perspectives

*Perspectives* is the third volume in Nehad Selaiha's *Egyptian Theatre* series, after *New Directions* and *Plays and Playwrights*.

Here the focus shifts to performers, directors, dramaturges, critics and managers, and they are presented through their work, in accurate, sympathetic portraits which combine the personal and artistic. The portraits shed light on the stresses, constraints and challenges of pursuing a career in theatre in Egypt and place them in a wider ideological and socio-economic context.

Accurately researched and highly informative, *Perspectives* is written with passion, humour and uncompromising honesty. Highly informative and entertaining.

Nehad Selaiha is professor of drama and criticism at the Postgraduate Institute of Arts Criticism at the Cairo Academy of Arts. She is also the drama critic of *Al-Alhram Weekly*, the leading English newspaper in Egypt.

Salwa Mohamed Ali and Mohamed Abdel Azim in *Anguished Dreams*.

Price EGP .10

www.ingramcontent.com/pod-product-compliance
Lightning Source LLC
Chambersburg PA
CBHW050336230426
43663CB00010B/1880